THE AUSCHWITZ GOALKEEPER

A Prisoner of War's True Story

THE
AUSCHWITZ
GOALKEEPER

A Prisoner of War's
True Story

Ron Jones

with Joe Lovejoy

Gomer

Published in 2013 by
Gomer Press, Llandysul, Ceredigion, SA44 4JL

Reprinted 2013

ISBN 978 1 84851 736 3

A CIP record for this title is available from the British Library.
© Copyright text: Joe Lovejoy, 2013

This book is published with the financial support of the
Welsh Books Council.

Printed and bound in Wales at
Gomer Press, Llandysul, Ceredigion

This book is dedicated to the POWs who didn't survive captivity or the Death March, and to the British Legion, who have done, and continue to do, so much good work for our gallant servicemen.

Acknowledgements

As anybody who knows me, or knows of me, will be aware, I have been a sports journalist, specialising in football, these past 45 years, and although a keen interest in the Second World War was fostered by my father (an ex-Royal Navy man), I would not claim to be an authority on such matters.

A great deal of research was therefore needed before venturing into print about Auschwitz, and although Ron Jones was obviously my first and richest source of information, it would be remiss not to acknowledge a major debt to the real experts.

Foremost among these has to be Piotr Setkjiewicz, chief historian at the Auschwitz-Birkenau State Museum, who has written the definitive book entitled *The History of Auschwitz IG Farben Work Camps*, and who was most helpful, always receptive to my inquiries, however uninformed. Further forensic detail was provided by *Anatomy of the Auschwitz Death Camp* by Yisrael Gutman and Michael Berenbaum (United States Holocaust Memorial Museum).

Laurence Rees's *Auschwitz: The Nazis and the Final Solution* is essential reading for anyone with an interest in this most daunting of subjects, while *Hitler's Scientists* by John Cornwell provides a comprehensive reminder of the often overlooked dual function of the concentration camps, as producers of ersatz raw materials, as well as extermination centres.

Grateful thanks are also due to Guy Walters, the journalist and author who, in the best traditions of investigative journalism, has questioned the accounts of Charles Coward, Denis Avey and other British POWs who were held captive alongside Ron Jones. Duncan Little, the esteemed author of *Allies in Auschwitz*, has raised similar doubts, and was of great assistance. Ditto Ben Barkow, director of the Wiener Library for the Study of the Holocaust and Genocide. My thanks also to Alan Bowgen at the National Archives, Kew, London.

I am additionally indebted to John Barnie, a conscientious and considerate editor, who corrected my many errors. Any that remain are entirely my fault. Also to Ceri Wyn Jones of Gomer Press who embraced the project so enthusiastically at a time when other publishers vacillated.

Finally, thanks to my IT guru, David Smith, and my long-suffering wife, Lesley, for tea and sympathy.

Contents

Preface

This was not a book I ever intended writing, until Joe Lovejoy persuaded me to do it as a joint project. I never spoke about my experiences in Auschwitz, and the "Death March" that followed, until I was in my eighties, and would not do so now but for the need to set the record straight, because suspect testimony is seized upon by the Holocaust deniers to further their wicked attempts to prove that Hitler's "Final Solution" never happened – that it is no more than a Jewish myth.

The Nazis' extermination of millions of people whose only "offence" was their race, *did* happen, and I was a horrified witness to how it was done. The story has been told before, of course, and I would not want anybody to think I am retelling it with any financial motive. At 96 I have no need of, or desire for, "blood money".

I have chosen to speak out 70 years after the event because I am concerned by other accounts which focus on personal heroism and downgrade the conduct of honest, less fanciful prisoners.

One such account is that of Denis Avey, author of, *The Man Who Broke into Auschwitz*. In 2010 he was fêted by the Prime Minister in Downing Street and acclaimed a "Hero of the Holocaust". Perhaps Avey believed that any witness to what really happened would be dead by now, so there would be no one to contradict his fabricated tales; but I'm still here; I knew him in the camp and I don't believe him.

Charlie Coward was another one who laid it on thick. He published a book which was made into a film, *The Password Is Courage*, in which Dirk Bogarde played Coward's supposedly heroic role.

Arthur Dodd, who I knew and liked in the camp, has also had a biography published, *Spectator in Hell*. This one is a good book, with plenty of accurate, valuable information, but unfortunately there are a couple of important passages where he falls into the same self-glorifying trap as Coward and Avey.

I have no envy of any of these men, they were comrades in suffering, and in no way do I wish to belittle what they endured, it is merely my intention to tell it exactly as it was. The fact that British POWs ended up in Auschwitz needs no embroidery and receives none here, although my own story is more extraordinary than some, in that I should not have been in the Army in the first place, having been called up from a reserved occupation due to clerical error.

It was a truly terrible time, and I witnessed things I wouldn't wish my worst enemy to see, but I take comfort from the knowledge that we British did as much as we could to help those poor, suffering Jews. This was acknowledged by *The Jewish Chronicle* in February 2012:

> *As many as 1,400 British prisoners arrived at Auschwitz towards the end of 1943 and hundreds were forced to work at the IG Farben chemical factory. Each one of these men was a witness to The Shoah* [the Hebrew name for the Holocaust]. *Their story has never been fully told, nor has the British government paid full tribute to the dignity and humanity these men demonstrated in helping the Jewish inmates in the camp next door.*
>
> *At times the "kriegies", as the POWs were known, and the "stripeys", as they called the Jewish prisoners, worked together, formed friendships and exchanged information.*
>
> *Detailed research carried out into E715* [our POW

camp] *by the American academic Joseph Robert White, for the Centre of Advanced Holocaust Studies, shows the British POWs in a genuinely positive light. Their response to incarceration was not to identify with their captors and turn a blind eye to the mistreatment of their fellow human beings, but to help where they could with clothing, food and information.*

Over the 68 years since the camps were liberated, there have been many attempts to tell the story of the British prisoners of war at Auschwitz.

This is my belated attempt to do just that. No exaggerations, no lies. As they say in court, this is the truth, the whole truth and nothing but the truth, so help me God.

Ron Jones, October 2013

Foreword

A nation that forgets its past has no future.

Sir Winston Churchill

Auschwitz is still a word to resonate with those of a certain age, a place synonymous with all that is worst in human nature – bestial brutality and unimaginable evil. It was the largest and most lethal of the Nazi concentration camps, responsible for the systematic annihilation of 1.1 million prisoners, 90 per cent of them Jews.

It owes its place in the satanic dictionary to the murder of these poor souls by inhuman SS guards and the cruel "kapos", turncoat prisoners or criminals who mercilessly forced their fellow inmates to work, or to file naked into the gas chambers.

What most people still don't realise today is that Auschwitz was more than a charnel house for the implementation of Hitler's infamous "Final Solution". It was three camps in one: an extermination facility, a slave labour factory serving the German war effort and a POW camp. The first of these, Birkenau, is all-too familiar. The latter two were called Bunawerke and Monowitz E715 respectively.

Situated next to the Jewish slave labourers, who had a camp of their own in Monowitz, the E715 prisoner of war facility held between 600 and 1,400 British POWs at various times. These were accommodated in a sub-camp, situated next to the Jews, and worked alongside them in an enormous factory complex. Among other things, this housed a chemical processing plant, financed and run by an internationally-renowned German company, IG Farben. It was established to produce synthetic petrol and rubber from coal, but it also manufactured Zyklon B, the pesticide used in the four gas chambers. There were some 40 satellite camps at Auschwitz (including coal mines) radiating up to 50 miles away.

Many of the Nazi horrors have been well documented down the years – the recycling of clothes, hair, spectacles and gold fillings from the corpses, the "showers" for "delousing" that were sick euphemisms for the gas chambers, and the crematoria that disposed of the "debris". The inhuman medical experiments carried out by Jozef Mengele and his acolytes are also common knowledge.

The fact that the SS and their business partners from IG Farben set out to earn millions from the exploitation of slave labour, and that this became Auschwitz's *raison d'être*, as much as the extermination of Jews and other "undesirables", is less well known. Likewise, the fact that the industrialists responsible for working prisoners to death got off so lightly at the end of the war that most of them were back in the boardrooms of major German companies by the 1950s.

In setting this book in its proper context it is necessary to remind ourselves, and especially, perhaps, younger readers, of the specifics of this hideous scar on European history.

It was in May 1940, eight months after occupying Poland, that the Germans decided to establish a concentration camp around the small Polish town of Oswiecim, some 30 miles south-west of Krakow. Oswiecim, which had a pre-war population of 12,000, had its name changed to Auschwitz when the Germans invaded in 1939. Incredibly, the camp was initially classified as a detention centre for prisoners whose offences were "relatively light and definitely correctable".

This soon changed, however, and soon at least a million Jews were murdered on arrival, without ever being registered as camp inmates. The initial "selection", dictating who lived and who died within hours, was made by SS doctors on a ramp at a railway siding outside Birkenau, from where the elderly, the sick, pregnant women, young children and anyone else classified as unfit for work, were marched straight to the gas chambers. Roughly 15 per cent survived this process, only to be worked to death, usually within six months.

Increasing demand caused by the seizure of Jews from all over Europe (in order of arrival, Poland, the Soviet Union, Czechoslovakia, France, Holland, Belgium, Yugoslavia, Norway, Germany, Greece, Austria, Italy, Latvia, Estonia and Hungary) saw constant expansion, and from March 1943 until the end of 1944 there were four gas chambers and crematoria working at full capacity, capable of "processing" 4,400 victims every twenty-four hours.

Auschwitz 1, the original camp, was an old Polish cavalry barracks comprising 16 single-storey buildings. From May 1940 to January 1942 it accommodated 36,000 prisoners – 26,000 civilians and 10,000 Russian POWs. This was clearly not enough for what the Germans had in mind and a huge new camp, Birkenau, was built to implement the official policy of *Vernichtung Durch Arbeit*, Destruction Through Work.

As this suggests, the extermination of European Jews and others was not the Germans' sole objective. They intended to gain useful work from the inmates before they died of starvation, exhaustion, brutality or disease, for Auschwitz was to be a profitable "business". Apart from the appropriation of prisoners' personal effects, including costly jewellery, the SS charged factories that had been purpose-built next to the camp four marks a day for skilled labourers and three for unskilled. The prisoners received none of this and at the end of 1943 the state's monthly earnings from slave labour reached two million Reichsmarks. Between 1940 and 1945 it is estimated that Auschwitz made a profit of 60 million marks.

The embezzlement of some of this money saw the camp's first commandant, SS Obersturmbannführer Rudolph Hoess, sacked in November 1943 – only to be reinstated later when the SS found his two successors to be less effective administrators.

The living conditions of the British POWs, whose numbers reached a peak of 1,400 in January 1944, were far superior to those of the Jewish inmates, but they worked in the same factories and, unlike German POWs held by the Allies, were never paid for their labour. Furthermore, unlike the Jewish survivors, they were not compensated for their suffering, which remains a bone of contention to this day.

The construction of Birkenau by POWs and civilian prisoners began in October 1941, and by March 1942 Auschwitz was fully operational as the focus of the Final Solution of the Jewish Question in Europe, complete with its first gas chamber at Birkenau. This abomination, a converted cottage, was referred to by Germans working at the camp as "The Little Red House". For 18 months, until September 1944, Jews and other "asocials" from all over the continent were transported to this hell on earth by cattle-truck.

Most of the various 40 satellite camps, miles from Auschwitz but under its jurisdiction, worked for the German armaments industry. Companies that used their slave labour, in foundries, coal mines, chemical plants etc included Krupp and Siemens, as well as IG Farben.

Monowitz (formerly the Polish village Monowice) became operational in October 1942. Situated four miles from

Birkenau, it was built alongside, and set up to service, IG Farben's giant synthetic rubber and petro-chemical works. It became known as Buna Camp. The IG Farben factory was built at enormous cost, 776 million Reichsmarks, with the aim of producing synthetic rubber and oil, though in the end neither was manufactured in any significant quantity.

The attempt to do so was overseen by German engineers who had a workforce of 29,000 by late 1944, including 8,000 German civilians, 13,000 foreign workers, 7,000 concentration camp inmates and 600 British POWs. The latter's story, and specifically that of Corporal Ron Jones, is the focus of this book.

That Ron Jones was ever in Auschwitz was the result of a double dose of extraordinarily bad luck. His job as a specialist engineer was a reserved occupation and his Army call up was due to a clerical error. Once enrolled in the South Wales Borderers misfortune struck again when, due to his absence on a drill course, he missed out on a job as Physical Training Instructor which would have kept him safe in the gym at Brecon throughout the hostilities.

Instead, captured by the Germans in North Africa, he was condemned to nearly three and a half years in captivity which left him a broken man, mentally as well as physically. Moreover, his suffering did not end with the Russian army's advance on Auschwitz at the end of January 1945, for the worst was yet to come during a horrific forced march that became known as the "Death March."

Unlike at least 200 of his comrades, Ron survived and went on to live a remarkable life. At 96 he still drives a car (he is one of a handful of nonagenarians in Britain to hold a licence), works part-time for an estate agent and continues to maintain a large, immaculate garden. His sterling efforts on behalf of the British Legion put men half his age to shame, and in February 2012 he was honoured by Newport Council for selling more than £10,000-worth of Remembrance Day poppies in local supermarkets.

The man is truly "one in a million", as his beloved football club, Newport County, have dubbed their longest-serving supporter, and his story deserves the widest possible audience.

This book also includes substantial testimony from some of Ron's former comrades in Auschwitz, notably Brian Bishop, who is still going strong at 93. Brian, who lives in Chard, Somerset, provides corroboration, amplification and in some cases a contrast to Ron's experiences.

Joe Lovejoy, October 2013

Chapter 1

"You're Next"

The belief that British prisoners of war at Auschwitz were protected by the Geneva Convention was shattered in shocking fashion within feet of Ron Jones on 20 February 1944, when a lance-corporal was shot dead by a camp guard at point-blank range, and Ron was told that he could be next.

Describing an event that was the stuff nightmares for decades later, Ron says: "I was working at the plant that was designed to make synthetic petrol from coal. This process involved big iron cylinders 60 to 70 feet high, full of clay filters for the fuel to run through. The Germans built three of them so that they could use two while cleaning the other. On this occasion I was there alongside a fella named Leslie Reynolds, from the RASC, with our usual supervisor, 'Meister' Beave, in charge.

"There were three of us there, and he asked Reynolds to go up top and clean. Reynolds didn't speak enough German to explain that he suffered from vertigo, and didn't have the right footwear for the icy conditions anyway. He knew that if he went up there, he'd fall off.

"Not understanding, 'Meister' Beave, who was actually a good boss, sent for a guard, and this *Unteroffizier*, Benno Franz, who nobody liked, arrived, pulled out his Luger pistol and signalled Reynolds to get up top immediately. When he didn't, the German shot him dead. Then I was told to do it, and I clambered up there like a bloody monkey. Poor Reynolds was just 27, no age really. It was terrifying to behold, and I've never been able to get it out of my mind, but of course it was the sort of thing that was happening to the Jews 24 hours a day.

"We never saw Franz again. Fair play, the German army guys weren't like that towards us. It was a one-off and there was hell to pay over it. They got rid of him straight away and I heard later that he was packed off to the Russian Front where it seems he died because there was no trace of him when they wanted to prosecute him after the war.

"Of course at the time, and for a while afterwards, there was a hell of a fuss about Reynolds' death. The mood was murderous when we got back to the camp that night, with fellows threatening to do all sorts. Nothing came of it, as far as I know, but I'm sure it would have done if Franz hadn't disappeared."

Ron was in shock at the time, and did not fully take in the event, but Lance Corporal L.J. Anderson, of the Military Police, put the murder on record in a statement given on 18 August 1947. He wrote:

"I was working in Arbeitskommando 711A from approximately February to June 1943. This was a working *kommando* of Stalag 8B and we were employed in the I.G. Farben factory at Auschwitz.

"The man in charge of the *kommando* was named Rittler and under him there were two *Unteroffiziers*, one of whom was named Schmidt and was a big man, the other, a small man, was unknown to me by name. This latter was half German and half Polish, was about 5ft 9ins in height, had a round, fresh-complexioned face, was of medium build with thickish shoulders and about 26 years of age. He was a good-looking man and always wore a superior air. In future he is referred to a Uoffizier X.

"One day when a working party returned from the factory they told us that one of their number had been shot. They said that they had been told to climb a scaffolding and that they had refused as it was icy and they were wearing wooden-soled shoes. Uoffizier X lost his temper as they would not obey his shouts and he turned and fired at one of them. He hit L/Cpl Reynolds in the chest. Two of our men then carried him into the workshop outside which they were standing and laid him on a bench. He was dead. The Uoffizier then marched the rest of the party back to camp.

"Two days later I saw Uoffizier X again when he came to visit the party with which I was working. We were causing some trouble as the manager was trying to make us do some work we did not want to do. Uoffizier X arrived and spoke to us by means of an interpreter from among our group. He said: 'I shot one of your comrades the other day and if you are not careful I'll shoot one of you.' He then said words to the effect that nothing would happen to him.

"Uoffizier X was only at the camp for about two more months."

The murder was not Franz's only war crime. He was investigated after the war for bayoneting Private "Jock" Campbell and a lengthy investigation saw various Germans interrogated by the British Army's War Crimes section. On 3 January 1947 Group Captain F.N. Potts, of the section's legal staff, wrote the following:

"Unteroffizier Benno Franz shot and killed Reynolds with his revolver when a party of prisoners of which Reynolds was a member refused to work because of dangerous weather conditions and lack of proper equipment. The accused also stabbed Private Campbell in the back whilst the latter was assisting a Polish girl to carry a pail of soup from the cookhouse.

"The killing of Corporal Reynolds took place at the IG Farben Chemical Works at Auschwitz, where the party was employed on constructional work."

Group Captain Potts added: "Dr [Lothar] Heinrich [of IG Farben] was employed at the factory and was responsible, among other things, for the provision of safety belts for men employed on constructional work."

The Army's War Crimes section authorised searches for both Franz and Heinrich, to no avail. An early lead to the effect that Franz had been transferred from Poland to Yugoslavia proved to be a red herring. Either he died before the war's end, or he literally got away with murder. Heinrich, too, was never found. For a time, the legal section of the War Crimes group pursued the wrong Lothar Heinrich – a chemist instead of a construction engineer.

The case file, the original of which is held by the National Archives, at Kew, was closed on 20 January 1948 with the following final entry:

"Killing of Cpl Reynolds:

"The present position in this case has now been carefully considered and as it would appear that Benno Franz is unlikely to be traced it is agreed that Doctor Lothar Heinrich may be released. It is not considered that any further action can usefully be taken in this case."

Another atrocity, in which six British POWs were said to have been killed for refusing to work properly, is mentioned in two books. Both *The History of Auschwitz IG Farben*

Work Camps, published by the Auschwitz-Birkenau State Museum, and *Death Dealer*, the memoirs of Auschwitz camp commandant Rudolph Hoess, state that on or about 16 April 1944 the six were shot "for not working hard enough", and that the rest of the POWs downed tools and left the site in protest.

However, no names are given in either book, and there is no trace of such an incident in the comprehensive records held at the Imperial War Museum, or the National Archives, and the Ex-Prisoners of War Association has no knowledge of it. Ron Jones says he has "never heard of it", adding "I certainly would have done in there."

Benno Franz escaped justice, but another German did get his just deserts at the time. Ron explained: "One of their lot was murdered in the camp. A new prisoner, named Miller, arrived on his own one day, which was unheard of, so we were wary of him from the start. Then he started asking questions all the time, which made him all the more suspicious. I was never in contact with him myself, but we all knew about him. He said he was from the Green Howards, but inquiries were made back at Stalag V111B, where he was supposed to have come from, and nobody there from his regiment had heard of him.

"It was all so obvious that in the end some of the lads took him over to the toilets, which were just a hole in the ground, and dumped him in, where he drowned in the cess pool. Nasty, but no nastier than what the SS were doing to the Jews.

"We never heard anything about it from the guards, which we certainly would have done if a genuine POW had gone missing, so that was a giveaway. He was one of theirs all right, their spy in the camp."

In view of all of this, it was regarded as a sick joke when the Germans invited British POWs to rejoin the war – on their side. The Nazis, however, didn't do humour, they were in deadly earnest.

With their situation steadily deteriorating, and manpower losses critical, Hitler's armies needed all the help they could get, especially on the Eastern Front, and *in extremis* they sought assistance from the most unlikely of sources.

In late 1943 a traitor by the name of John Amery toured the camps, seeking volunteers for what was to be known as the British Free Corps. In advance of his visits, the Germans had distributed a leaflet, which read as follows:

"As a result of repeated applications from British subjects from all parts of the world wishing to take part in the common European struggle against Bolshevism, authorisation has recently been given for the creation of a British volunteer unit. The British Free Corps publishes herewith the following short statement of the aims and principles of the unit.

1. The British Free Corps is a thoroughly British volunteer unit, conceived and created by British subjects from all parts of the Empire who have taken up arms and pledged their lives in the common European struggle against Soviet Russia.

2. The British Free Corps condemns the war with Germany and the sacrifice of British blood in the interests of Jewry and international finance, and regards this conflict as a fundamental betrayal of the British people and British Imperial interests.

3. The British Free Corps desires the establishment of peace in Europe, the development of close friendly relations between England and Germany and the encouragement

of mutual understanding and collaboration between the two great Germanic peoples.

4. The British Free Corps will neither make war against Britain or the British Crown, nor support any action or policy detrimental to the interests of the British people."

The unit, formed on 1 January 1944, was intended to be part of the Waffen SS, but it never saw any fighting. Its maximum strength was 27 malcontents and malingerers, with nobody deemed suitable for officer rank. Amery, its recruiter, was the louche son of the then British Secretary of State for India, Leo Amery, who was part of Churchill's war cabinet. Amery junior was hanged as a traitor in Wandsworth Prison on 19 December 1945, aged 33.

Chapter 2

You're in the Army Now

The onset of the Second World War found the British Army totally unprepared to fight the German Wehrmacht. Conscription had been scrapped in 1918 at the end of the First World War, and in 1937, with renewed hostilities increasingly likely, Britain's army was just 200,000 strong.

The Prime Minister, Neville Chamberlain, was an appeaser rather than a fighter, but even he realised a more effective impediment was needed if Herr Hitler, as he called him, was to be deterred from his ambition to conquer the whole of mainland Europe.

Accordingly, the Emergency Powers (Defence Act) was passed in August 1938, calling up military reservists and expanding the Territorial Army and RAF Volunteer Reserve. It was not enough, however, and with Hitler's aggressive intent increasingly evident, Parliament passed the Military Training Act in April 1939, requiring all men aged 20 and 21 to undertake six months military training. Even so, when war broke out, on 3 September 1939, Britain had an army of 897,000 to Germany's 2.5 million and France's 5 million.

Further legislation was needed to address the disparity, and the National Service (Armed Forces) Act rendered all men between the ages of 18 and 41 liable for conscription. As a result, by the end of 1939 just over 1.5 million men had been called up, with 1.1 million going to the army and the rest divided between the Royal Navy and the RAF.

There were exemptions to conscription, with certain jobs deemed essential to the war effort designated as "reserved occupations". These included merchant seamen, dock workers, miners, farmers, scientists, railwaymen and water, gas and electricity workers. As an engineering specialist, working for a company that produced steel forgings for tanks and aircraft, while pressing millions of army helmets, Ron Jones was considered one of these. He says:

"When war broke out in 1939 I was newly married and working as a wire drawer at Guest Keen in Cardiff. They used to call us the 'soapy holes' because we used to draw the wire through soap which used to get under your gloves and make a little hole in them, burning your hands. It was a specialist job, and I was the only one out of 40 of us that ever got called up. They brought women in to do other jobs, to free up men for the services, but women couldn't do ours because the work was too heavy for them. We were moving around great coils of wire, that sort of thing.

"In my case, getting called up was all down to a mix-up. Everybody had a medical examination, after which you had a form to fill in every six months to explain your call-up status. Your employer had to sign it to state that you were in a reserved occupation. I was working nights and at home in bed when my wife, Gwladys, came in and said: 'There's a letter here for you from the War Office.' I opened it and it was my call up papers. That woke me up all right! I got out of bed and went straight down to the works.

"It was a cock-up. According to the personnel manager, my last completed form got put into the incoming mail instead of the outgoing, so there was no record of it at the War Office. There was nothing he could do about it. 'Thanks very much,' I said to myself. When I ended up in Auschwitz, I often thought: 'Bloody hell, this is ridiculous. I shouldn't have been in the Army anyway.'

"To join up I got on the train on the old Brecon and Merthyr Railway (what was my station then is now Junction 28 on the M4), and went to Brecon under protest to report to the South Wales Borderers. I arrived in September 1940 and during the first six months I was there, the firm made three attempts to get me back, but each time the company commander found an excuse not to let me go. The first time he said: 'You've got to do three months basic training first, then we'll see about it.' Then it was: 'Oh no, you're in now and it's been extended to six months.'

"I could see he wasn't going to release me, and next he sent me on a cadre course and made me a lance-corporal. The course lasted six weeks and taught you how to train others and how to give drill commands and get everybody moving quickly and in unison. We had to shout so much that they gave us Vaseline for our throats.

"Once I had completed the course, the C.O. said: 'Oh no, we're short of NCOs, we can't let you go.' I never appealed against the decision, but my firm did. They wanted me back. I'd been with them a long time, first of all in Rogerstone, where I was born, then in 1937 they moved everything to the docks in Cardiff – from the smelting to the finished article.

"Like me, Gwladys thought my call up was all a mistake that would quickly be rectified, and when it wasn't she was terribly upset. We hadn't been married that long and parting was the last thing we wanted. But all my mates were getting called up, and we thought we had to accept it.

"My twin brothers, Melvyn and Leslie, were also called up. Mel was working in a brickyard in Risca at the time and smashed his fingers badly on one hand – they had to be amputated – so the Army discharged him almost at once – straight after basic training. Les was in the Territorial Army before the war so he was drafted in to join the regulars straight away. He was in Malta when I was in Africa. He served all over Europe and I got my discharge before him.

"Once I was in the Army, they paid me two shillings [10p] a day, half of which went direct to Gwladys. When I got made up to lance-corporal I think my money doubled.

"Different regiments worked different ways, but with the war coming, the Army decided everybody should be trained the same way, to make changing your unit easier. So the South Wales Borderers picked two NCOs, me and a fella named Jenkins, who was from Pontypridd, and sent us to the Scots Guards barracks in London. There they taught us how to drill so that we could go back to our regiment and teach them do it the Guards' way.

"While I was with the Guards, in Chelsea, sergeant-major Reardon, who was in charge of the gymnasium back in Brecon, retired and they were looking for someone to take over from him in the fantastic gym they had there. Someone who had seen me working in the gym recommended me, but I was up in London, and they couldn't find me quickly enough so they gave the job to Corporal Phillips, from Cardiff, who stayed there all through the bloody war! I didn't find out until I came back. Instead of Auschwitz, I could have spent the war in Brecon. Fate, eh?"

The change of unit, which lay behind the homogenizing of drill etc, occurred in 1941, after the army's defeat in Crete. In April that year Hitler gave the go ahead for Operation

Merkur, which saw the invasion of the Greek island by the parachutists of General Karl Student's X1 Fliegerkorps.

Britain had occupied Crete in November 1940 and Brigadier O.H. Tidbury, the first commander there, had identified potential airborne drop zones, including Heraklion and Maleme. Intelligence intercepts then confirmed that the Germans would indeed be using Heraklion and Maleme.

Major General Bernard Freyberg VC, commander of the New Zealand Division, arrived to take charge of the island's defences on 29 April. Fatally, he deployed only a single New Zealand battalion to defend Maleme airfield, which was the Germans' main objective. On 6 May further intelligence revealed that the Germans were planning to land two airborne divisions – double the force Freyberg had been briefed to expect.

The operation was launched on 20 May, when 40 gliders landed at Maleme, followed by Junkers Ju52 transport planes dropping parachutists along the coast. Forewarned of the attack, Freyberg's men reacted well. Many of the transport planes were shot down and the Germans who did land suffered the sort of casualties that bordered on massacre.

At 12th Army headquarters, in Athens, Field Marshal Wilhelm List, who was in overall command, favoured aborting the operation but General Student ignored his superior and reinforced the beleaguered invaders with every available reserve to be dropped near Maleme, where Allied defences were at their weakest and quickly overwhelmed.

Freyberg, who had thought the invasion would come by sea, refused to sanction a concerted counter-attack, holding back his strongest unit, the Welch Regiment, because he still expected a seaborne attack. When such an attack did come, it was annihilated by the Royal Navy, and the general believed the island was safe. He could not have been more wrong.

Having taken control of Maleme airfield, the Germans poured in reinforcements at the rate of 20 planes per hour, and the defence of the island was doomed. British reinforcements, in the form of a commando brigade, arrived at Suda Bay, in time to learn that Crete was being abandoned.

The regimental history of the South Wales Borderers records the débâcle as follows:

"Undeterred by heavy casualties, the Germans continued to send in wave after wave of fresh airborne troops, and within a week they were virtually in control of Crete. The 1st Welch losses were equally heavy... The battalion's last stand came on 28 May when, virtually isolated in their Suda Bay position, they were overwhelmed by the onslaught of nine German battalions.

"After a desperate fire-fight the remnants withdrew in scattered groups, but not all of them managed the 40-mile mountainous trek to the British base at Sphakia, where the Navy was organising evacuation.... On 1 June 1941 all that remained of 1st Welch disembarked at Alexandria. They numbered seven officers and 161 other ranks.

"They had left behind in Crete some 250 dead, while 400-odd had been marched into captivity. In September the strength was made up with a draft of 700 officers and men from home."

Ron Jones takes up his story as follows: "That was how I came to join the Welch Regiment. With the Borderers, I went out to Egypt in August 1941. The 1st Battalion of the Welch Regiment had been shot up badly in Crete, the remnants were brought back to Cairo and a contingent of Borderers was sent to make them up to full strength again.

"We were shipped out from Liverpool on a luxury liner called the *Orcades*, sailing in convoy, protected by Royal

Navy destroyers and cruisers. We went via Nova Scotia then across the Atlantic to Freetown and then Durban. At Durban we boarded a Dutch ship that took us up to Port Taufiq, the entrance to the Suez Canal. The whole journey took nearly two months because we had to zigzag to avoid enemy submarines. I heard that a lot of convoys ran into trouble, but fortunately we didn't.

"While we were on board ship we were training all the time – weapons training mainly. I also remember being part of a team that won a tug-of-war competition, and the captain gave the eight of us cigarette cases, embossed with a carving of the *Orcades* crossing the Blue Lagoon. The ship was a cruise liner, but modified for our purpose. They filled the cabins with three-tier bunks, but it was a luxury ship and we were well looked after – very well indeed.

"I was in Cairo, training, for about a month, in a place called The Citadel. After that the 1st Battalion the Welch regiment went 'up the blue', as we called it, into the desert, where the conditions were dreadful. It was boiling hot in the day and bitterly cold at night. And there was always a shortage of water. We got a litre per day, for washing and everything. You didn't drink all your tea, you had to keep some of it to shave with in the morning. What water we did get was almost undrinkable. Terrible.

"We slept in little bivouacs, which were fold up tents. We had to cope with scorpions and sandflies, but worst of all were the persistently aggressive desert flies, which swarmed all over you and your food when you were eating or going to the toilet. Dysentery was a problem because of those buggers.

"We were attached to the 4th Indian Division, so most of our rations were the same as theirs. We had a lot of Indian food. Because of their religion and its peculiar hygiene, we were issued with an additional small bottle of water every day. The Indians used it to clean their backsides, they wouldn't use toilet paper. The water situation was always desperate, made worse by the weather. We used to get sandstorms. It would get very hot and windy, and all of a sudden the storm would be on us and the sand would get everywhere, inside your clothes, everywhere.

"I don't remember it raining at all, not once, but I do remember mirages. You'd see a line of troops or a line of armoured cars in the distance, surrounded by mist. They weren't there really, it was a mirage. We used to get a lot of them, they were frightening until you got used to it.

"But the flies were definitely our worst plague. We'd whitewash the toilet walls and within minutes they were black with swarms of the buggers. Most of the fellas had vaccinations against the diseases you could get out there, but I never had any jabs. My father didn't believe in vaccination and passed that view on to me.

"When we were youngsters there was an outbreak of diphtheria locally and everybody was getting inoculated but my father wouldn't have it and none of us caught it. Then there was a scarlet fever epidemic, and everybody went to the infirmary for jabs. Not us, and again we never had it. My father would say to mother: 'Daisy, they won't catch it. I think the injections can cause it by giving a small dose of it.' We never had measles, whooping cough or all the other things kids were vaccinated for.

"When I got called up it was part of the process that you were vaccinated against all sorts but, because of my father, I didn't have the jabs. I got somebody else to sign my paybook to say I'd had it done. On the ship, going out to Egypt, it came over the tannoy to take our paybooks to prove we'd been vaccinated against malaria and everything else and again somebody else signed for me. I think dad was right.

"Out in the Middle East, fellas who'd had the injections were going down with malaria and all sorts, but I never caught anything. It was the same when I was a POW, prisoners were going down with dreadful illnesses, but not me. Touch wood, I've never even had 'flu. I get a letter every year, asking me to have a 'flu jab, but I always say: 'No thanks.' I'll never have one.

"While I was out in the Middle East, I received some bad news. I got a letter saying my parents had been bombed out of our home in Rogerstone. A landmine fell in Park Avenue and my mother and father had their house wrecked. The family sheltered under the stairs when they heard the air raid sirens and after a while my father said: 'I'll go and see what's going on.' As he came out from under the stairs the landmine dropped and the back door was blasted off and hit him on the back of the head. He was laid out, unconscious. He came round and recovered, but about ten years after the war he started suffering with terrible headaches.

"Eventually I took him to see a surgeon who operated on him and found a tumour over the brain. In those days there was none of the treatment you get now and they couldn't do anything about it. He died six months later, only 62. The surgeon said to me: 'Your dad must have had a terrible blow on the head at some time to cause that' and my mother told him: 'I know what that was, it was when we were bombed out.' So my dad was gassed in the First World War and died as a result of an injury received in the Second. My mother lived to the age 89.

"Of course war doesn't stop because your parents have been bombed, and we advanced to Bardia, then Tobruk and eventually to Benghazi. The 5th Indian Brigade had left the 4th Division by this time; they were detached to go and fight in Syria. Fortunately the Italians we were up against had so little stomach for it that I never came under fire at any stage in North Africa, so I never fired a shot in anger in the war."

For the Allied "Desert Rats", accustomed to easy successes against the poorly equipped, low morale Italians, a nasty shock was coming. General (later Field Marshal) Erwin Rommel arrived in North Africa in February 1941 with his Afrika Korps, briefed to seize the Middle East and its oil. To his disgust, he found that his retreating Italian allies had thrown away their weapons, intent only on escape. Rommel stiffened their resolve by deploying them between German units and launched his first major attack in April, when the Italian Brescia Division took Benghazi and the Germans besieged Tobruk.

In June, Prime Minister Winston Churchill replaced General Sir Archibald Wavell with General Claude Auchinleck as commander-in-chief and demanded a more aggressive prosecution of the war in the desert. After building up his forces, Auchinleck attacked on 18 November with Operation Crusader, which saw the newly-constituted Eighth Army, under Lieutenant General Sir Alan Cunningham, cross the Libyan frontier with the intention of raising the siege of Tobruk.

General Freyberg's New Zealanders distinguished themselves, partially restoring their commander's reputation, which had been tarnished in Crete, but Allied tanks took a terrible battering from the German artillery. Cunningham wanted to withdraw, but Auchinleck overruled him and on 26 November the tide turned and the New Zealanders captured key airfields at Sidi Rezegh and Lambut, thereby denying the

Luftwaffe forward bases. That same day the Tobruk garrison broke out and joined up with Freyberg's men.

With the Afrika Korps in disarray, Auchinleck replaced Cunningham who was deemed too timid, with Major General Neil Ritchie, who took up the attack westward. In December, however, Hitler transferred troops from the Eastern Front to reinforce Rommel and the balance of power changed again.

Ron says: "We got to Benghazi in December 1941 and had our Christmas dinner there, but by the second week in January we knew there was trouble coming. There were a lot of rumours. Typically, the Italians stayed behind when Rommel made his move on 21 January '42, with 50 tanks in two columns.

"The General they called 'The Desert Fox' was a genius, and with a clever feint he deceived our lot into thinking that his target was to cut the coast road at Mechili, to the east of Benghazi, and not the city itself. Fooled by his deception, we began evacuating the 4th Indian Division on the 27th. That left our defences depleted when he made his real move.

"On the 29th Sergeant-Major Cogbill came to me and said: 'Corporal Jones, take a section up the road and see what's going on.' So ten of us went, and what should come down the road to meet us but a bloody great tank with a black cross on it. There was an officer up on the turret who said in perfect English: 'Come on boys, the war is over for you.' I had a sub-machine gun, the rest of the lads had rifles, and none of those were any use against armoured vehicles, so we dropped them in the ditch by the side of the road and surrendered. One of the lads, a fella called McGuffock, was a bit slow doing it, so the tank fired a warning shot over his head. That did it – he dropped his rifle then all right!

"The irony of the situation was that in normal circumstances

I was part of a two-man team operating an anti-tank rifle. An officer, Second Lieutenant Phillips from Newport, used to carry the gun and I had the heavy iron tripod. I remember the thing had a hell of a recoil. Unfortunately on this recce we didn't have the weapon or the officer with us, and I went 'into the bag' at the end of January '42. I think we were among the first to be captured. The Indian 7th Brigade escaped in the nick of time.

"Up to this point we'd been fighting only Italians, no Germans. Rommel's arrival with the Afrika Korps changed everything. With the Italians, you just had to point a rifle at them and they gave up by the thousand. In a two-month period during 1941 they lost 150,000 men, 800 pieces of artillery and 400 tanks, mostly surrendered. We lost just 2,000 men. When our lot first came up against them, we took 38,000 prisoners in three days for the loss of 624 of our own.

"The Italians marched happily into captivity, glad to be out of danger, but the Germans were totally different, real fighting men. They captured the entire battalion, then handed us over to the Italians, who put us on some trucks and took us to Tripoli. The journey was over 600 miles and seemed to take forever.

"I had some good mates in Africa, but a couple were killed and when we were captured the rest of us were split up. The only one I stayed with was a fella called Albert Mellish, whose father kept the Tredegar Arms in Bassaleg in those days. He survived the war in other camps to me, then the poor man went on holiday and had a heart attack.

"The Italians had very little discipline, they were scared of us until we were disarmed, then they became bullies. The Germans took us by truck to Tripoli, where they handed us over to the Italians. They had us in a camp for a week or so, before we were put on small cargo boats and taken to the Italian mainland. During that first week they lined us up one day, looking for rings and watches. I had a signet ring on one hand and I couldn't get it off. An Italian was going to cut my finger off to get it, but a German officer spotted him and tore into him. He went wild. The German Wehrmacht wouldn't tolerate things like that.

"From then on, every time there was a search by the Italians I'd take the ring off and stick it up my arse. I had nowhere else to hide it and not even the Italians would go there! It wasn't just me, the other lads were doing the same.

"I managed to keep that ring all through the prison camps, Auschwitz included, until I got home. Then someone pinched it off me in work, back at Guest Keen – my own bloody workmates – after all I'd been through."

Brian Bishop was born and raised in west London and followed in his father's footsteps by joining the Regular Army in 1938, aged 18. He originally favoured the Royal Marines, but when he went for their medical examination he had a heavy cold, and was told to come back when he was fully fit. In the interim he was advised to join a regiment that would teach him a trade, for later in life, and so chose the Royal Corps of Signals.

Evacuated from Dunkirk on 1 June 1940, on one of the last small boats to leave, he was posted to Aldershot to retrain for the only motorised division left after the retreat from France. Like Ron Jones, he was then sent to North Africa and captured by the Germans in one of Rommel's encirclements, some 20 miles south of Tobruk.

The Wehrmacht passed these prisoners on to the Italians

in circumstances that seemed amusing at the time. In an interview for this book, Brian said: "Rommel got up on his command vehicle and addressed us all. He apologised for handing us over to the Italians and explained that they had taken no prisoners of their own, and were getting us to raise their morale!"

Brian subsequently followed much the same route as Ron, from north Africa to Italy, then to Germany and finally to Auschwitz. There was one notable difference. "I had no trouble with the Italians," Brian said. "The commanding officer at the second POW camp I was sent to in Italy had a son who had been captured by our lot and was a POW in Canada, so he treated us well in the hope that we would be doing the same for his boy."

Ron Jones takes up his own story: "On 14 March 1942 Gwladys received a telegram that frightened her half to death and had her weeping uncontrollably. It was from the Army and came in standard printed form, with the names and dates filled in by a clerk, in ink. It read as follows:

I regret to have to inform you that a report has been received from the War Office to the effect that No 3914334, Lance Corporal Ronald William Godfrey Jones, the Welch Regiment, was posted as 'missing' on the 28th January 1942 in the Middle East

The report that he is missing does not necessarily mean that he has been killed, as he may be a prisoner of war or temporarily detached from his regiment.

Official reports that men are prisoners of war take some time to reach this country, and if he has been captured by the enemy it is probable that unofficial news will reach you first. In that case I am to ask you to forward any postcard or

letter received at once to this office, and it will be returned to
you as soon as possible.

Should any further official information be received it will
be at once communicated to you.

"Of course Gwladys feared the worst. She thought I was dead and she got herself into a terrible state. She heard nothing to ease her pain for two months, and when she found out that I was OK and a prisoner of war it came not from the Army but from what the telegram had called 'unofficial news'.

"A woman from Scotland wrote to Gwladys, saying she had heard Lord Haw Haw mention my name on the radio in one of his propaganda broadcasts from Germany. So Glwadys learned that I was alive that way, a week before she received a letter from the War Office, confirming that I was a prisoner of war. Bloody ridiculous.

"Before we were transported to Italy, they separated us according to rank. They had four small cargo boats for the purpose, and of the four of them only two made it to Naples. The private 'squaddies' were on one and the NCOs on the other. The two for warrant officers and officers were sunk by our own navy.

"A few years ago I went on holiday to Denia, in Spain, and Gwladys and I went into the restaurant one night and sat at a table for four. An elderly couple came and took the other two places, and we hit it off and sat with them at dinner every night, and during the entertainment afterwards. It turned out the husband had been a petty officer in the Royal Navy, serving on a submarine in the Mediterranean when those two boats were sunk, and he thought he could remember them doing it. Small world, eh?

"Anyway, we were in Naples for a couple of nights, then

they took us to a POW camp at Alta Mura, down in the heel of Italy [30 miles south-west of Bari], where we were held from May 1942 until April '43. It was a transit camp, holding about 1,000 POWs on a stony piece of ground, exposed to the elements. The conditions were dreadful. There was no heating in our barracks in winter, so the lads would light fires using wooden slats from the beds, and rain turned the place into a sea of mud. The toilets were outside, just a bar over a trench. Local people passing by would laugh at us doing our business in the open air.

"The Italians gave us no work to do, we were just lolling about all the time, bored, so I had to find something to occupy myself and started sewing. When our socks were worn out and fell apart, the Italians gave us squares of white calico to wrap around our feet, and that material gave me something to sew with.

"A mate called Haydn John, from Pontypridd, had bought a wallet in Cairo which had the pyramids illustrated on it and, together, using threads I pulled from a groundsheet, we made two handsome-looking cloths, one with the Citadel, in Cairo, picked out on it and the other decorated with the crowns that the sergeant-majors wore – one in each corner and a big one in the middle. The Italian C.O. in charge of the camp came round and saw me doing it one day and gave me a bottle of wine, as a prize.

"I kept the two cloths in Auschwitz and on the long march to freedom, but lost them the day after we were liberated. The Americans sent us for de-lousing and I left them in my kitbag, along with a pair of binoculars and a Luger pistol which I'd pinched off the German guards when they cleared off, right at the end. Then, when I was free, our own men stole them from me."

Meanwhile, back in north Africa, General Bernard Montgomery and his Eighth Army finally defeated the Afrika Korps at El Alamein in November 1942, throwing the Italians into something approaching panic. Fearing invasion in the south, they wanted all POWs out of the way, to obviate the threat of a rising in support of an Allied landing, and hurriedly transferred them to the north of the country.

Ron says: "They took us to a place called Macerata [near Monte Cassino], which was also known as Sforzacosta, by train, and I had a nasty accident on the way up. We used to make what we called a blower, to cook on. The Italians gave us no cutlery, no plates and nothing to cook with but a lot of us were engineers and we devised a way to make our own. From nothing, really, we made a square metal plate-cum-cup which you could both eat off and drink out of. We used to make plates by flattening a tin. For mugs, we'd fit a handle to a Klim [powdered milk] tin.

"Cooking, or making tea, was a more difficult proposition. What we did have, from our Red Cross food parcels, was packets of tea and Klim, 'Klim' being 'milk' spelled backwards. Of course we needed something to boil the tea, so we came up with the blower. We'd take a piece of wood from a bed, about a foot long and six inches wide, and use a couple of Klim tins. We'd fasten one upside down and have the other the opposite way, with a piece of groundsheet wrapped around it, secured with a piece of wire that we'd get off the bales of straw we slept on. Then we'd cut a hole in the top and fasten a piece of the tongue, from our boots, in there. When you blew down, the tongue sealed the hole, when you opened it, the air rushed in, so you had a bellows. Then you'd take a piece of tin, again from the Red Cross parcels, and make a pipe from a fruit tin to connect the two. To seal the pipe we'd roll it in mud.

"On the other side of the contraption we'd use two oval-shaped pilchard tins, put one in the bottom and the other in top and ram it in tight. Knock nail-holes in one and you had a furnace. It used to take about a week to force the things in tight enough, using a stone. Job done, we'd pinch some charcoal from the cookhouse and that was our blower. Now we could brew our tea and coffee. The Italians wouldn't give us any hot water, so when the cook wasn't looking we'd shovel some of the hot coals into a tin for use in the blower.

"I don't know who made the first one, but eventually I made one myself. It took me about two months. Don't forget, we had no tools. I had a knife made from a metal tent peg, which was an aluminium pipe. I flattened one end into a strip, using a heavy stone, and to sharpen it I honed it, again against the stone. That took about a week.

"Anyway, we had one of these contraptions on the train to Macerata and I was laying on the luggage rack, having a kip, when someone shouted 'Brew up, Taffy'. Being Welsh, I was always 'Taffy' in the Army, no one called me Ron. So I jumped down with my bootlaces undone, just as the train went into a curve, and the whole lot went down into my boot. Red hot charcoal. I had a blister so big it was hanging down and touching the floor either side of my leg – huge it was.

"When we got to Macerata we had to march two or three miles to the camp and my mates tried to help me, but the Italian guards wouldn't let them, and pushed them away, using their rifles. I couldn't get my boot on, so I had to walk with the boot hanging around my neck.

"When we got to the camp there was no hospital, just a medical room. Our own lads took all the blistered skin off and wrapped my foot in something called Aquaflavin, which was olive oil mixed with some other stuff. I had my foot up, wrapped in that, for about a fortnight, and it worked a treat. I haven't got a scar of any sort – no marks there at all. Acquaflavin. Marvellous stuff."

Ron's less than favourable impression of the Italians is shared by Charles Rollings in his book, *Prisoner of War*, where he writes: "There was a great deal of difference between the behaviour of the two [Axis] armies towards their prisoners. The Afrika Korps tended towards chivalry while the Italians inclined towards brutality... much to the annoyance of the German troops, who had often to intervene. Italian camps were often sub-standard – even more so than the worst German camps – and the commandants and guards were generally more capricious than their Axis counterparts in the Greater Reich."

Ron says: "We were in Macerata until late July '43. Then the interpreter came round and said: 'Anybody here with engineering experience?' I asked why, and their guy said: 'We need people for the car factories in Milan.' By this time we were all physical wrecks. All we got to eat was what they called a 'piccolo panni', which was a little bit of bread, and a small piece of cheese. Sometimes there was potato soup, which was just like water.

"It was barely enough to keep us alive, but we had no strength. If we lay out in the sun it took us about ten minutes to get up, we were so weak. You'd get up on one knee and everything would go black, then on to the other knee and nearly pass out.

"Our treatment by the Italians was in breach of the Geneva Convention, there's no doubt about that, and I've never really understood why some of those responsible weren't prosecuted as war criminals. Perhaps it was because Italy changed sides midway through the war and became our allies. The Geneva Convention was properly interpreted by the British when dealing with German and Italian POWs, as follows:

1. From the moment of surrender, [enemy] soldiers are regarded as POWs and come under the protection of the Geneva Convention. Accordingly, their military honour is fully respected.
2. POWs must be taken to assembly points as soon as possible, far enough from the danger zone to safeguard their personal security.
3. POWs receive the same rations, qualitatively and quantitatively, as members of the Allied armies, and if sick or wounded, are treated in the same hospitals as our troops.
4. Decorations and valuables are to be left with the POWs. Money may be taken only by officers at the assembly points and receipts must be given.
5. Sleeping quarters, accommodation, bunks and other installations in POW camps must be equal to those of garrison troops.
6. According to the Geneva Convention, POWs must not become subject of reprisals, nor be exposed to public curiosity. After the end of the war they must be sent home as soon as possible.

"The Italians showed us no respect, as regards our 'military honour'. Quite the contrary, they tried to humiliate us whenever they could, especially in front of the local population. They did nothing to safeguard our personal security, gave us scraps for food, denied us proper medical treatment and our accommodation was a dump by comparison with their quarters. It was a disgrace.

"A lot of the Italian POWs ended up in Wales, and I've seen one of the camps used, near Bridgend. Not only did they have much better accommodation than us, they were treated a lot better, too. They worked on farms locally and were allowed out to meet the Welsh people. Quite a few married Welsh girls and stayed on after the war.

"We all knew we had to get away from Macerata if we could, so when we were offered the chance to work elsewhere a couple of hundred volunteered. We were put on a proper passenger train and travelled overnight before pulling up in a station, presuming it was Milan. Then we heard shouts of 'Raus, Raus!' and one of the lads said: 'Hey, that's German.' We'd stopped in the Alps, at the Brenner Pass, which separates Italy and Austria, and the Italians were handing us over to the Germans."

After the Allies had invaded Sicily in July 1943, and the Americans had bombed Rome for the first time, the Fascist Grand Council met on the 24th and passed a motion for the return to a constitutional monarchy and a democratic parliament. The dictator, Benito Mussolini, was ousted in favour of Marshal Pietro Badoglio, who became Prime Minister the following day. Badoglio promised Hitler that Italy would continue to fight as his ally, but the Germans were not convinced and seized the Brenner Pass and its environs with eight Wehrmacht divisions.

They were right to be sceptical. Italy surrendered on 3 September, at which stage they held some 70,000 Allied POWs. It was in August 1943, shortly before it happened, that Ron Jones and his mates were delivered into German hands – a fate shared by 53,000 of the 70,000.

Ron says: "Naturally the Germans didn't want us to be liberated to fight against them again, so they took us prisoner. Some of our lads elsewhere, in the south of Italy, did get away – they were allowed to walk out when the Italians gave up – but not us. No such luck. We were among the majority who were handed over to the Germans before the surrender.

"Back home, everybody thought the Italians' prisoners must have been released. Gwladys only found out otherwise from the local paper at the end of August, when a report in the *South Wales Argus*, under the headline "Newport Man in New Camp" read:

'It was announced in London last week that a preliminary report from the Swiss Government stated there was no confirmation of any British prisoners of war having been transferred from Italy to Germany since the Badoglio regime was set up.

'At the weekend a letter received in Newport proved that there has been movement of British prisoners of war from Italy to Germany, but in this case it seems to have been anticipatory – or it must have been done with remarkable speed.

'The fall of Mussolini was announced on Sunday night, July 25th. On July 28th Lance Corporal Ronald W.G. Jones wrote to his wife at Rosemead, Pye Corner, Newport from Stalag 1VB, Germany. The postmark on the letter was August 8th and it was received on August 27th. Previously he was at P.G. 53, eastern Italy, and he wrote from there on June 26th to say he was recovering from a foot scalded on the train journey from P.G. 65, southern Italy.

'The letter stated: "As you will note by the address, I have moved from Italy to Germany and I must say we are being treated by the Germans much better than the Italians. Of course our mail and parcels will be held up again for a while, but we will have to be patient. I can't tell anything about the journey that I would like to, but I saw some marvellous sights that I should never see in 'civvy street'.

"We have had a vaccination and an inoculation. It is against such things as smallpox etc. Under new conditions we are allowed two letters and two cards per month, so if people don't hear from me you can tell them the reason." '

Ron now says of that letter: "The reality wasn't quite as pleasant as I was suggesting to Glad because I didn't want to worry her. In Germany immediately things were very different. Everybody must have seen pictures of the Jews getting transported in cattle trucks, well we had the same treatment. They crammed 40 of us into each truck, and we were in there for two days before they let us out for some food. There was a lot of bombing going on, so they'd park us in sidings overnight.

"Eventually we arrived at camp Stalag 1VB at Muhlberg, north-west of Dresden, where the first thing they did was shave all our hair off. And I do mean *all* our hair – not just on our heads. They did it with a machine, like sheep shearers, then they daubed us all over with a dark disinfectant that smelled like creosote. I can still hear the guy that did it now. To every one of us he said: 'Come here', then 'Go away' when he'd finished. They were the only English words he knew! They put our uniforms through a delousing machine to kill the lice because by this time we were covered in the bloody things after the dreadful conditions in Italy.

"After a couple of months there, we were put in the cattle trucks again in October 1943 and it was four or five days before we arrived in Poland. Because of the poor food, we all had the runs and there was no toilet. We had to use one corner of the truck for that. There was no toilet paper, so we had to wipe our backsides on our shirt tails. The humiliation and degradation was appalling. We stunk to holy heaven.

"By the time we got to Lamsdorf [previously Lambinowice in Poland, the nearest town Krakow] I was a physical wreck with a long beard. We had no razors in Italy, they wouldn't allow it. Lamsdorf was a big holding camp, where you could clean yourself up before moving on. It was also a rest area, where the sick were sent from other camps. It had been used for the same purpose in the First World War."

At the start of the war Germany had 31 POW camps, but by late 1943 this figure had risen to 148. Lamsdorf was the largest, accommodating 10,537 British POWs in December 1943. In his excellent reference work *Prisoner of War*, Charles Rollings describes it as "One of the worst German camps, where there were repeated outbreaks of typhus and where POWs suffered from dysentery, diphtheria, tapeworm, lice and fleas."

Ron was only there for a matter of weeks. He says: "There was not much there to lift the spirits, but I did have one bit of luck. There was a butcher's shop in Newport market run by the Clayton family, and when I was walking from the train to the camp I heard a shout: 'Ron!' It was Jack Clayton, from Newport, so I had a mate, which was a big plus, psychologically.

"In fairness, the Germans gave us clean uniforms and razors, so at least we looked decent again. They also took photos of us with POW numbers (mine was 221728) underneath, like America's 'Most Wanted'."

The interview process to which the prisoners were subjected was like something from the FBI, too. Lance-corporal Maurice Jones, of the King's Shropshire Light Infantry, was curious when one of the camp's interpreters, who were all German-

Americans, asked him for his mother's maiden name. He stopped laughing when a Czech prisoner explained that the Nazis wanted to know if he might have any Jewish blood.

For the most part, however, the questions were to ascertain what sort of work suited each individual. In the German camps, every prisoner who wasn't an officer had to earn his keep. It was only the officers, who were held in different camps, called Oflags, who were excused work.

Lamsdorf, designated Stalag V111B, was a remarkable place. At one stage it had its own dance band (signature tune "The World is Waiting for the Sunrise"), an even bigger military band and a string orchestra. The 11-piece dance band, the Rolls Roysters, comprising two guitarists, a drummer, double bass and brass section, was pictured on stage, complete with bow ties, in the Spring 2010 newsletter of the National Ex-Prisoners of War Association. It was accompanied by the following rueful comment:

"These photos were marvellous propaganda for the Germans. They did not show any photos of us on night shift in the freezing cold, working on a building site, or at the coal face 300m below ground. Well they wouldn't, would they? I showed some to a friend and she thought I was at Butlins. There is no answer to that."

All the bands played in a theatre with seating for 600, and there were long queues for tickets. One show for which there was great demand was a concert featuring Beethoven's *Fifth Symphony*, played by a 50-piece orchestra that included a fair number of professional musicians.

Denholm Elliott, later to become a celebrated actor, was a prisoner at one time. As a wireless operator in the RAF, he had been shot down on his third mission. Incredibly, the POWs' production of Shakespeare's *Twelfth Night*, in which

Elliott played the part of Viola, was allowed out on tour, using costumes provided by the Breslau Opera. The venues they visited included Auschwitz.

The standard of entertainment may have been high, but the food, as ever, was both dreadful and in pitifully short supply. During an inspection of the camp by senior SS officers, one asked if the prisoners had any complaints, and Charles Waite, a private in the Queen's Royal Regiment, said more food would be welcome. The German looked him up and down with disdain before replying: "Grass is good enough for you people."

Ron Jones takes up his story: "I was only at Lamsdorf for the couple of months it took them to sort us out – who was going where and so on. There were 200,000 POWs in Poland, including the Russians, us, and the Americans, working in coal mines, on the railways, on farms etc. A mate of mine went to work in a coal mine in Katowice."

Brian Bishop, who was at Lamsdorf at the same time as Ron, recalls the circumstances in which he was sent to Auschwitz as follows:

"I hadn't been there [Lamsdorf] long and I was sitting on my own, looking miserable, when this bloke came up for a chat and asked me: 'What's the matter?' I said: 'I'm bloody hungry' and he told me: 'You want to go out on one of the working parties, they get better grub. If you get on one of the farms, you'll be well fed.' I said: 'Nah, I'm not working for the bloody Germans.'

"Anyway, the following day he came looking for me and said: 'They want names for a working party. Want to go?' I was still hungry and I changed my mind and put my name down. The next day we were loaded on to cattle trucks and where did we end up? Auschwitz."

Ron Jones says: "I was one of 280 sent to work in the IG Farben factory. Again we got on a train with no idea where we were going, and when we got off we were marching down the road when we came to all these barbed wire fences, sentry posts and men in pyjamas digging trenches. It was October, very cold, and they were in striped pyjamas. So one of us said to our guards: 'Who are they?' and I remember plainly a guard saying '*Juden*'. We said 'Who?' and he shouted: 'Jews!' – as if we should have known.

"They were all bound for the gas chambers; we were looking at dead men walking. We had arrived at a final destination, in more ways than one."

Chapter 3

How it all Began

Had his father had a different attitude to secondary education, Ron Jones could well have been an officer in the Army, in which case he would never have been sent to Auschwitz. Captured Allied officers were held in Oflag camps, non-commissioned ranks in Stalags, and officers were not made to work.

Obviously he didn't know it at that time, but Bill Jones did his son a terrible disservice when, against the teachers' advice, he took his son out of grammar school where he was an A stream pupil, at the age of 14. Ron, who was keen to stay on and pass the exams required to become an accountant, remembers being "very upset" by the decision.

He tells the story of his early life as follows:

"My dad, Bill, was an industrial blacksmith at GKN and my mother, Daisy, was a self-employed tailoress. She worked from home and there was always a crowd in our house, people having things made or altered. When I was a kid she used to pay me a shilling to clean the house every Saturday morning. I had to hang the rugs and matting on the line outside and pick all the bits off. I'd go over them with a magnet to get all mum's pins off.

"Dad wasn't into the domestic chores at all, he did nothing

at home. He'd been a regimental sergeant-major in the First World War, in the London Rifles. He was a big, robust man, but got invalided out of the Army after being gassed by the Germans at Ypres. I've still got his ceremonial cane.

"Because of the gassing, dad was ill for years with a bad stomach. I remember my mother steaming a lovely piece of fish for him for lunch, and on his way back to the factory he had to go to the toilet and bring it all back up. That sort of thing was a common occurrence, but he remained a big, strong man – certainly no invalid. He used to tell stories about his time in the First War. My favourite was how the Gurkhas used to go out of the trenches at night and come back with a few German heads they'd killed with these terrifying knives, called kukris.

"I had a decent education, going to Pontywaun grammar school. When I passed the entry examination, the headmaster came to see my parents to congratulate them because I was the first pupil he'd ever had who produced an all-correct maths paper. At 14 I was doing pretty well in school, seventh in the class, but my parents went to see the governors to get me out. They wanted me to go to work. They had four children younger than me, twin boys and two girls (they are all dead now), and my parents said it was time I was earning. So my father got me an apprenticeship at Guest Keen (GKN), working with him.

"I wanted to stay on at school, and having to leave really upset me. I wanted to be an accountant because I was good at figures, but there you are – life was hard in those days. My father was a tradesman and he wanted all his kids to have a trade, he wasn't interested in the professions. One of my brothers was a decorator, his twin was a brickie. One sister was a hairdresser and the other went into the print.

"They were wonderful parents, don't get me wrong, but factory work definitely wasn't what I wanted to do. After the war, when I had my own son, Leighton, I was so incensed about what had happened to me that I said to my wife, Gwladys: 'If I've got to go out scrubbing floors I'll do it to give Leighton the chance I never had.'

"When he was seven I sent him to a private prep school, called Rougemont, and he did so well there that they told me they wanted him to sit the entrance exams for public school. They gave me a list of six and I chose three. I took him to Christ College, in Brecon, to the Hereford Cathedral School and to Haberdashers, in Monmouth. He passed the exams for all three and said: 'Dad, I'd love to go to Monmouth', so at ten-and-a-half he became a boarder there. He was a natural at school and could have gone to Cambridge University, but chose Liverpool instead. He went on to make a name for himself as the managing director of a major international company, travelling all over the world, so it all paid off. He's achieved what I might have done, which is wonderful.

"As a lad, my big interest was football. My father had been a goalkeeper and I played for the local team in goal, winning a competition called the Woodcock Cup. I was also a fanatical fan, supporting Newport County. I've watched County for 87 years. The first time I went down to the old Somerton Park ground in Newport was on the crossbar of my father's bike. I was seven and I've been a supporter ever since. I've followed them to every ground bar two – Newcastle and Sunderland. That was a bit far in the old pre-motorway days! The County have had me on their website, calling me 'One in a Million'.

"At one time Newport and Cardiff City never played at home on the same day, so I'd go to Newport one week and Cardiff the next. I couldn't always afford to travel away with

County, but I've always been an ardent supporter. I was there when they got to the quarter-finals of the old European Cup-Winners' Cup and were knocked out by an East German team, Carl Zeiss Jena, who went on to lose the final. Jena were a bloody good team – the best I've seen County play. And I was at Wembley when they played there for the first time, in the 2012 FA Trophy final. For seven years, in the Sixties, I was secretary of the supporters' club, but then Gwladys had a breast removed because of cancer and I had to give it up for her sake.

"I met her when she was 16 and I was 17, so we were almost childhood sweethearts. I saw her for the first time after she'd been to the Girl Guides. There was a guy with us, Wally Scouse, who fancied himself as a bit of a wit, and he said to Gwladys: 'You've got your dark blue bloomers on tonight, have you Glad?', referring to her uniform. That gave us a laugh and broke the ice.

"After that first meeting, if there were any social evenings, nine times out of ten it was me and Gwladys who paired up. We started courting properly when I was 18, and it was soon getting serious. Glad was very insistent on the extra letter, W, in her Christian name. It had to be spelled the Welsh way; she was a proud Welsh speaker. Her mother came from west Wales, Ystradgynlais, and we used to go down there for weekends.

"Anyway, at first I was going back and forth to see her on my bike. It wasn't far as she was a Bassaleg girl, which is pretty close to Rogerstone. Her father, Tom, had a brother, Fred, a policeman in Newport whose wife had died, and Fred said to Tom one evening: 'You're lucky to have a daughter looking after you.' Gwladys had been a nurse, but by this time she was staying at home to look after her mother, who was an invalid. Tom said: 'You can have her if you want to.' He was only joking, but Fred took him at his word and said: 'Do you mean it?' Then he said to Glad: 'You come and live with me as my housekeeper – you can have the front bedroom and I'll go in the back – and I'll give you £1 a week.' We're talking about 1937, when £1 was quite a lot of money, so Gwladys moved in there.

"This meant I was back and forth to Edward Street, in Newport to see her, which is a much longer journey, and one day her uncle Fred said to me: 'Why don't you two get married and live here?' So I asked Glad, but she wasn't interested in getting married at that stage. I wasn't put off, I kept on about it, and one Friday night I said to her: 'Come on, what about this marriage?' A friend of hers, Ann, was getting married the following day and Glad was going to the wedding, so my mother had made her a smart suit for the occasion. Glad told me: 'I'll tell you what I'll do. If it rains tomorrow I won't go to the wedding in my new outfit, I'll keep it back to wear and we'll get married.'

"When I went to work the next morning the bloody sun was shining, but then by 9 o'clock it was pissing down! I started to laugh, and the boys I was working with asked: 'What's up with you?' I said, 'I think I'm going to get married because of this pissing rain!' Anyway, I went home, had a shower, got changed and went down to Edward Street, only to find out that Gwladys had gone to the wedding after all.

"She came back at about 7 o'clock and I asked her if she'd worn her new outfit. 'Of course not,' she replied. So I said, 'Are you going to keep your promise?' and she told me, 'Yes, all right then.' So we ran into town and bought an engagement ring from a jewellers at the bottom of Stow Hill.

"When we told my mother that we were engaged and

going to get married, she was overjoyed. 'Don't get married in that suit,' she said to Glad. 'Keep it for your honeymoon.' My mother made her a lovely wedding dress and we were married in 1938. For our honeymoon we went to Dudley Zoo. Glad's sister was married to a keeper up there, Harry Young, and they had a house inside the grounds. So we spent our honeymoon among the animals! We didn't have the money to do anything else.

"When we got back we went to live with Uncle Fred, but Glad was never very well in Newport. She didn't have a strong constitution and always seemed to have something wrong with her. In Edward Street she constantly had a cold and eventually our doctor told her, 'Gwladys, you want to get back into the Bassaleg fresh air. Living here is no good for you.' The problem was that Edward Street in Newport was one of those narrow terraced roads. To see the sun you had to go out the back and look for it, and Gwladys wasn't used to that.

"Fortunately this woman we knew in Bassaleg, Mrs Jobbins, offered to split her house into two to accommodate us. She went to live upstairs and we had the downstairs. That was fine for us, and that's how things were when I got called up.

"Before that, though, I was in the Home Guard, of *Dad's Army* fame, from when the war started in September 1939. Our unit was supposed to protect the factory from the German invasion everybody thought was coming, but the only action we saw was at the cards table in the canteen. I won quite a lot of money one night, playing cards, so I went into town the next day and paid £5 or £6 for a Westminster chiming clock. We had that clock for 40 years or more before it ended up in a box in the attic.

"It went wrong and I couldn't get it repaired properly. Eventually this shop in Newport mended it, but at 12 o' clock it struck 13 and Gwladys didn't like that, so it went up in the attic. She thought we'd had enough bad luck."

Chapter 4

Welcome to Hell

Everyone who arrived at Auschwitz, guards and prisoners alike, were agreed – the first thing they noticed was the smell. The nauseating odour of burning flesh, from the crematoria, was something they would remember for the rest of their lives, be that a matter of hours, days or decades.

Seventy years on, Ron Jones still gets flashbacks from the aroma of meat cooking. It has been a common complaint. Jack Stevens, a Grenadier Guardsman in Monowitz, told the story of how his next-door neighbour burnt the Sunday roast, forcing Jack to leave his house and go for a walk in nearby woods because the smell brought back terrible memories.

Jack, like Ron, was taken prisoner in North Africa and ended up a slave worker for IG Farben. During the Allied bombing raid when 38 POWs were killed, he received injuries to his eyes which left him scarred for the rest of his life. The years in Monowitz left him a physical wreck, his extreme anxiety manifested in tremors and convulsions, diagnosed as motor hysteria.

Brian Bishop said: "If the wind was blowing in the wrong direction, you could smell this awful sickly smell. That upset me more than anything I think. For the smell alone I would have preferred to stay in the Italian POW camps."

The SS garrison (and their families) were spared the awful odour when they were off duty. Like the camp administrators and secretaries, they were allowed to live in the town.

Witnessing the persecution of the Jews was harrowing to the point of psychological damage and being forced to work for the enemy intensely demeaning, but for Ron Jones it was another aspect of his confinement that troubled him most deeply. He says: "For me, the worst thing about being incarcerated in Auschwitz was not the horrific treatment of the Jews, the starvation rations or the work I was forced to do for the German war effort, which was against the Geneva Convention. All that was dreadful, and the cause of nightmares for years afterwards, but worse still, personally, was the sheer humiliation of being a prisoner of war. It was absolutely terrible, it made me feel worthless.

"I was no use to my wife and couldn't fight for my country. I'd lie in bed at night worrying about my wife back home, and I used to hate working for the Germans. I went sick as often as I could.

"Nothing could prepare you for arriving at what was hell on earth. The shock knocked us all sideways, we were just stunned. We hadn't heard anything about the Germans' persecution of the Jews, we'd never heard of gas chambers, but it didn't take us long to find out what was going on. It was horribly ironic that while fighting in the war I had not seen a single person die, but from the so-called safety of a POW camp I was to witness plenty – death by beating, gassing, burning, hanging and all forms of the worst brutality, as well as shooting.

"When we got to our original camp, which was called E711, the first thing we noticed was this horrible sweet, sickly smell. It was revolting and we soon learned what was causing it. The stink was from the crematorium, and its burning flesh."

Ron and Brian Bishop arrived in October 1943 – the month when 1,200 Jewish children, all Poles, arrived with 53 guardians, including doctors. All were killed in the gas chambers the same day. Also in October, 1,700 Jews arrived from another camp, Bergen-Belsen, which led to an incident described as follows by the Panstwowe Museum, Oswiecim:

"They had been told that they were being transported to Switzerland. As they were being unloaded and assembled to go into the undressing chamber, SS Lieutenant Hoessler, playing the part of a representative of the Foreign Ministry, informed the people that the Swiss government insisted that everyone be disinfected before entry into Switzerland was permitted.

"He was very polite, and with the most reassuring voice even told them that their train was scheduled to leave at 7.00 a.m. Most of the people in the undressing chamber were doing what they were told, but there were a number just standing about and watching the process, or looking for a way out. The SS now had to use stronger tones in their commands, yet some people were obviously not undressing.

"The SS, now armed with clubs and even undoing the flaps on their holsters, began beating those who were not undressing. Many people were already being moved through the corridor into the gas chamber. The beatings stopped.

"SS soldiers named Walter Quakernack and Jozef Schillinger both were attracted to a beautiful, black-haired woman who began a seductive striptease act when she realised that she had caught their attention. As she lifted her skirt and exposed her thigh to them she glanced around to see what was going on near to her. She removed her blouse, then leaned up against the pillar to remove her high-heeled shoes.

"The two SS stood in awe, with their eyes glued to her body. In a flash she struck Quackernack with the heel of her shoe, leapt on his falling body and snatched the pistol from its opened holster. Quackernack was holding his bleeding face in both hands as a shot rang out. Schillinger screamed in pain and fell to the floor. A second later another shot was fired, narrowly missing Quakernack.

"The young woman ran and disappeared into the crowd, which by now was in panic. One by one the SS began creeping out of the undressing chamber, since they could not see where she was. As an SS guard tried to pull Schillinger out, another shot rang out. He left Schillinger there as he limped up the stairs.

"The lights went out for some time. Everyone groped in the dark, especially the Sonderkommando, who were trying to get to the door to the corridor. Moments later, machine-guns and blinding spotlights were being set up in both doorways. The doors were flung open and the Sonderkommando trapped inside were ordered out.

"Kommandant Hoess pulled up in his car just as the machine-guns opened fire inside the undressing chamber. The people unable to hide behind the pillars were caught in the vicious crossfire of the machine-guns. The few who survived the hail of bullets were themselves shot later.

"The young woman's body was removed and put on display for the SS to view as a warning of what happens when they relax their vigilance. Sergeant Schillinger died on the way to the hospital."

Arthur Liebehenschel replaced Hoess as commandant less than three weeks later. Quakernack, a guard renowned for his brutality in the camp, was tried as a war criminal and executed by the British in 1946.

Ron Jones, who had just arrived, was billeted some three miles away and was mercifully unaware of the incident. Of his early days in camp he says: "I was among the first POWs to get sent there. In all, 1,400 Brits arrived, but 800 were transferred elsewhere.

"Auschwitz had three main camps, and most of the Jews who worked alongside me at the IG Farben factory didn't come from the extermination camp, which was Birkenau. They came from Monowitz, down the road, next to where we were kept. The Jews' lifespan in the IG works was three or four weeks. After that they were too weak to work and were sent to the gas chambers.

"Our POW camp was separate from the one that held the Jewish slave workers at Monowitz, and we didn't actually witness what was being done in Birkenau, which was three miles away, but the Jews who were working in our factory soon told us."

Apart from Birkenau, the extermination camp where the Jews were systematically killed, there was a large industrial complex adjacent to Auschwitz to sustain the German war effort. There, contrary to the Geneva Convention, British POWs were made to work alongside the Jews, who were forced to labour beyond human endurance until they were too weak to do so any longer. The SS term for this process, *Vernichtung durch arbeit* (Extermination through work) was subsumed in another which expressed the Nazi attitude to Jews in general, who were *Lebensunwertes Leben* (Life unworthy of life).

Construction of the Buna factory complex had begun in April 1941 and when the Brits arrived in September 1943 much of the building work was unfinished. At first, the prisoners' work consisted of installing machinery. Ron Jones and company laboured alongside a cosmopolitan gang of non-Jewish workmates, including Germans, Poles, Ukrainians and Italians. At its highest point, in late 1944, there was a huge workforce of 30,000-plus, including 13,000 foreign workers, 8,000 German civilians and 7,000 concentration camp inmates, supposedly making synthetic petrol and rubber, margarine, methanol, carbide – all manner of commodities the German economy needed. Unbeknown to all but a few prisoners, the plant also manufactured Zyklon B, the gas used in the gas chambers.

When the Nazis first set about exterminating the Jews it was by mass shooting, which saw countless thousands murdered by specially formed death squads. Later they resorted to carbon monoxide poisoning, using the gas from motor vehicle exhaust redirected into sealed compartments in vans. Then in July 1941 a group of prisoners, under SS supervision, were disinfecting clothes and bedding with the Zyklon B pesticide when a cat that had entered the room was quickly killed by the cyanide gas the chemical produced.

One of the guards suggested that the chemical, in larger doses, could have the same effect on humans and in September it was tried on 600 Russian POWs and 250 camp inmates. The experiment was repeated later the same month on 900 Red Army prisoners. All those subjected to the gas died, and two gas chambers were in action shortly afterwards.

The highest number of British POWs engaged in factory work was 1,150 at the end of 1943. Transfers to other camps had brought that down to 574 by the final roll call on 20 January 1945. IG Farben's chief engineer, Maximilian Faust, said of their contribution: "The guards at our disposal are too few in number, and to some extent lacking in moral fibre, for which reason they are unable to impose any discipline on those under their charge, or encourage them to work.

"Moreover, the English prisoners of war are showered with gifts [he was referring to food parcels]. They hand out chocolate and cigarettes to Poles, inmates, and probably the guards as well. They take on a quarrelsome stance, and though there are so many of them their output is quite below average."

Ron Jones says: "I only worked on the synthetic fuel side, where much of the time I was moving machinery around by hand. In fairness, they gave us gloves to wear – otherwise your skin would stick to the metal and tear off in the extreme winter cold. I remember looking through the wire and seeing kids going to school on skis. The summer weather was very different, we used to go to work stripped to the waist.

"At first our living quarters were reasonably comfortable. We were in E711, which had previously housed the Hitler Youth, so it was a huge improvement on what we had been used to before, in Italy and at Lamsdorf. There were flush toilets, good showers and proper bunk beds. We had no high guard towers surrounding us, like there were around the Jews' camps – just the barbed wire. We had to march only four blocks to and from the works.

"As it turned out, we weren't in E711 for long. In November 1943 Auschwitz 3 and 40 sub-camps were reorganised, and not long after that we were moved to E715, which was much nearer IG Farben's Buna works and only 400 yards or so from the Monowitz concentration camp. We were housed in three separate barracks, numbered 4, 6 and 8. Mine was only about 300 yards from the factory. There were 150 German civilian workers in a separate barracks next to us.

"Now we marched to and from work every day in plain

sight of what was happening to the Jews in their Monowitz camp, which was just horrific. We'd see bodies hanging from a gibbet in the mornings and hear screams and shootings at night."

It is estimated that between 23,000 and 25,000 labourers died in Monowitz, from gassing, shooting, hanging, lethal injections or just plain exhaustion. Many of them died on the job at the IG Farben factory where they were routinely beaten or worked to death.

Ron says: "Russian prisoners of war had been held in E715 before us, and it was a bit of a dump by comparison with 711. We had to clean it up to make it habitable. We lived in wooden huts, 18 sleeping in double tiers in each section of a building that had four sections in all. There were no more flush toilets, just a big, stinking hole in the ground. On the bunks we didn't have mattresses, we had palliasses, a grand name for bagfuls of straw. When the straw got compacted and became flat, we used to change it from bales we were given for the purpose.

"It was never comfortable, but we made the best of everything. I've read others saying it was freezing in our huts, but it wasn't. We had a big stove in the middle of ours and we were supplied with wood to keep it going. For anyone who has seen the film *The Great Escape*, I'm talking about the sort of stove they dug their tunnels under.

"We had blankets and the huts were insulated with asbestos, so we were never freezing cold. The Germans weren't idiots, they kept us in decent shape to work. I've heard others say they couldn't sleep because of the stress or the noise, but I never had much trouble – not after a full day's hard labour. It wasn't that I was hard-hearted, just plain exhausted.

"The toilets and washing facilities were crude but

serviceable. We did our business either in a long trough or sat on bars over a cess pool, but that wasn't much different from what we had been used to in our own army, in north Africa. There were showers, so we were able to keep ourselves clean, and we were allowed a knife, fork and spoon, which the Italians hadn't let us have. There wasn't much to eat with them, mind. There was no mess hall, not even a dining table in the hut, but that didn't matter. You had so little food you could easily eat it off your lap. I didn't have a proper meal in the camp the whole time I was in there.

"The Jews, Russians and others were guarded by the SS, but we weren't, thank God. The German Army, the Wehrmacht, guarded us. The SS came around occasionally, conducting searches and I remember them coming in, looking for our radio. They ripped the floorboards up and gave the hut a right going over, but they never found it because it wasn't there. It was hidden in the store where the Red Cross parcels were kept. Generally, though, the SS didn't bother us. We usually found out they were coming, so they didn't find much. If they did find some cigarettes or whatever they'd just confiscate them, there was no violence. I don't remember anything like that.

"We always had the impression that the Germans, including the SS, had more respect for us than any other category of prisoner, and I think statistics bear that out. More than half the Russian prisoners taken by the Germans died in captivity but not many of ours did."

Of the POWs' guards, Ron says: "The Wehrmacht in charge of us on a daily basis were mostly old men, or soldiers who had been wounded in action, 90 per cent of them weren't fit enough for active service any more. The young, fit soldiers were away at the front and if you got the guards on their own, many were sympathetic, they couldn't believe what was going on either. I found the German army fellas were all right – no different to us."

Brian Bishop found there were exceptions to that general rule. He said: "One or two of the Wehrmacht guards could be nasty. There was one we called 'Leatherhand'. He'd been wounded on the Russian Front and had the whole of one arm permanently encased in leather. He'd whack us with his leather fist. You had to be careful with some of the guards, but others were OK. I got quite friendly with a couple of them. They'd get me things in exchange for cigarettes."

Even the "real bastards", as Brian called them, could crack and be human occasionally. A guard named Rittler was a particularly nasty individual who would take pleasure in inflicting punishment for the most inconsequential of transgressions, and his work detail feared the worst when one of their number was caught with a dead duck hidden under his greatcoat. The culprit was heading for a spell in solitary confinement, at least, but when he explained that the duck had attacked him viciously, and that he had killed it in self-defence, even Rittler saw the funny side and allowed him to keep the duck.

The Germans gave their prisoners all sorts of propaganda to read, including *Mein Kampf*, Hitler's notoriously turgid political testament. Brian recalled an occasion when one of his mates was late on parade, for which he would normally have been punished, but when asked why he was late, he replied that he had been engrossed in *Mein Kampf* and hadn't noticed the time. Even the guard commander laughed at that and let him off.

Ron Jones says: "The SS, of course, were a totally different proposition. Evil bastards. They had the death's head emblem on their uniforms and were proud of being ruthless killers. They'd shoot a Jew as soon as look at him, and beat them for nothing, but we seemed to be off limits as far as they were concerned.

"We didn't come into contact with those *kapos* who knocked the Jews around so cruelly all the time. I saw them walking about with their clubs and whips doing their worst, but they had nothing to do with us. They weren't allowed to. Don't get me wrong, we didn't have it easy, far from it, I had a bayonet jabbed up my arse for not marching quickly enough, but prisoner of war life wasn't too bad, compared with what was happening to those poor Jews.

"If we were sick, the Germans saw to it that we were looked after. It was even possible to pretend that we were ill and get a day off. We had two doctors with us in the camp, named Spencer and McFarland, and if we weren't well we'd go to one of them. Mind you, they had no access to medicine or drugs, so they couldn't help with anything serious. I remember one treating me when a length of railway line was accidentally dropped on my toes.

"If one of our lads was seriously ill, the Germans would take him to the civilian hospital in the town, but that was rare. The horrible, debilitating thing we all used to suffer from was boils. I was covered in the bloody things, and when I say that I mean they were everywhere. One lad had one down his throat, which was really nasty. We all had them, and abscesses, because of malnutrition.

"Even when I came home I was like it for all of 12 months. Then the local GP, Desmond Hull, who I went to school with, called to see me one day, because we were friends, and said: 'You have to come to the surgery about those Ron.' I went and he gave me a bottle of tiny grey tablets. He said: 'Take 14 the first day, then 12, then ten until you've had the lot.' I don't know what they were, but I've never had a boil since. Mind you, I've still got the marks from where abscesses were lanced."

The OKW (Wehrmacht High Command) had issued the following directive regarding POWs: "Every prisoner of war liable for work and able-bodied is expected to exert himself to the full. Should he fail to do so, the guards or auxiliary guards are entitled to take rigorous action. Guards who fail to take such action will themselves be held responsible and severely punished. They are entitled to enforce their orders by force of arms." At its highest point, in February 1944, there were 80,000 POWs working for the Third Reich.

Ron says: "At IG Farben we worked six days a week, 12 hours a day, with every Sunday off. On a working day we were up not long after 5 o' clock to do our ablutions and have what passed for breakfast before roll call at 6.00. The guards then marched us to work and handed us over to a civilian boss, a German we called a 'Meister'.

"For my gang of nine men, all Brits, it was a German engineer called Meister Beave. He had to be careful what he said, but you could tell he wasn't a Nazi and that he didn't like what was going on. He didn't approve of Hitler and his crowd, and we were very fortunate to get him. Other 'Meisters' would actively encourage the *kapos* to give their workers a beating, and some carried pistols and weren't afraid to brandish them and push our lads about, but Beave wasn't like that. I was very lucky there.

"To give you an idea how decent he was, he'd give us a list of things to do and say: 'As soon as you've finished you can go back to camp and rest.' Probably once a week we'd finish by 2 or 3 o' clock in the afternoon and he'd let us go, when we should have stayed until 6.00. He was a very fair man.

"On Sunday mornings we had our version of a church service, conducted by a lay preacher. I wouldn't say I was a particularly religious man, but I was a member of the church back home, where I was Confirmed. Put it this way: I Believe. When I went to bed at night in there I prayed, and I still do. Now, when I go to bed, I thank God for looking after me, because he certainly has. In there, of course, it seemed all the more important. A lot of the other men didn't pray, or attend service. I suppose I was that way inclined because my wife played the organ in the local chapel at Rogerstone. She did that for a long time, so we were active members of the church.

"I think maybe my faith gave me mental strength in the camp – helped to keep me going. There was definitely something like that, supporting me in my hour of need. It was a grim place, but I was pretty strong, mentally, and unlike some I was never reduced to tears or serious depression, never suffered the sort of breakdown which had some of the men spend every spare minute in bed."

Maurice Jones, a lance-corporal in the Kings Shropshire Light Infantry, said: "Sometimes after roll call a chap would go straight back to the hut and get back into bed and stay there until the roll call in the evening. When that was noticed the treatment was to pull him out of bed and make him walk around the compound with everybody else. After a few days, the mood wore off and he got back to something like normal again. If you were allowed to lie in bed all day like that, you'd lose your marbles."

Ron was never that bad, but says: "I have to admit, though, that the separation from Gwladys did get me down. Even with the best wife in the world, you were bound to wonder what was going on back home after you'd been away for years, and I suppose that's summed up by what I wrote after receiving a letter in which Glad said she'd been out to a dance. This was my reply (Ga-ga was a pet name for Glad which came about because it was what our little niece and nephew called her, they couldn't say Gwladys):

Tuesday 25th June 1944

Dearest Ga-ga,

I have just received two letters and I must say I am surprised to hear you are not getting my mail as I write every week and I receive yours regularly. Still, you'll get them all at once just now.

You must look after Ivy darling, now she is in trouble, and if anything happens to Oliver, Denise will have a home.

I don't know about that second honeymoon in Yorkshire as I have had so much travelling this past three years that I am afraid it will take a lot to move me from our fireplace.

I suppose you did enjoy yourself at the dance on the 27th November under the circumstances (I suppose that means other men's arms). Dear heart, if you only knew what heartache you give me when you mention dances, you wouldn't go. Surely there is other entertainment for you without having to be held in others' arms? There are thousands about better than I, and what if you met one, as most probably Peggy will if she goes on like that. What will happen to me then?

If it wasn't for the thought of coming back to you some day I shouldn't have stood the life as long as I have.

You have been without a man for three years, and having been in contact with them, such as dancing... well.

Darling please be careful, I love you so.

Yours for ever,

Ron.

Like everybody else in confinement anywhere, Ron lived in constant dread of the "Dear John" letter.

Even on days off, it was important to keep the mind off such things and the body busy. Ron says: "Apart from our service, we'd spend Sunday maybe doing a bit of sewing, cleaning ourselves up and in summer playing football or cricket, or sometimes just walking around, chatting. When the snow was on the ground, recreation meant card games or reading.

"The mates I remember best in the camp were Cyril Quartermain, from Nottingham, and Charlie Evans, who came from Carmarthen. I've still got Cyril's address. We used to correspond with one another, and when Gwladys died he wrote to me a couple of months later to say his wife, Lily, had just died, too. I've always had a Christmas card from him, but that stopped a couple of years ago, so I suppose he must have passed away. Charlie was a fellow Welshman and I got on well with him; he'd been captured at Dunkirk. I can remember the local council giving him the freedom of Carmarthen. Sadly he died a few months later.

"The prisoner who had had the most publicity was Charlie Coward whose nonsense I will analyse later. He got himself elected as our 'Man of Confidence', which was a role created by the International Red Cross. Every POW camp had one. Their job description was laid down like this: 'The prisoners elect their own leader, who acts as camp leader and "Chief Man of Confidence" in negotiations with the prison authorities, the International Red Cross and the representatives of the protecting power (Switzerland). In a camp for other ranks, it is a sergeant major. He speaks for the men.'

"As it turned out, Coward spoke mostly for himself.

One of the other lads came out with a good line about him after the war. I think it was Arthur Dodd who said: 'E715 veterans regarded Coward less a "Man of Confidence" than a confidence man, due to his gift of the gab and spotty relations with other POWs.'

"There were many nationalities in the works – civilian workers as well as POWs. I wouldn't say ours was particularly hard work, physically, but then I'd been used to heavy engineering. Sometimes there were heavy materials to pick up, but a few of us would share the load. If there was any digging of drainage trenches or whatever to be done, the Jews usually did it. We had none of those *kapos*. They were in our works, with their armbands on, but not involved with us. A lot of them were Jews themselves, and they were real bastards, treating the other Jews as badly as the SS did, knocking them around with terrible savagery. If they killed them, the attitude was 'So what?' The *kapos* ruled the roost, no doubt about it."

The so-what attitude about the death of the Jews was spoken of at the Nuremberg war crimes trials by Charles Hill, of the Royal Artillery, another prisoner in E715. Hill, from Manchester, said: "Those who collapsed or were hurt one way or another would often be left there until evening. One case I remember very clearly. One of the inmates fell from a building at about 2.30 in the afternoon. As a result of the scream, one of the Germans went out to see what had happened. When he saw it was only an inmate he said: 'It's only a Jew'. When we left at about 6.15 in the evening after finishing our work, we passed the inmate and he was still there, propped against the building."

Ron Jones says: "Officially, we weren't allowed to talk to the Jews in the works. If we did, they'd get beaten up by the *kapos,* so we learned to do it surreptitiously, without being seen. The Polish civilian workers, who came in from outside the camp, worked all over the place, as fitters, electricians, whatever. There was one in particular I got friendly with, swapping cigarettes for bread and eggs. I even got a watch from him. Joseph, or maybe Jozef, was his name.

"We used to get Red Cross food parcels occasionally – not as regularly as we should have done because the Germans used to steal them. Anyway, a food parcel came one day and I had a piece of sausage, about six inches long, which I took to the works and gave to Joseph. He was all over me after that. A couple of days later he gave me a signet ring he'd made out of a metal pipe – I still wear it today. About a week after that he disappeared so I asked one of his mates where Joseph had gone and he told me: 'Gas chamber. *Kaput.*' The poor bugger was dead.

"That never happened to any of us. For the most part, the Germans stuck by the Geneva Convention in dealing with us. There were one or two who could be nasty, but that was true of our lot, too, and basically we were treated OK – better than when we'd been when prisoners of the Italians, certainly. In Italy we weren't allowed anything they thought might be used as a weapon. The Germans gave us knives and forks and razors, and we had to shave every day.

"Discipline was maintained in the camp as it would have been in the Army anywhere. You weren't allowed to grow a beard. If you didn't shave, there was trouble. Believe it or not, I still use the same safety razor now that I had in the camp, nearly 70 years ago! We kept ourselves clean and tidy, as proper soldiers. Our uniforms did get very tatty, but that was hardly our fault. Mine had deteriorated badly in Italy. The first thing the Italians did was to put identification patches on the back of our clothes. By the time I got to Lamsdorf, mine were in a bit of a state, but the Germans rigged us out with fresh uniforms. They sewed a blue diamond on the back of our tunics and trousers to identify us as POWs That was the only uniform I had until I was picked up by the Americans at the end of the war.

"Apart from the two doctors, who were captains, there were no officers in the camp. We had Coward, a colour sergeant from the Royal Artillery in charge. He got promoted to sergeant major while we were there. I don't know how that happened, maybe the rank went with the 'Man of Confidence' job. Anyway, if there was anything you wanted, you went to Charlie, he was Mr Fix It.

"I didn't have much to do with him, I hardly saw the bugger – only at roll call really, and occasionally at night-time. We had roll call twice, once in the morning and again at night. It was like a formal parade – fall in, come to attention and fall out. Coward brought us to attention and the Germans would count us. Whoever was sick would fall out and the rest of us marched to the works. Coward never took us there. Once we went through those gates, the guards were in charge of us. Once we were in the factory, the guards disappeared into a hut and handed us over to the overseers, or *Meisters*. In the works, I was never told what to do by anybody other than Beave.

"When we came back at night, we got to the gates again and marched in with our hands held over our heads in the surrender position, ready to be searched. The guards would then run their hands down you. It wasn't the most thorough of searches, the whole process taking not much more than ten minutes. It was very different for the Jews, who could be kept on parade for hours at a time.

59

"The one positive thing I remember Coward for was our radio. We had a shed-cum-store where the Red Cross parcels were kept and that's where it was hidden. We made it ourselves – put it together from valves and other bits and pieces stolen from the works. We were all searched every time we got back to our huts, but the radio components were quite small and they were hidden under false bottoms to our haversacks.

"In a camp like that you get all sorts – mechanics, engineers, electricians etc – and it hardly took two minutes to put it all together. I made the box for it. Charlie Coward used to go to that storeroom every night, get the BBC news from the radio and come round all our huts and tell us what was going on. Nothing was ever written down, it was all done by word of mouth, but we were kept well informed – we knew all about the Second Front after D Day and heard that the Russians were coming before the Germans did!"

Keen to win the propaganda war, even if they were losing the real thing, the Nazis countered the POWs' celebrations over the Normandy landings with the front page of the camp newspaper which carried a big red V to trumpet the news that their V1 flying bombs were hitting London.

The prisoners' radios (they made more than one) were a constant source of irritation to the camp authorities, who never managed to find them. Ron says: "Searches of the huts were carried out quite often, to no effect. Our lads were quite clever about it. A small piece of equipment would be left somewhere that was easy to find and as soon as the Germans found it they'd go – 'Found it!' and off they'd go.

"The guards were hardly the cream of the German army, and not the brightest. If they were looking for radio sets they didn't see knives or anything else we shouldn't have had. Radio sets were all they were interested in."

The British were amused by that, but not by the nature of their daily labours. Ron Jones explains: "The work we were doing was for the German war effort which was contrary to the Geneva Convention, but when a deputation went to complain, the IG Farben manager on duty, a man named Gerhard Ritter, produced his pistol, saying the Luger was his Geneva Convention. We were also told that anyone who refused to work in the factory would instead be sent to work as a coal miner, and conditions in the mines were much worse, so we had no choice but to carry on. Not that it meant we had to work properly.

"I was an engineer so they presumed I was a fitter, and I used to work changing the pipes and filters on the synthetic petrol plant. Because it was for the Germans, there was a lot of sabotage. When I went up to work on the top of the filtration towers I used to take a handful of sand to drop into the filters. Luckily, the guards never tumbled. If they had caught me it would have meant solitary confinement, at the very least.

"I did spend three days in the Auschwitz jail once. In the works I swapped some cigarettes for half a dozen eggs and I put them in my gaiters, thinking the guards searching us wouldn't go down that low. This guard did and said: '*Eier, mein lieber!*' He squashed the bloody eggs and I got three days in clink on bread and water.

"From the top of those cylinders in the works we could see the trains arriving, the infamous 'selections' being made and could see down into Birkenau. You couldn't hear anything, we were too far away, but it looked hideous. I saw Josef Kremer (adjutant to the camp commandant) strutting around with his shiny jackboots and his stick, and if a Jew got in his way he would shoot him without even pausing for thought. I saw him do it in our works on two occasions – kill men just for being in his line of sight. Other than that he'd kick out at them, and of course the poor buggers were dying in front of him anyway. They were in such a state they couldn't get out of his way. They couldn't walk, they stumbled along. The pure hatred and utter contempt the Germans had for the Jews had to be seen to be believed.

"I saw it from Irma Grese, the female guard who was hanged after the war. One day she brought a gang of women into our camp with a horse-drawn wagon to empty our cess pool. They pumped the human waste into a big tank, then took the horse and cart into a field at the back of our camp where the bung was knocked out of the tank and they went up and down, emptying our sewage on to the field. Then these Jewesses arrived with bags wrapped around them, full of seed potatoes. They had to wade through our shit, planting the potatoes. I have to admit we weren't interested in the muck, we were looking at the first women we'd seen for a long time, but what a disgusting, degrading thing to make them do."

Even by Auschwitz standards, Grese was a particularly nasty piece of work. Born to an agricultural family in 1923, she left school at 14 and worked as an untrained nurse at an SS hospital. From 1942 she was a telephonist, then a guard at Ravensbrück women's concentration camp. She was assigned to Auschwitz in the spring of 1943, when the first impression she made was with her blonde good looks. Because of these (adjutant Jozef Kramer was among her lovers), as much as her ferocious enthusiasm for the work, she was quickly promoted to a position which enabled her to do her sadistic worst.

One Hungarian survivor said of her: "There was a beautiful woman called Grese who rode a bike. Thousands of us would be on our knees, suffering in scorching heat, and she took delight in watching us." A doctor in the camp recalled that it was Grese's ambition to become an actress: "She gazed at herself in the mirror for hours and constantly made a seamstress sew her new dresses. She had lovers, even prisoners among them, and when she got pregnant she made a prisoner who had been a doctor in Hungary abort her baby."

Grese became renowned more for her brutality than her good looks – she would whip the faces of female prisoners and deliberately blinded one girl for speaking to an acquaintance through the wire fence.

A woman named Ackermann, from Budapest, said of her: "Grese had a rubber baton and would beat you up if you did not stand erect. We were beaten for all possible, and impossible reasons. When Grese came we had to stay on our knees for hours."

When Auschwitz was evacuated Grese was transferred back to Ravensbrück and then to Bergen-Belsen where she carried on torturing her victims. When the war ended, she was apprehended by the British Army and tried at Krakow, after which she was executed as a war criminal on 13 December 1945, aged 22. When the hangman called her forward she looked around her contemptuously and said only one word: "*Schnell*".

Grese may have been one of the worst, but her inhumanity was typical of the SS. Ron Jones says: "When the Jews became too weak to work, we'd see them carted off to the gas chambers in an open lorry, poor buggers. Seeing that gave me and most of the other lads nightmares. We always thought we'd end up like that, gassed if the Germans reacted badly when they realised they were losing the war. That unspoken threat was hanging over us all the time."

The British POWs relieved this apprehension and the grim routine of camp life as best they could. Ron says: "Obviously Auschwitz was a hellish place, but for us it wasn't all doom and gloom and hopelessness. Life was grim, no doubt about it, but we made the best of things. We improvised. We didn't have a pack of playing cards, so we saved our cardboard cigarette packets and made cards out of them. Some of the lads even managed to brew alcoholic booze. I never touched the stuff because I didn't drink, but they'd get raisins and potato peelings in a bucket, heat it up with a pipe over the top and it all produced some sort of liquor. The saying was that if you drank too much it would make you blind! They called it methanol, after what we were making.

"Some of the lads even found love, or perhaps we should call it lust. There were girls working for IG Farben and one of our boys fell for a female Ukrainian welder called Natasha. To be honest, she was as glamorous as she sounds! They were big, strong girls, who always had heavy, industrial clothing on, with bodies to match. There was another popular one, a Pole called Maria, who used to sing a lot. I certainly didn't find any of them attractive, but I wouldn't have been interested anyway. I was a happily married man. Some, though, found romance, if we can call it that!"

Brian Bishop remembered a Russian woman by the name of Olga. He said: "We had all sorts in the factory, including Russian POWs and a couple of French guys who always mystified me. I didn't speak their language so I never found out how they got there, but they definitely weren't POWs. Some of the Russians were women, and one of them was this big girl called Olga. She was lovely looking, but big all over. Her arms were enormous. She worked as a welder's assistant, and the oxyacetylene cylinders the Germans used were half as big again as the ones we had in Britain. When we moved the empty ones, it took two of us, but Olga would carry a full one on her own, she was that strong.

"Anyway, she took a fancy to a mate of mine and used to come looking for him, but he was scared of her and used to hide. She didn't want to know me, unfortunately. I stayed a virgin until I was 25 – there was not much chance of 'the other' in Auschwitz. These French guys always had their eye on Olga, and one day when she had to bend over in front of them, one of them ran his finger down her backside. She turned in an instant and knocked him out cold with a big right-hander – broke his jaw in two places. Some item, that Olga."

Less exotic entertainment was available, courtesy of a prisoner named Wally Martin, who was a BBC producer before, and after, the war. Ron Jones says: "Wally was a hell of a character. In December '44 he put on a play, *Sweeney Todd*, in which I played the part of a police sergeant. Charlie Coward said he found it all too frivolous, the miserable bugger! The Germans turned out in force to watch – they always took the front seats for anything we did like that and they'd be laughing and clapping as much as our lads. You'd be surprised how many of them could speak English – it was their second language, they all took it at school – and we had to be very careful what we said if they could overhear it.

"Apart from amateur dramatics, we had books to read when we weren't working. They were sent us in parcels and I got a biography of Genghis Khan, which came to me by mistake. It should have gone to an officer from Newport, but there was a mix-up and he got my book and vice-versa. We all swapped, so there was always something to read. We even had our own small orchestra. I don't know where they got the instruments from – presumably the Red Cross. I know the Jews had one that used to play classical stuff as they went to work every day, but I never heard them.

"Lights out was at 10 o' clock every night and Wally, who was always up to something, managed to contrive a laugh even then. There were 18 of us to each room, and when the lights went out we'd always be yarning about what we were going to eat when we got home. We were all going to good restaurants for a slap-up meal. Mind you, if we weren't too hungry, the talk was about women.

"One night Wally was bored with all the food talk, got a box of matches and said: 'Does anyone want to fart?' As we did, he lit a match under us and the gas flared into a blue light. Schoolboy stuff, I know, but it gave us a good giggle at a time when there wasn't much else to laugh about.

"I had a lovely surprise meeting with Wally years after the war. I lived in a flat for a time, opposite a garage at Pye Corner, and the garage owner used to get me to keep an eye on things out front while he took deliveries or whatever. One of the mechanics who worked at the garage was called Armstrong, and one day he turned up at the house I had moved to and said: 'I've got someone in the car, looking for you.' I went out to see who it was and there was Wally. He was on his way from London to BBC Wales in Cardiff, passed a road sign for Bassaleg and thought of me. He drove to the garage, asked if they knew me, and ended up staying the night here. The following day he took me to the BBC studios and showed me around. A smashing man. Years later, it upset me when I had a letter from his wife, saying he'd died from lung cancer.

"Apart from whatever Wally was up to, the main relief we had in the camp came from our letters from home. Only letters from next of kin were allowed, which in my case meant

Gwladys. I've still got all the letters I sent to her, she kept them and I've got them all in a big chocolate box. Whatever I wrote to her, and *vice versa*, was censored at both ends, and if there was the slightest information that was regarded as sensitive in any way, it was blacked out.

"Apart from the letters, Gwladys was allowed to send me what were called next-of-kin parcels. She told me she sent seven and I think I received three. She sent me a pair of brogues once. At home I'd worn them with plus-fours. Brogues in Auschwitz – you couldn't make it up! I wore them in the camp, but not in the works, they were too soft for the factory, where you needed your boots.

"Not all the Germans were as monstrous as they have been portrayed. That Meister Beave couldn't say Jones, he used to call me 'Yonas'. He said to me one day: '*Kommen Sie hier*, Yonas. You get tins of meat in those Red Cross parcels, ja?' I confirmed that we did, and he said: 'Bring in the meat tomorrow and we will go to my cottage for a meal.' So he got some bikes and three of us went to his cottage about half-a-mile from our camp. It was one in a row of bungalows that housed the German civilian bosses – all property confiscated from Polish families, of course. He had vegetables in the garden – we were still surrounded by the electrified perimeter fence, mind – and with our tin of 'Bully' he made a big stew.

"I'm a keen gardener and the thing I remember most about the visit was a German vegetable I'd never heard of called kohlrabi. It's a cross between a turnip and a cabbage. Delicious it was. He was all right was Beave, a decent man. I used to wonder what happened to him at the end. I guess I'll never know. The last time I saw him was the day before they marched us out.

"One or two of the Wehrmacht guards were just as

friendly. On one occasion two of us were taken to the dentist in Katowice by an old boy – too old for the front – who took us for a meal at his house afterwards. When we got him on his own, he'd call Hitler all the names under the sun. The 'Führer' was a stupid bugger, he said.

"The dentist out there didn't do me much good. By the time I got home my teeth were in such a state that I had to have seven out and a plate full of new ones. Then another couple came loose and my dentist at home added two more to the plate. Anyway, it kept happening and he said to me one day: 'Ron have the bloody lot out, I can't keep adding to the plate like this', so I had a full set of false teeth by the time I was 35. There's something else the war cost me – when I was called up I had perfect teeth.

"The dentist we went to in Katowice had a scam going. He used to open a drawer, and if you put a pack of cigarettes or a bar of soap in there he'd say you had to come for a follow up visit which got you out of the camp again. It was on one of those second visits that the guard took us to his house and his wife cooked us a meal. I didn't realise what he was doing. I'd been to the dentist before, so I knew the route, but this time the guard took us up another street. I asked him: 'Where are we going?' and he said: 'To my home.' When we got there, his wife cooked the three of us a spaghetti bolognese. Very nice too, when you were as hungry as we were."

Brian Bishop also had reason to remember a visit to the dentist. He said: "I went to Katowice once to have a tooth out. I walked into the surgery and the bloke had me sit in what was an ordinary armchair. This woman came in with big boobs, stood behind me and took my head between her boobs as he pulled the tooth out. The boobs were the only anaesthetic I got!"

Food, or the lack of it, was always an issue and the main topic of conversation. Ron Jones says: "Apart from the Red Cross parcels, the rations we got from the Germans every day were barely enough to keep you alive, and nowhere enough to stay healthy. Before we went to work, breakfast was a cup of ersatz coffee, made from burnt acorns and a piece of black bread. We got a large loaf which we had to slice up between 18 of us, which meant we had a small piece each. It was supposed to be 350 grams, but of course we had no way of weighing it to make sure. To go with that there was ersatz margarine and sometimes a piece of cheese which was rubbish. It smelled like hell and always had fish scales in it. And there was a large sausage between the 18 of us.

"When we came back in the evening there was always a soup. There was a ladleful of that, usually potato soup, every day. Apart from the awful coffee in the morning, all they gave us to drink all day was water, but we did have our tea from the Red Cross parcels.

"The soup in the works at lunchtime was so bad it was undrinkable. It was disgusting – the smell made you heave. We used to give it to the Jews if we could. I never had any of it."

Brian Bishop said of the ubiquitous soup: "It was foul. You took the lid off the container and the stink was disgusting. Once one of the blokes told us he'd seen a girl from the cookhouse pee in one of the big containers. I said: 'Find out which can it is, it's got to taste better than the usual stuff!' We gave all the soup to the Jews. They were really starving so they drank it all. As I remember, anything the Germans gave us tasted bloody awful."

Ron Jones said: "If it hadn't been for the food parcels we wouldn't have survived. It was like a real feast when they came. In them you'd get a tin of bully beef or Spam, a packet of biscuits, butter, sugar, coffee, tea, a tin of that dried milk called Klim and a Heinz tinned pudding. There would also be a bar of chocolate and a bar of soap. We had a room near the toilets where we could go and cook stuff and boil up a cup of tea.

"The Red Cross parcels weren't addressed to us individually, and there were never enough for one each, so we shared the food around. You couldn't sit there eating while mates looked on, hungry. More often than not, you shared one between two or three of you, but towards the end, when the deliveries dried up, it was one between four or more.

"How often we got the parcels varied tremendously. You wouldn't get one for a couple of months, then you'd have one a week for a month. The Germans used to steal a lot because their food was pretty poor, too. The near-starvation diet got so bad that some of the men took up smoking, just to reduce the hunger pains.

"People ask me if there was any chance to escape. The answer is no. Our lads did form an escape committee, but married men were excluded from joining, the organisers didn't want the responsibility of having family men shot, which was the likelihood. This wasn't like any other POW camp. Apart from the Wehrmacht soldiers guarding us there was a battalion of SS men next door, who would kill you as soon as look at you – and probably torture you first. If you got out wearing civilian clothes, they'd treat you like a partisan, or a spy.

"The only way to escape was wearing German uniforms, but the Jerries knew that. We weren't allowed to have lead pencils because they'd found elsewhere that POWs were using them to dye our khaki clothes their field grey. It's surprising

– one pencil would provide a whole vat of liquid for the purpose.

"I don't know of any of our POWs escaping from Auschwitz. If you did get out there was nowhere to go really. Deepest Poland was so far from friendly territory, and the fact that none of us could speak the language was a hell of a giveaway. All of us became resigned to sitting tight and waiting it out, but even that was fraught with fears."

Ron is right. According to the official history of the camp, no British POWs did escape. Between 1940 and 1945 the 802 prisoners who did get out and away comprised 396 Poles, 195 Jews and 179 Russians, plus a few others, none of whom were British.

Chapter 5

The Auschwitz Cup

It was in the Germans' interests to maintain the physical wellbeing of their strongest slave labourers, and also to portray their concentration camps in the best light possible whenever they came under international scrutiny through the inspection visits carried out by the Red Cross. Theresienstadt, in what is now the Czech Republic, was the Nazis showpiece, supposedly reserved for "prominent" Jews, but in reality it was no more than another ghetto. Presented as a model Jewish settlement, it housed nearly 60,000 prisoners in barracks designed for 7,000 Czech troops. More than 33,000 inmates died, from hunger, sickness or sadistic treatment by the SS.

A deliberately deceptive gloss was put on Auschwitz, too, whenever the Red Cross came calling, and it has to be said that their inspection teams allowed themselves to be fooled much too easily.

At Auschwitz part of the illusion was the provision of a football pitch of sorts for the British POWs. Ron Jones and the others realised it was all a Nazi ruse, but were certain that nobody back home would be fooled and chose to seize what was a rare chance of recreational enjoyment.

Ron says: "The Red Cross came for an inspection visit one

day and they'd been told that we played football on a Sunday afternoon, so they came with four sets of shirts, English, Scots, Welsh and Irish. I was goalkeeper for the Welsh team. I had a mate who could draw and he drew the Prince of Wales feathers, from which I embroidered them on my shirt, using an old sock. The England goalkeeper was a mate of mine, a Londoner by the name of Doug Bond. Doug died in December 2009.

"I'd played in goal in the Newport area before the war and with one team in Rogerstone, called The Night School, I'd won the Woodcock Cup. My claim to fame is that I won seven caps for Wales – in the Welch Regiment in Cairo.

"In Auschwitz we had a decent pitch, which was a field between our camp and the Jews in Monowitz. No crossbars, just sticks for posts. The guards would come out to watch, shouting and cheering, and we had quite a crowd – not just the POWs but the locals who worked in the factory. We're talking about hundreds. The Germans never joined in mind. We did try to persuade them to get a team together and play us, which would have been like the film *Escape to Victory*, but they wouldn't. Don't forget most of the guards had been invalided back from the front line or were aged 50-plus.

"Most of the matches were played in the summer of 1944. We couldn't play football in winter of course. In Poland it snowed in October and you wouldn't see the ground again until April. But when we could, we had a bit of fun out of it."

Ron does not agree with Denis Avey about much, but he has to admit that his controversial contemporary had a point about football in Auschwitz when he wrote: "The chance of a game had been hard to turn down and, right or wrong, I enjoyed it enormously, [but] looking back, we were perhaps naive. We were lined up for team photos afterwards and we can all be seen smiling into the lens.

"Now I think we were part of an elaborate propaganda exercise. Around the same time we received some fresh uniforms. They weren't new, but they were smarter than what we had and many of the lads were lined up and photographed in those, too. It was a gift to the Germans. It helped the Wehrmacht to put some distance between their treatment of us and the methods the SS used on the Jews. I have no doubt it also helped the camp commanders to keep the visitors from the Red Cross off their backs.

"They [the Red Cross] had proved to be highly gullible. Some of their reports into conditions in our camp bore little resemblance to the truth. They suggested we had been able to play football whenever there were enough guards. It was utter balderdash. One Red Cross report claimed that the work was not hard and that there were no complaints about it. They said we had hot running water and, even more ridiculous, that they had seen inmates playing tennis."

Elsewhere, other POWs understood the Nazis' propaganda motive and refused to share a pitch with them. At Lamsdorf, where the inmates included pre-war professional players, the Germans wanted to play a match against them. Peter Morrey, from Melbourne, Australia, was told of the approach by his father, William, who had been captured in Crete while serving with the Royal Artillery, and who was awarded a medal by the Swedes for organising sporting activities in the camp. Peter said: "There were many English and Scottish League players among the POWs, and one of the guards was an Austrian international. One of the English POWs, Charles Bisbie, had played against him before the war.

"The Nazis wanted a team from the POWs to play a

German team, to be broadcast to England, but the POWs refused. The German radio van remained in the camp until the planned date, just in case they changed their minds."

Ronald Redman, of the Royal Hampshire Regiment, received the same Swedish medal for organising six-a-side football at E715. He said: "The idea was to relieve the tension caused by the American and Russian bombing raids, but I found it difficult to get players off their bunks in their free time in the evenings, or on Sundays, and also to arrange the German guards necessary to supervise.

"Unfortunately my medal, along with my other meagre possessions, was looted in one of several Russian field hospitals I was forced to be in during the evacuation from Auschwitz. It was not of any value, except as a memento, but one got no sympathy from the Russians."

Ron Jones comments: "Apart from football, we played basketball. There was quite a decent space between our huts and somebody rigged a couple of hoops up between two of them and we kept ourselves as fit and active as possible by playing that, too. I've never been tall, but I got quite good at it. Mind you, I still wear a reminder of those games. We all used to suffer from boils and abscesses because of the lousy diet, and I played basketball with a big abscess on my left forearm. What happened? I went to shoot, someone tried to stop me and his hand cracked down right on the abscess. I've still got the scar, right down to the bone, today.

"There was no real treatment for things like that. We had the South African doctor with us, but he had no access to drugs or medication and all he could do was fill the hole in my arm with a roll of bandage. The stuff that used to come out of that wound is indescribable. It didn't half hurt.

"When the Red Cross came for their inspections they

went right through the camp, checking everything, but of course the Germans knew they were coming and made sure everything looked right. They had the Polish prisoners, who always got the worst jobs, clean up everywhere and put the best possible gloss on things.

"Football or not, we weren't very fit. The malnutrition gave us a lot of trouble with our teeth, which would chip easily and come loose. We had no dentists in the camp so they'd let three or four of us go, with a guard, into Katowice, to a Polish dentist. Those trips happened virtually every week. I had four teeth pulled out with what looked like a set of pliers. No anaesthetic, mind. One of the camp's characters, Wally Martin, was there with me one day. The guard knocked on the dentist's door, a Pole opened it and there were two German soldiers sitting there, waiting their turn. Immediately they stood and gave the 'Heil Hitler' salute and the guard answered the same. Wally, quick as a flash, clicked his heels and said 'Larry Adler!' At our reunions after the war, that was our salute, 'Larry Adler'.

"It was a few years after the war before I was fit enough, or interested enough, to start playing football again. When I did it was for the works team at GKN, in the Steel Cup. I played in goal for them until I was 41. At that age I thought it was time to retire and concentrate on supporting Newport County."

No. 6as/A/41
(If replying, please quote above No.)

Army Form B. 104—83

...............Infantry..............Record Office,

...............Exeter...............

...............14th March...............1942.

Sir or Madam,

I regret to have to inform you that a report has been received from the War Office to the effect that (No.) 3914334 (Rank) Lance-Corporal (Name) Ronald William Godfrey JONES (Regiment) THE WELCH REGIMENT was posted as " missing " on the 28th January 1942 in the Middle East

The report that he is missing does not necessarily mean that he has been killed, as he may be a prisoner of war or temporarily separated from his regiment.

Official reports that men are prisoners of war take some time to reach this country, and if he has been captured by the enemy it is probable that unofficial news will reach you first. In that case I am to ask you to forward any postcard or letter received at once to this Office, and it will be returned to you as soon as possible.

Should any further official information be received it will be at once communicated to you.

I am,

Sir or Madam,

Your obedient Servant,

Mr. Jones

Jn. Wearle Lieut-Col

for Officer in charge of Records.

IMPORTANT.

Any change of your address should be immediately notified to this Office.

Wt. 30051/1249 400,000 (16) 9/39 KJL/8812 Gp 698/3 Forms/B.104—83/9

Bad news for Gwladys Jones. The telegram she received informing her that Ron had been captured in North Africa and was a prisoner of war.   (*Author's collection*)

In May 1940 the Germans started converting a Polish cavalry barracks near the small town of Oswiecim into a detention centre for prisoners whose offences were "relatively light and definitely correctable." It was not until March 1942 that it became the focus of the "Final Solution of the Jewish question in Europe". *(Auschwitz-Birkenau State Museum)*

Heinrich Himmler (second from the left), the head of the SS, is accompanied by IG Farben engineer Maximillian Faust (in civilian clothes) on an inspection of the Auschwitz expansion in 1942. *(Auschwitz-Birkenau State Museum)*

The IG Farben factory known as Auschwitz 3, or Monowitz, in which British POWs were made to work alongside Jewish slave labourers. *(Auschwitz-Birkenau State Museum)*

History's cruellest lie? The infamous gate at Auschwitz bearing the legend "Arbeit Macht Frei", which translates as "Work Will Make You Free". No worker was ever freed until the Russians liberated the camp in January 1945. *(Auschwitz-Birkenau State Museum)*

British POWs pictured in front of their barracks.

(Author's collection)

The Welsh football team at Auschwitz. Ron Jones is in the middle of the back row.

(Author's collection)

Amateur dramatics were staged by the POWs to relieve the purgatory of camp life. In this production of "Sweeny Todd" Ron Jones played the part of a police sergeant.

(Author's collection)

Ron Jones in the goalkeeper's jersey he wore in the Welsh football team.

(Author's collection)

The Welsh feathers Ron embroidered for his football jersey.

(Author's collection)

Poasent lga-ga   Tues 25th Jan 44.

I have just received two letters and I must say
I am surprised to hear you are not getting my mail
as I write every week and I receive yours regular.
Still you'll get them all at once just now. You must
look after Iny darling now she is in trouble and if
any thing happens to Oliver, Danine will have a home
I don't know about that record honeymoon in Yorkshire as I have had so much travelling this last three
years that I am afraid it will take a lot to move
me from our fireplace. I suppose you did enjoy
yourself at the dance on the 3rd Nov. under the
circumstances (I suppose that means other men's arms).
Dear heart if you only knew what heart ache you
give me when you mention dances you wouldn't go.
Surely there is other entertainment for you without
having to be held in other's arms. There are thousands
about better than I, and what if you met one as
most probably Peggy will if she goes on like that.
What will happen to me then. If it wasn't for the
thought of coming back to you some day I shouldn't
have lived this life as long as I have. You have been
without a man for 3 years and being in contact with them
such as dancing-well. Darling please be carefull I love you so-Ron
(Yours-ever

Ron's worried letter home in 1944, in which he urges his wife, Gwladys, to be careful
of the company she is keeping when out dancing.   (Author's collection)

Slave labour by "stripeys", as the POWs called Jewish inmates on account of their distinctive clothing.
(Vad Yashem)

Jewish slave labourers queue for the daily ration of soup that the British POWs considered foul and inedible.
(Vad Yashem)

The railway to hell. A chilling view of the tracks that led more than a million Jews, and others, to terrible deaths in the gas chambers. *(Auschwitz-Birkenau State Museum)*

The railway spur and unloading ramp where the life or death "selections" were made. Those deemed unfit for slave labour went sent straight to the gas chambers.

(Auschwitz-Birkenau State Museum)

Chapter 6

To Bomb or Not to Bomb?

How could it be that the governments of the two great Western democracies knew that a place existed where 2,000 helpless human beings could be killed every 30 minutes, knew that such killings actually did occur over and over again, and yet did not feel driven to search for some way to wipe such a scourge from the earth?

(David S. Wyman,
The Abandonment of the Jews: America and the Holocaust)

The question whether or not the Allies should have bombed Auschwitz to put an end to, or at least seriously disrupt, its diabolical work persists to this day. The issue has moral, practical and emotional aspects which complicate the debate. There is no doubt that it could have been done, and some of the reasons why it wasn't are deeply concerning; on the other hand, it would have been impossible to bomb the gas chambers without causing casualties among prisoners housed in their close proximity. On one occasion in August 1944, when the Americans bombed the IG Farben factory, three miles from Birkenau, 38 British POWs were killed and many more seriously injured. That same month, when the United States Army Air Corps bombed a factory next to Buchenwald concentration camp, 315 prisoners were killed and 525 badly injured.

The first request for the RAF to bomb Auschwitz came in January 1941, from the Polish general staff. Air Chief Marshal Sir Charles Portal, chief of the Air Staff refused, stating that British bombing techniques were not accurate enough for the task. There was much – too much – obfuscation at the time, but we now know that the Allies were aware of the nature of the camp from May 1941, when the Polish government in exile, in London, informed them of what was going on. It became public knowledge in July 1942, when a newspaper in London listed 22 camps, including Auschwitz, where atrocities were taking place, and on 17 December the British Foreign Secretary, Anthony Eden, read a statement to Parliament, condemning the murder of the Jews.

On 1 June 1943 *The Times* carried an article about "Nazi Brutality to Jews" at Auschwitz and in January 1944 a Polish agent, codenamed Wanda, arrived in London and reported that "children and women are taken to the gas chambers and there they are suffocated with the most horrible suffering lasting 10 to 15 minutes." The report added that "10,000 people daily" were being murdered in "three large crematoria", and that 650,000 Jews had already been exterminated.

Auschwitz was first flown over by an Allied reconnaissance aircraft on 4 April 1944, during a mission to photograph the synthetic oil plant at Monowitz, after which Jewish leaders asked the Americans to bomb the railway lines that supplied the camp with victims, but in Washington the War Department decided against it in July, claiming it was impractical because "It could be executed only by diversion of considerable air support essential to the success of our forces now engaged in decisive operations."

A War Department internal memo stated: "We must constantly bear in mind that the most effective relief which can be given victims of enemy persecution is to ensure the speedy defeat of the Axis." Colonel Thomas Davis, of their Logistics Group, is on record with the callous statement that: "We are over there to win the war, and not to take care of refugees."

Sir Winston Churchill was approached in July, and was in favour of the bombing. He wrote to the Foreign Secretary, Anthony Eden, saying "Get anything out of the Air Force you can, and invoke me if necessary", but on 15 July the Air Ministry wrote to Eden, saying it was "out of our power" because the targets were too distant for the RAF's heavy bombers to reach. To his eternal disgrace, one of Eden's Foreign Office subordinates, Armine Dew, wrote in September 1944: "In my opinion, a disproportionate amount of time at the Office is wasted on dealing with these wailing Jews."

In *The Abandonment of the Jews: America and the Holocaust*, David S. Wyman writes that "The US War Department consistently turned down proposals to bomb Auschwitz and the rail lines leading to it. The chief military reason given was that such proposals were 'impracticable' because they required 'the diversion of considerable air support essential to the success of our forces now engaged in decisive operations elsewhere'." However, as Wyman goes on to observe: "From March 1944 on, the Allies controlled the skies over Europe. Beginning in early May, the Italy-based 15th Air Force had the range and capability to strike the relevant targets."

Professor Wyman points out that the Allies only became interested in bombing Auschwitz when they turned their attention to the disruption of Germany's oil supplies as the best way to win the war, after which the IG Farben works became a target. "Loss of oil gradually strangled the Third Reich's military operations," he states.

"In late June the 15th Air Force was about to move the 'oil war' into Upper Silesia, where Germany had created a major synthetic oil industry based on the vast coal resources there. Eight important oil plants were clustered within a rough half-circle 35 miles in radius, with Auschwitz near the north-east end of the arc and Blechhammer near the north-west end.

"Blechhammer was the main target. Fleets ranging from 102 to 357 heavy bombers hit it on ten occasions between 7 July and 20 November. But Blechhammer was not the only industrial target. All eight plants shook under the impact of tons of high explosives. Among them was the industrial section of Auschwitz itself."

David Wyman insists that "The United States could readily have demonstrated concern for the Jews", adding, "There is no doubt that destruction of the gas chambers and crematoria would have saved many lives. Mass murder continued at Auschwitz until the gas chambers were closed in November 1944. Throughout the summer and fall, transports kept coming from many parts of Europe, carrying tens of thousands of Jews to their deaths."

He claims it would have been straightforward to identify the extermination facilities from the air. "The four large gassing-cremation installations stood in two pairs. Two of the extermination buildings were 340 feet long, the others two-thirds that length. Chimneys towered over them. Beginning in April 1944 detailed aerial reconnaissance photographs of Auschwitz-Birkenau were available to the U.S. Air Force headquarters in Italy. And descriptions of the structures and of the camp's lay-out, supplied by escapees, were in Washington by early July 1944."

Professor Wyman accepts that heavy bombers, operating from high altitude, could not have been accurate enough to prevent many casualties among the camp's inmates, but suggests an alternative:

"A small number of Mitchell medium bombers, which hit with more accuracy from lower altitudes, could have flown with one of the missions to Auschwitz. An even more precise alternative would have been dive bombing. A few Lightning P38 dive bombers could have knocked out the murder buildings without danger to the inmates at Birkenau. P38s proved they were capable of such a distant assignment on 10 June 1944 when they dive-bombed the oil refineries at Ploesti.

"The most effective means of all for destroying the killing installations would have been to dispatch about 20 British Mosquitoes to Auschwitz – a project that could have been arranged with the RAF. This fast fighter-bomber had ample range for the mission and its technique of bombing at very low altitudes had proven extremely precise. In February 1944, for instance, 19 Mosquitoes set out to break open a prison at Amiens to free members of the French Resistance held there for execution.

"The first two waves of the attack struck with such accuracy, smashing the main wall and the guardhouses, that the last six planes did not bomb. A November appeal for bombing Auschwitz pointed out the similarity to the Amiens mission. The War Department denied that any parallel existed, but in fact the Amiens attack required greater precision and had to be carried out in very bad winter weather."

David Wyman concludes: "It is evident that the diversion explanation was no more than an excuse. The real reason the proposals were refused was the War Department's prior decision that rescue was not to be a part of its mission. To the U.S. military, Europe's Jews represented an extraneous problem and an unwanted burden."

In his international best-seller *Auschwitz: The Nazis and The Final Solution*, Laurence Rees also observes that "The bombing question has become much bigger than a debate about practicalities and has taken on a symbolic dimension – proof that the Allies could have prevented Jewish deaths but chose not to." However, he continues, "Because of the collateral damage to the barracks, only metres from the crematoria, it would probably have killed hundreds of the very prisoners the raid was designed to save."

This argument is backed up by the inaccuracy and comparative ineffectiveness of the Allies' four major air raids on the Monowitz complex. Thousands of bombs were dropped by hundreds of aircraft but the power plant was never hit and the Buna factory never destroyed.

The first raid took place on 4 May 1943, when the camp commandant, Rudolph Hoess, reported to his superiors that "several" enemy planes dropped bombs, nine of which exploded "near Buna". They had also strafed (machine-gunned) one of the watch towers.

As a consequence of that action, Hoess asked for a battery of 12 anti-aircraft guns, and by August 1943 the military had provided 27 AA guns and 126 barrage balloons. Bomb shelters were built at the factory and anti-shrapnel ditches dug.

On 12 May 1944 the United States Airforce targeted the factory and other targets in Upper Silesia in strength, with 935 heavy bombers. The damage was slight, but a week later Albert Speer, the Nazis' Minister for Armaments, told Hitler: "The enemy has attacked one of our most valuable sectors. If this time they persist, soon we may lack an effective means of producing fuel."

Allied air reconnaissance had identified the synthetic fuel

and rubbers plants and on 27 May 1944 the British War Cabinet's sub-committee on Axis Oil warned: "Once work on the hydrogenation part of the Auschwitz plant is completed, as will soon happen, its production capability may reach 180,000 tons of fuel, with the prospect of reaching even 500,000 tons per annum in the future."

With that in mind, the bombers returned on 20 August 1944, when 127 American Flying Fortresses, escorted by 102 Mustang fighters, were committed to the latest raid. At 10.00 a.m. sirens sounded the alarm and a further prearranged warning was given by a large yellow basket hoisted on the roof of the Carbide tower. The air defences performed poorly. Twenty-five German interceptors were chased off by the Mustangs, smokescreens were spread too late, the barrage balloons failed to rise to an effective level in time, and the AA fire was inaccurate.

Consequently only one Allied plane was lost when, from a height of 30,000 feet, 1,336 bombs were dropped, weighing a total of 334 tons. Unfortunately, the raid was notable more for the prisoners it killed than for the minor damage done to its target. Ron Jones takes up the story:

"My worst moment in Auschwitz came when we were bombed that Sunday. In all, there were four occasions in late 1944 when the Americans carpet-bombed the factory. They always did it on a Sunday morning because they must have known we didn't work on Sundays and that we'd be back in our camp.

"We'd get warning that the planes were on their way. An air raid siren would sound off up to half an hour before they arrived, usually at about 11 o' clock. You could see them coming, we used to stand there and watch them making their attacks from every direction – all four corners. Our compound was very close to the factory and we could see the bombs all the way down. There were no fighters to stop them, the German Luftwaffe was on its last legs by then.

"The first time it happened was on a lovely sunny day, so a lot of us were out and about for some recreation. The first we knew something was up was when the Germans lit their smokescreens, which meant it was time to take cover. The number of planes was incredible – Flying Fortresses escorted by Mustang fighters. They were bombing the factory, not the camp, but we were dangerously close to the works and the Germans had allowed us to dig zig-zag trenches and gave us some corrugated sheeting and concrete slabs to put over the top. The earth we had dug was piled on top of that – the same principle as the Anderson shelters back home.

"The air raid sirens were going but we hadn't been bombed before, just had a few false alarms, and a lot of the lads thought this was another of those and stayed out in the open. I'm a bit claustrophobic and I wouldn't go in the shelter so I was lying on the ground outside when the bombs started falling.

"Thank God for my claustrophobia. A stray bomb dropped right on the shelter and killed all those poor lads who had been caught in a last-minute rush to get in. Of course, there were a lot injured as well as the dead and the scene was horrific. The blast had blown bodies all over the place and there were dead and dying and body parts everywhere. The call went up for anyone with mining experience to get the injured out, and in desperation the lads clawed away at the rubble with their bare hands. The casualties – and there were some terrible injuries – were taken out of the camp to the infirmary in the village. Those who died were buried in the cemetery at Auschwitz, then the coffins were moved to a church graveyard in Katowice after the war.

"It was an appalling, traumatic end to what started out as a day of celebration. We'd all heard about the success of D Day and the progress of the Second Front, so we organised what we called a gala, a bit of a tea party with fun and games – I remember a coconut shy – and a good old sing-song on a stage we'd put up."

Brian Bishop was unwell when the fatal bomb fell, but left his sick bed to help the survivors. He said: "When the bombing happened I was in the sick bay. I had a fever which the doctor said was brought on by drinking contaminated water. So when the bombing started I was in bed. When the raid was over the medical officer came in and said: 'We need your help to get the wounded in.' Most of them weren't too bad. The worst one was a big sergeant whose head had split and his scalp was hanging over one ear. All I could do for him was lift it back into place and tell the doctor, who did what he could."

Another prisoner in E715, Ronald Redman, from Brighton, recalled the afternoon's tragic events as follows:

"Our camp was just off the perimeter road around the IG Farben factory, as were the Ukrainian forced labourers, French volunteers and Jewish camps. It was a beautiful sunny day when the Germans suddenly lit their smoke screens with the news of large bombing formations leaving Italy and heading towards Silesia.

"The balloon was going up – literally. This was a red and orange basket hoisted in stages on the tallest chimney stack to warn of the planes. If the balloon was at the chimney top, the planes were overhead! This time they were American.

"We had dug zig-zag trenches and covered them with large concrete slabs. The entrance was a concrete slope at one end. We'd had some false alarms when I'd noticed that near the entrance pools of water made it undesirable, and that further in the trenches it was drier. Therefore I resolved to go deeper in the trench as the sirens were sounding.

"Sadly, many of the lads were reluctant to go in, despite the shouting of the guards. It was so fine and sunny, and maybe this was another false alarm.

"I heard the whoosh as the first stick of bombs came down and the blast blew me upside down in the shelter. When we finally emerged from the rubble we learned that there had been a last-minute rush to enter from the ramp and a lot of the men had been too late.

"The area around the ramp was devastated. It looked like a direct hit and the blast had flung the bodies far and wide. I remember one guard noisily suggesting it was 'a pity it wasn't all of us' as we were recovering the bodies."

It wasn't only the British POWs who suffered. Another Monowitz inmate, Alfred Ehrlich, recalled how a bomb had fallen on a different workers' camp. He said:

"Our reinforced concrete hall was cut in two by the bomb. Huge pipes and other heavy objects flew in the air as if they were made of paper.

"All of a sudden an oak railway sleeper was hurled into the air and, falling from a great height, it landed on my left leg, crushing it into the sand. Cautiously I bent and dug it out with my left hand. My tormented groans could only be heard by those laying closest to me as the din of the bombers drowned out all other noises.

"There was indescribable chaos when two bombs exploded very close to some pipes stacked alongside a ditch in which work squads were cowering. You could hear the groans and cries of these unfortunate prisoners with ripped and crushed arms and legs, while many others lay slowly dying beneath the subsided pipe stack."

Ehrlich described how one badly injured prisoner, carried away on an improvised stretcher, exulted loudly in his mistaken belief that the factory had been destroyed. Thirty inmates were killed and 250 treated for injuries in the camp hospital. Those maimed too badly to work were sent to Birkenau and certain death.

Again damage to the factory was slight and the raid deemed unsatisfactory, so the process was repeated on 13 September 1944. This time 96 B24 Liberators dropped 943 500-pound bombs from lower attitude, in search of improved accuracy. On this occasion, however, the Germans were better prepared. The smokescreens did their job and anti-aircraft fire was intense, with the result that the bombs were dispersed even further afield. Some fell on Auschwitz town, destroying several buildings and killing 15 inhabitants. Two fell on Birkenau, demolishing an air raid shelter, and one on an SS barracks. Forty-three prisoners, 30 civilian workers and 15 SS men were killed.

Three bombers were brought down over the target and 51 damaged, but again damage to the factory was small and the post-operation reconnaissance report admitted: "The fresh damage is not likely greatly to delay the work of completing the synthetic oil plant."

The poor results were bordering on the embarrassing and the USAAF tried yet again on 18 December 1944, when 47 Liberators and two Flying Fortresses dropped 436 500-pound bombs. They repeated the mission on Boxing Day when 95 Liberators dropped 679 bombs. By now the bomb loads delivered ought to have obliterated the factory, but large parts of it, including the power plant, remained undamaged.

Statistics tell us that barely one-third of the bombs dropped by the United States Air Force during the war fell within 300 yards of their target – they even bombed towns in Switzerland when targeting Germany. In view of this serial inaccuracy, the official *History of Auschwitz IG Farben Work Camps*, published by the Auschwitz-Birkenau Museum, concludes:

1. The heavy B17 and B24 bombers used against the IG Farben factory were quite unsuitable for the bombing of Birkenau gas chambers and crematoria. The large dispersion of bombs dropped from these planes would have undoubtedly resulted in huge losses among the inmates without providing any guarantee that the actual target would be hit. There was therefore no sense in some of these bombers leaving the main force that was attacking the Monowitz factory for the "opportunity" of attacking the Birkenau crematoria.

2. The use of a few Mosquito squadrons to bomb the crematoria (as suggested by David Wyman) would have required the organising of a quite separate mission, for the Mosquito was much too fast to be able to escort the slower B17 and B24 bombers. On the other hand, a separate mission would not require a fighter escort as the Mosquito was faster than any German fighter.

3. The entire Auschwitz air defence system was organised to protect above all the IG Farben factory. For Mosquitoes attacking Birkenau crematoria at low altitude the only serious obstacle would have been the anti-aircraft guns, but even their fire would probably not have seriously hindered the accurate dropping of bombs. In such a case, one could still not ignore the possibility of inadvertently hitting several barracks inhabited by prisoners, but 15th USAAF Command

had to take into account far greater prisoner losses in the Monowitz camp and still went ahead with the decision to drop bombs.

Given the earlier reluctance, why did the air raids start in August 1944? It was nothing to do with the Holocaust. The Allies decided to concentrate their aerial bombardment on the Nazis' oil-producing facilities as a way of shortening the war, in the knowledge that the lack of oil was seriously hampering the German military. It was in August that Romania, one of Hitler's allies, sued for peace and changed sides, costing Germany its last access to conventional fuel.

Eight synthetic oil plants were within a 35-miles radius of Auschwitz and the American 15th Air Force bombed them all, including Buna, on 10 occasions between July 7 and November 20.

Ron Jones says: "The factory was bombed several times, first by the Americans, and at the end, as they closed in, by the Russians. In a raid three weeks after the one that killed our lads, the Americans hit the factory again. This time bombs destroyed an SS barracks, killing 15 of them and seriously injuring 28, but Birkenau was also hit, killing 40 prisoners and injuring 65, so the bombing caused more casualties among the prisoners than the Germans.

"That raid was shown on television many years later in a documentary. I thought: 'The cheeky buggers are boasting about killing the SS, but they don't mention how many of us they killed.' I had a letter published in the *Daily Mail* about it, saying how annoyed I was that they conveniently overlooked our 38 dead and the many more who were badly injured.

"I know the Allies were criticised for not bombing the

gas chamber and crematoriums, but the reason for that was obvious. If they had done it, they would have killed all the prisoners in its vicinity. They bombed the factory instead, but still with tragic results on that one awful occasion.

"Should they have bombed the gas chambers? I don't think so. There would have been too much 'collateral damage' as they call it today. But I know Jewish leaders in Hungary pleaded for air strikes on the railways to prevent the transportation of Hungarian Jews, who were the last to be rounded up, in March 1944. Surely that could have been done?"

Chapter 7

IG Farben and the Factory of Death

It is a little-known fact, even today, that IG Farben, not the Nazi government, financed and was therefore responsible for Auschwitz and all its works, including Dr Josef Mengele's inhuman medical experiments.

The Nuremberg court found that Auschwitz was paid for and owned by IG and that their use of slave labour was a crime against humanity. The evidence against them included the following testimony from a former SS doctor by the name of Hoven: "The SS did not have notable scientists at its disposal. The experiments in the concentration camps only took place in the interests of IG. They let the SS deal with the dirty work in the camps. It was not IG's intention to bring any of this out into the open, but rather to put up a smokescreen around the experiments so that they could keep any profits for themselves. It was not the SS but IG who took the initiative for the concentration camp experiments."

At the conclusion of the trial, the company was told to pay compensation to its Jewish victims, then go into liquidation.

Georg von Schnitzler, an IG Farben director, made the following damning admission: "IG took on a great responsibility and gave, in the chemical sector, substantial and even decisive aid for Hitler's foreign policy, which led to war and the ruination of Germany. I must conclude that IG is largely responsible for the policies of Hitler."

The size of the company's operation is staggering. They had accommodation for a workforce of 27,000, sleeping in 11 barracks camps, another 364 in barracks belonging to private construction companies, 164 in their own housing estate for German civilian workers and 58 homes in a nearby village for senior staff. They built a railway spur to transport slave labourers the four miles from Auschwitz to the Monowitz factory, and when that failed to cope with the ever-increasing numbers involved they spent two million marks on creating a new sub-camp, next to the works.

The journalist and author, John Cornwell, wrote that "IG Farben would emerge in the period of the Third Reich as one of the most formidable, and easily the most corrupt, multi-national in the world. [It] brought together the German chemical 'Big Six' – Bayer, BASF, Agfa, Hoechst, Casella and Kalle – into an '*Interessengemeinschaft*' (community of common interests). Hence 'IG' Farben."

In the early Thirties, before Hitler came to power, IG Farben had been the largest single donor to the National Socialists' election funds. When leading German industrialists met with Hermann Goering and Heinrich Himmler on 20 February 1933, IGF contributed 400,000 of the three million Reichsmarks raised for the Nazis' campaign. By 1935 they were contributing five million marks to party funds. They were well rewarded for their contribution, becoming the largest and richest company in Germany, producing poison and nerve gas for the Wehrmacht (never used) as well as orthodox armaments, the Zyklon B gas used in the gas chambers, and the chemicals used in Mengele's medical experiments. These were all financed by IG Farben.

When the war began, in 1939, the Germans had only two months supply of rubber in stock with no means of producing the real thing, so the need to manufacture it synthetically was a key element in the Nazis' Economic Four-Year Plan which was overseen by Goering. The plan required a buna (synthetic rubber) plant to be built, and IG Farben were allocated the concession. The synthetic rubber was to be made by a process called hydrogenation, which involves passing hydrogen gas over coal at a high temperature. Coal and water are essential raw materials, and their existence led Dr Otto Ambros, the executive in charge of rubber and plastics for IG Farben, to choose a site between three and four miles from Auschwitz.

Synthetic fuel was more than twice as expensive as normal oil refining, and had to be artificially stimulated and sustained by government orders and subsidies. IG Farben produced synthetic rubber using the molecule butadiene and the element sodium [Na], hence "buna."

Ambros needed a factory which required more than 500,000 cubic metres of water an hour and 1.2 million tons of coal per year in a region with good rail connections. After an exhaustive search, conducted mostly in Silesia, he settled on the conjunction of three rivers. The closest town was Oswiecim, which was renamed Auschwitz. The Germans expelled the Jewish population of 14,000 from the area and confiscated their homes. Any houses not required for the staff imported from Germany, or for construction workers from other parts of Poland, were demolished, with no compensation paid.

It was originally envisaged that Germans would be resettled to provide the workforce, so the possibility of using slave labour from the camp was not a major factor behind the siting. It was not until 6 February 1941, by which time huge numbers of German workers were being drafted into the army, that Carl Krauch, an IG director, had Goering ask Himmler to supply labour from prisoners at the concentration camp. By early 1942 there were 11,200 men working at the site, 2,000 of them from the camp.

On 18 February 1941 Goering instructed Himmler, and his SS, to supply all possible assistance. Goering wrote:

In order to acquire a workforce and provide it with accommodation in time for the construction of the Buna-Auschwitz plant to start in early April, the following measures are to be implemented as fast as possible:

1. *The Jews of Auschwitz and the surrounding areas are to be promptly expelled from their homes to provide living quarters for Buna plant construction workers.*
2. *Poles living in Auschwitz or the surrounding areas who can be employed as construction workers are to remain in their place of residence until the construction work is completed.*

By April 1941 all remaining Jews in the Auschwitz area had been deported.

Rudolph Hoess, the camp *kommandant*, found his own involvement taxing in the extreme. In his memoirs, written while awaiting trial as a war criminal, he wrote: "Before the war, the concentration camps were used to protect Germany from its internal enemies, but because of the war Himmler ordered that their main purpose now was to serve the war effort. Every possible prisoner was to become a defence plant worker. His [Himmler's] announcement during his visit in March 1941 was clear in this respect.

"The following plans for the camp spoke clearly enough:

Preparation of the camp for 100,000 POWs, the remodelling of the old camp for 30,000 prisoners and the allocation for the Buna factory of 10,000 prisoners. At that time, these numbers were unheard of in the history of concentration camps. Before, a camp containing 10,000 prisoners was considered tremendously large.

"The emphasis that Himmler put on the ruthless, quickest possible acceleration of the construction, while at the same time ignoring the existing and anticipated difficulties, which I doubted could be eliminated, made me suspicious. The way in which he dismissed the considerable objections led me to believe that something very unusual was in the works."

"Something very unusual" is quite an understatement. What Himmler was doing was paving the way for the Final Solution of the Jewish Question, and at the same time planning to make a fortune for the SS from hiring out slave labour. Because of acute labour shortages, Germany's major industrial companies employed both foreign workers and slave labourers from the concentration camps.

At Auschwitz, the camp authorities undertook to maintain the productivity of prisoners at 75 per cent of that of the German civilian workers but in reality, because of their starvation diet and the physical abuse they had to endure from their supervisors and guards, the slave workers never attained anything approaching that level. IG Farben, who complained frequently, estimated the true figure between 30 and 40 per cent.

German workers were always in the minority in the Monowitz factory. Apart from Poles, Auschwitz inmates and POWs there were large numbers of French, Italians, Czechs and Croats, plus Dutch, Belgians, Spaniards, Danes, Slovaks, Lithuanians and even Arabs from north Africa. On trial at

Nuremberg Otto Ambros testified that the company had paid over 20 million marks for the hire of prisoners to work at the Buna factory.

The ultimate work on the subject, *Anatomy of the Auschwitz Death Camp*, states that:

"During every year that Auschwitz was in existence, prison labour was assigned to outside businesses. In 1941 about 1,000 prisoners out of a total of 10,000 worked for the only firm in the vicinity, IG Farbenindustrie. In 1942 about 4,600 prisoners of 24,000 worked for outside establishments. In 1943 about 15,000 prisoners out of 88,000 worked for outside firms and in 1944 about 37,000 out of 105,000.

"The largest employers of prisoners were chemical plants. In 1944 chemical plants employed over 18,000 prisoners, nearly 50 per cent of all those who worked outside the camp. The largest employer was IG Farben. In the summer of 1944 it had 11,000 Auschwitz prisoners at its disposal. The second largest employer of Auschwitz prisoners was the mining industry, which employed over 7,000 in 1944."

Hoess said of the use of Jewish labour:

"Originally all the Jews transported to Auschwitz were to be destroyed, without exception, but during the arrival of the first transports of German Jews the order was given that all able-bodied men and women were to be separated and put to work in the arms factories. The sorting process went as follows:

"The railway cars were unloaded one after another. After depositing their baggage, the Jews had to pass individually in front of an SS doctor, who decided on their physical fitness as they marched past him. Those who were considered able-bodied were immediately escorted into the camp in small groups. On average between 25 and 30 per cent were found fit for work, but this figure fluctuated considerably. The figure for Greek Jews, for example, was only 15 per cent while there were transports from Slovakia with a fitness rate of 100 per cent."

The reality was that those under the age of 16, mothers with children, the sick, the old and the weak were "selected" on arrival, loaded on to trucks and transported straight to the gas chamber. Those deemed fit enough to be worked to death were taken to the camp, tattooed with a serial number on their left arm and registered. Regular "selections" were made inside the camp, and those no longer fit for work were dispatched to the gas chamber. At least half the registered prisoners died, from malnutrition, disease or exhaustion.

By the end of March 1941 the IG factory was ready to start work. The intention was that it should produce 30,000 tons of synthetic rubber per year. A month earlier a feasibility study had been commissioned into the practicality of incorporating a synthetic fuel plant into the factory complex, with the aim of producing 75,000 tons of fuel per year.

At first, the Jews working at the Buna factory had to rise at 3.00 a.m. and march four miles from their camp before a 12-hour shift, but from 29 July 1941 they travelled by train, to nearby Dwory station. Their work was both heavy and dirty – digging drainage ditches and roads, extracting gravel, laying cables and the like. At midday each slave labourer received a mug of soup, which was no more than a few scraps of cabbage or turnip in hot water. In the evening it was soup again, this time with bits of rotten potato or swede.

Of the Jewish slave labourers working out of Monowitz, between 70 and 80 died each month. A nurse working in the camp hospital made the following entry in his diary: "14 April. Today 18 were brought to the hospital from Buna – one has already died. They had been working without being given any lunch. Since dawn I can hear the groans of the sick and the dying. One of those from Buna who died was well built and tall, it wasn't exhaustion that killed him. His entire back and buttocks were bruised. It seems that they dislodged his kidneys."

The Jewish prisoners became almost bestial in their desperation to survive and it was not unusual for one to kill another for a piece of bread. Hoess wrote: "They were no longer human beings, they had become animals, who sought only food." The Germans called these poor unfortunates *"Muselmänner"* (i.e. 'muslims') which was their derogatory name for the walking dead.

The collaboration between IG Farben and the SS was built on cruelty and violence. As Maximilian Faust, the engineer in charge of construction, put it: "Achieving the appropriate productivity is out of the question without the stick."

IG, famed as the world leader in the creation of synthetic substances, was increasingly reliant on slave labour, and the largest company in Europe and the fourth largest in the world (after General Motors, US Steel and Standard Oil), became "morally bankrupt", as one historian has said. The inhuman experiments carried out by Mengele and another SS man, Dr Helmut Vetter, were financed by the company, and included the removal of organs without anaesthetic, deliberately infecting victims with diseases and the testing of new drugs manufactured by IG Farben's Bayer pharmaceutical division.

In the Auschwitz files, correspondence between the camp commandant, Hoess, and IG includes a letter from the company requesting the provision of 150 female prisoners for experimental purposes. Hoess demanded a fee of 200 Reichsmarks per guinea pig, but IG haggled: "We consider the price to be too high. We propose to pay no more than 170 RM per woman. If this is acceptable to you, the women will be placed in our possession. Please prepare for us 150 women in the best health possible."

The deal was agreed at 170RM each, and IG sent a receipt: "Received the order for 150 women. Despite their macerated condition, they were considered satisfactory. We will keep you informed of the developments regarding the experiments." A subsequent letter stated: "The experiments were performed. All test persons died. We will contact you shortly about a new shipment."

Meanwhile, at Monowitz the need for more workers at the Buna factory found the railway inadequate for the transportation of the numbers required, and the factory management decided to create a new sub-camp, next to the works. This was completed at the end of October 1942, with a prisoner population of 2,100. By the middle of 1944 this had been expanded to 10,000 and the Monowitz camp, at 270 x 490 metres, was bigger than the Auschwitz main camp (but not Birkenau).

Despite this increase, the company's use of sick, exhausted prisoners in their Buna factory saw production tail off to an alarming degree, and in January 1943 Richard Glücks, the SS economics administrator with responsibility for all the concentration camps, instructed camp commandants everywhere "to make every effort to reduce the mortality figure", in order to "preserve the prisoners' capacity for work". The following month the SS agreed, at IG's request, to the systematic replacement of those no longer capable of hard labour.

On 9 September 1943, the management agreed to set up a new sub-camp at Monowitz for 1,000 British POWs. This was surrounded by a barbed wire fence, but no watch towers. It was placed under the jurisdiction of the Wehrmacht, not the SS, and guarded by between 50 and 60 soldiers from a territorial battalion. The first consignment of 200 POWs arrived on 16 September 1943, another 600 a week later. Eventually the camp population increased to 1,200, the majority of inmates captured in North Africa.

IG Farben paid the SS 4.50 RM per day for unskilled POWs and six RM for skilled workers but, despite the superior physical condition of the British prisoners, they found that output was no better than for the Jews and other forced labourers.

By October 1944 IG Farben employed 83,000 foreign workers – 46 per cent of its total workforce. This included 9,600 POWs and 10,900 concentration camp inmates. Construction of the IG Farben factory continued until the first days of January 1945, by which time, with the Red Army's guns audible, the company had spent 524 million marks on the project, and estimated that full completion would cost another 250 million.

Methanol, used in aircraft fuel and explosives, was produced from March 1944, at a rate of 3,200 tons per month, which was 15 per cent of Germany's total output. Heating oil and tar were also produced in late 1944, at 400 and 200 tons per month respectively, but the Buna plant was never completed by the Nazis and produced only a token amount of benzine/petrol and no synthetic rubber. Full production was scheduled for the end of 1945.

When the Red Army arrived there was no heavy fighting, so the facility was captured virtually intact, and within four weeks it was being dismantled for export to the Soviet Union. The wheel had turned and the labour required was provided by German POWs, who were being held in the Auschwitz main camp. With unintended irony one of them, Ernst Dittmar, wrote on 6 July 1945: "Hard work at the IG Farben factory in Auschwitz. Long hours: 9.00 to 21.30. Hunger and exhaustion. Finally, free time in the evening. There is nothing to eat. No break at noon. It is the first time we have worked like this."

For six months the German POWs dismantled the factory and loaded the machinery on to railway freight cars, for dispatch to a chemical plant in western Siberia. In total the Red Army sent 300,000 tons of industrial material.

The Monowitz complex was finally handed back to the Polish authorities on 1 September 1945. It was 1948 before they were able to restore the factory to working order and 1949 before the first synthetic petrol was produced. It was soon discontinued on economic grounds, but synthetic rubber took over in the early 1950s. Today, the plant is still the largest synthetic rubber factory in Poland, operating as Dwory SA.

After the war charges were brought against 24 members of the board of IG Farben, Otto Ambros among them. In *Exorcising Hitler*, the historian Frederick Taylor vividly describes the "Who, me?" attitude of these war criminals. Taylor writes:

"Dr Georg von Schnitzler was a board member of the chemicals giant, closely involved in defence matters and an enthusiastic member of the Nazi party. Agents of the American Military Government finally tracked him down to a country estate north-west of Frankfurt. Von Schnitzler had been involved in the ruthless plundering of Europe through mass kidnapping of slaves and in organising the forced expropriation of foreign companies. A historian of IG Farben describes the meeting between the predatory lawyer and his nemesis:

'He received them wearing his trademark Scottish tweeds and English brogues, sitting in a room enhanced by a large Renoir over the fireplace. After offering them a brandy (which they declined), he said he was happy "all this unpleasantness is over", and that he was looking forward to seeing his old friends at ICI and DuPont again. When he was asked to accompany his visitors back to Frankfurt, he politely declined. As the SHAEF report of the meeting recalled: "He replied that he was unable to do so as the way was so long and he was so old (61)." The next invitation came from a sergeant with a tommy-gun. This time the Herr Direktor did come.'

The arrest of Von Schnitzler's boss, Hermann Schmitz, took longer. Taylor writes: "Schmitz was a director of IG Farben for 20 years, a Nazi member of the Reichstag from 1933 and succeeded Carl Bosch as chairman of the company in 1935. [He] unquestionably bore ultimate responsibility for every criminal act, every ruined life and agonising death the company inflicted. Nevertheless, unlike Von Schnitzler, Schmitz was not arrested immediately at his house in Heidelberg. Only after searching the building several times did American investigators find a trunk stuffed with hundreds of [incriminating] company documents.

"A British intelligence officer, Major Tilley, managed to extract from Schmitz the location of his [concealed] personal safe. The documents there included photographs of the branch of IG Farben's Buna Works in the Auschwitz industrial complex, the construction and operation of which cost at least 35,000 lives."

Schmitz, Von Schnitzler and the 22 other members of the IG Farben board were prosecuted for "waging war and plunder", but the crucial crime was "slavery and mass murder". The precise language of the indictment was as follows: "Farben, in complete defiance of all decency and human considerations, abused its slave workers by subjecting them, among other things, to excessively long, arduous and exhausting work, utterly disregarding their health or physical condition. The sole criterion of the right to live or die was the production efficiency of the said inmates."

The trial opened on 27 August 1947 at the Palace of Justice in Nuremberg, and typical of the testimonies was this from Rudolf Vitek, a doctor and inmate: "The prisoners were pushed in their work by the *kapos*, foremen and overseers of the IG in an inhuman way. No mercy was shown. Thrashings, ill treatment of the worst kind, even direct killings were the fashion."

The witnesses spoke of IG Farben's participation in selections that would mean death for those not selected, of company workers witnessing the hanging of prisoners and of Farben staff being aware of the gassing and cremation of inmates in other parts of Auschwitz.

To widespread disgust, the majority view of the Nuremberg tribunal of judges was that the cruelty and inhumanity at Buna was the responsibility not of the corporate people at Farben but of the Nazi regime which had imposed the regulations that led to those crimes. The sentences passed on the 12 IG Farben executives ranged from eight years (for Otto Ambros) to one-and-a-half years. Only five of the 12 were found guilty of slavery and mass murder, and all received sentences ranging from six to eight years. By 1951 they had all been released and most were soon back in executive positions in Germany industry.

The chief prosecutor, Josiah DuBois, said the punishments

were "light enough to please a chicken thief", and the one dissenting judge, Paul M. Herbert, commented: "It was Farben's drive for speed in the construction of Auschwitz which resulted indirectly in thousands of inmates being selected for extermination by the SS when they were rendered unfit for work. The proof establishes that fear of extermination was used to spur the inmates to greater efforts, and they undertook tasks beyond their physical strength as a result of such fear."

Earlier, another Nuremberg prosecutor, Telford Taylor, had commented: "These companies, not the lunatic Nazi fanatics, are the main war criminals. If the guilt of these criminals is not brought to daylight and if they are not punished, they will pose a much greater threat to the future peace of the world than Hitler if he were still alive."

IG Farben had manufactured a high percentage of the explosives used by the German military, and in 1938 IG scientists had produced two deadly nerve gases, which they called Sarin and Tabun. Both were in production near Breslau by 1942, and 12,000 tons of Tabun was in storage by June 1944. In the aftermath of D Day some of Hitler's more fanatical acolytes were urging him to use the gas to counter the Allies' advances, and he did consider using it against the Red Army, in the east. Fortunately for all concerned, Speer told him that the factories producing the ingredients had been too badly damaged by air raids.

With all this in mind, General Eisenhower said the war could not have taken place without IG Farben. He called for the company to be broken up "as one means of assuring world peace", but his plan to dismember the conglomerate was thwarted. Instead its various businesses were consolidated into three of the old companies: Bayer, BASF and Hoechst.

In September 1955 Freidrich Jaehne, who had been sentenced to a year-and-a-half at Nuremberg, was elected chairman of Hoechst and the following year Fritz ter Meer, the IG Farben director in charge of operations at Auschwitz, who had been convicted of plunder and slavery, and served four years in jail, was elected chairman of the supervisory board of Bayer. He held that position for seven years, and his grave, in Krefeld, is decorated with a large headstone, donated by Bayer.

Chapter 8

Auschwitz as Big Business

It seems incredible now, but the SS ran Auschwitz as if it was an entirely normal operation. Indeed "normality" was probably the key to how they shut their minds to the inhuman nature of what they were doing. When they were not murdering people on an industrial scale they returned to their "normal" quarters, away from the camp, and went about living a "normal" home life in Auschwitz town. The SS even had their own pub, the Deutsches Haus Inn, commonly known as the Ratshof.

The commandant had a lovely detached villa in substantial grounds, well out of sight and sound of the camp's cacophony of death. Commandant Hoess took pride in his garden, which he described as "a paradise of flowers", and revealed that his four children (a fifth was born in 1943) kept numerous animals in the garden, including tortoises and lizards. On Sundays he and his family would walk across fields to ride their horses, or in summer went swimming in the river that was the eastern boundary of the camp complex.

The SS officers and senior managers from IG Farben enjoyed hunting, and for other ranks, including the company's civilian workers, there was a brothel, staffed by ten prostitutes recruited from Germany, a German cinema and a casino.

Liebehenschel, who succeeded Hoess, was keen for all his men to take time out from a murderous occupation, and the following extracts from his printed Orders of the Day reveal the extent to which conventional life went on:

Entertainment of the troops
The following events will take place during the month of November 1943:

Tuesday November 23, at 20:00 hours:
Performance in the State Theatre of Der Strohm – *Play by Max Halbe*

Friday November 26 at 20:00 hours
Performance in the Operahouse Kattowitz of an opera by Walter Kollo, Die Frau ohne Kuss

Sunday November 28 at 15:30 hours
Matinee performance for the children of SS families of Der Gestiefelte Kater. *Admission 50 RM*

Monday November 29 at 20:00 hours
The Symphony Orchestra of the city of Kattowitz will perform "Beschwingste Musik", in addition to several vocal soloists

December 7, 1943
Christmas Trees
The commander's office of the concentration camp Auschwitz will be available to take orders for Christmas trees until 14:00 hours on December 12 1943; for the various companies, their departments and sections.

Prohibiting the shooting of stray dogs:
To go into effect immediately.

Horse-drawn carriages:
I have been made aware repeatedly that horse-drawn
carriages (sleighs at this particular time) have been driven
with extremely high speed, to the point of putting stress on
the horses, leaving them exhausted, which is not tolerable.
I request that all drivers act on my advice so that the
horses may be spared.

Apparently Commandant Liebehenschel had more concern for the welfare of stray dogs and horses than he had for his suffering prisoners.

The concentration camp network, and its dual function of harsh imprisonment and commercial exploitation of "undesirables" dated from 1938, when Germany's territorial expansion began in earnest. As the Nazis intensified their preparation for war, rapidly enlarging their armed forces, manpower shortages were increasingly evident, especially in the construction industry. To remedy this situation Heinrich Himmler, the head of the SS, established a state-owned company, DEST, which acquired quarries, mines, gravel pits and the like where concentration camp prisoners were put to work.

When the war started in September 1939, conscription of men capable of bearing arms created an even more serious manpower shortage which was damaging to the German economy. In the three years from May 1939 civilian employment fell by nearly eight million, with the shortfall in labour made up by foreign workers and POWs. Hitler himself ordered that the concentration camps should contribute to the war effort.

It was Himmler who decreed that the camps would hire out prison labour on the condition that the private companies involved paid any building costs. The expense of establishing new plants was a deterrent, however, to most industrialists. Only the very biggest concerns could afford the start-up costs and by the end of 1942 just two were in the slave labour business. These were IG Farben and Hermann Goering Werke, the latter set up by the head of the Luftwaffe, who was also Hitler's deputy. From April 1941 IG Farben used labour from Auschwitz in constructing its chemical works at Dwory, which was next to the camp.

The SS were now running the camp as a business. For every manual worker they provided for IG Farben they charged 3 Reichsmarks per day. For specialists, such as electricians or welders, the rate was 5 RM. The children were not spared. The rate for them was 1.5 RM. At the end of 1943, SS monthly income from the hire of Auschwitz prisoners reached 2 million RM. By the end of the war the total figure was 20 million RM. For their money, IG Farben received an endless supply of new labour, and were "relieved" of those who became unfit for work, who were immediately sent to the gas chambers. Some 180 million RM in cash and belongings was taken from those who perished.

By mid-1942 Germany's war on the Eastern Front had taken an alarming turn for the worse. All available manpower had been called up by the military and orders went out requiring the maximum exploitation of prison camp labour to compensate.

Altogether, during the course of the war, nearly 8.5m foreign workers were pressed into the service of German industry, of whom at least 500,000 died, when increased brutality in search of greater productivity accelerated prisoner mortality. There were 4,585,000 prisoners of war, of all nationalities, engaged in forced labour, of whom only 3,425,000 survived.

At Auschwitz, Hoess was appointed commandant on 29 April 1940 and arrived the following day, with five SS men, to supervise construction of the camp. His subordinate, Gerhard Palitzsch, chose 30 German prisoners from elsewhere, all criminals, to act as *"kapos"*, or supervisors, as part of the prisoner self-government concept. Fifteen SS from Krakow were assigned to Auschwitz as the camp's first garrison.

The original camp, with its *"Arbeit Macht Frei"* sign, was surrounded by a four-metre-high electric fence and consisted of red-brick barracks. In those early days it was an ordinary concentration camp, not planned with extermination in mind. The first inmates were 728 Polish POWs and political prisoners, who arrived on 14 June 1940.

The first executions took place on 22 November 1940, when 40 Poles, sent by the police in nearby Katowice, were shot and cremated in the first of the camp's crematoria.

On 1 March 1941 Himmler visited Auschwitz with representatives of IG Farbenindustrie, who wanted to establish a factory on camp grounds. Himmler immediately authorised expansion plans, ordering Hoess to enlarge the original camp to hold 30,000 prisoners and to build a new camp at nearby Brzezinka (Birkenau) for 100,000 POWs, plus an additional 10,000 to build and work at an IG Farben industrial complex, to become known as the Buna works. The maximum number of British POWs to work there was 1,150 at the end of 1943. By the end, in January 1945, transfers elsewhere had reduced this to 574.

IG Farben were a huge company based in Frankfurt. Their choice of the Auschwitz area for a major new plant was influenced by good railway links, nearby coal and salt mines and tax relief offered by the Nazis to companies that moved into their conquered territories. It was also, at the time, beyond the range of Allied bombers and there was the availability of cheap concentration camp labour.

Given all these advantages, IG Farben built its Bunawerk plant six kilometres east of Auschwitz, in the village of Monowitz. Work started on its construction on 7 April 1941, with the SS building a bridge and a rail spur to connect the camp to the new plant.

The company bought the land for next to nothing after the Nazis confiscated it from its Polish owners without compensation. The Polish Jews in Oswiecim were expelled and their homes confiscated and sold cheaply to IG Farben for the company to house workers transferred from Germany.

After the German invasion of the Soviet Union in June 1941 there was a huge increase in the number of new prisoners, and Auschwitz established a POW camp for them, under the control of the Waffen SS. Auschwitz 2, or Birkenau, was built nearly two miles from the original, to accommodate up to 200,000 new prisoners. It was enormous, 15 square miles, and the village of Brzezinka was demolished to accommodate it.

The construction of Birkenau began on 7 October 1941, but almost immediately the original plans were modified to enable it to function as a death camp. The first sections, with barbed wire fences, gates and watchtowers were completed in 1942, when a women's section was also established. A separate camp for Gypsies was created in February 1943.

According to the Auschwitz-Birkenau State Museum, Auschwitz had control over 40 satellite camps in Silesia, 28 of which worked either directly or indirectly for the German armaments industry. Nine were established near foundries and other metal works, six near coal mines, another six supplied prison labour to chemical plants, three others to light industry, one was situated next to the plant manufacturing construction materials and one near a food processing plant. Prisoners from other camps worked in renovation and construction, in forestry and on farms.

The largest of these satellite camps was Monowitz (Monowice) where, when Ron Jones started work in 1943, the workforce was 29,000 strong. By 13 January 1945, shortly before liberation, there were 29,806 inmates, of whom 9,054 were Jews.

The performance of prisoners working in harsh conditions and on a starvation diet fell far short of German requirements and in January 1943 SS General Richard Glücks, the inspector general of concentration camps, ordered camp commandants "to make every effort to reduce the mortality figure", thereby "preserving the prisoners' capacity for work".

The Buna plant, which covered 12 square miles and used as much electricity as the whole of Berlin, was never completed and never produced any buna (synthetic rubber). From October 1943 it did supply 3,000 tons of methanol per month, used in aircraft fuel and explosives, and by late 1944 it contributed 15 per cent of Germany's total output of the chemical. Synthetic rubber production had been scheduled to start in January 1945.

In 1942 Auschwitz became overcrowded and conditions worsened. That year Birkenau was designated by Himmler as the centrepiece for "the final solution of the Jewish question in Europe", which meant the camp was now used for extermination, and freight trains started arriving daily. On arrival, those not fit to work were immediately killed. There were four gas chambers, combined with crematoria, capable of killing 5,000 per day, and the camp population went from 25,000 at the outbreak of war to 525,000 in 1944. By January 1945 it was over 700,000.

By the time the Red Army liberated the camp, some 400,000 prisoners of both sexes from nearly every European country had been registered, tattooed with serial numbers and "processed". Roughly half of them died, but this figure does not include the majority of prisoners who were murdered on arrival, without being registered.

Prisoners were organised in work *kommandos*, controlled by SS men who were assisted by *kommando* leaders, the *kapos*. These were prisoners chosen by the SS to bully fellow inmates with beatings to accelerate work rate. If prisoners died as a result, no questions were asked. In return for their savagery, *kapos* received better food and living quarters, theoretically improving their chances of survival.

Heinrich Himmler said this of the *kapo*: "His job is to see that the work gets done, so he has to push his men. As soon as we are no longer satisfied with him, he is no longer a *kapo* and returns to the other inmates. He knows that they will beat him to death on his first night back. Since we don't have enough Germans to do this work we use others. A French *kapo* for the Poles, a Polish *kapo* for the Russians. We play one nation against another."

Oskar Schroeder was a German criminal prisoner who became a *kapo*, first in the Auschwitz main camp, then in Monowitz. After his post-war arrest, he confessed to the following: "I was armed with a crop which I used to make the prisoners work faster. These prisoners were already worn out as a result of mistreatment, the cold and the lack of food, so my beatings caused them to lose even more strength, for which reason I am to a large extent responsible for their deaths. One day at work, I beat a prisoner to death. Before I killed him I had ordered him to roll in the snow for a quarter of an hour."

One of the survivors, Rudolf Vrba, said this of the regime: "Men ran and fell, were kicked and shot. Wild-eyed *kapos* drove their bloodstained path through rucks of prisoners while SS men shot from the hip, like television cowboys who had strayed somehow into a grotesque, endless horror film. Adding a ghastly note of incongruity to the bedlam were groups of quiet men in impeccable civilian clothes, picking their way through corpses they did not want to see, measuring timbers with bright yellow folding rules, making neat little notes in black leather books, oblivious to the bloodbath.

"They never spoke to the workers, these men in the quiet grey suits. They never spoke to the *kapos*, the gangsters. Only occasionally they murmured a few words to a senior SS NCO – words that sparked off another explosion.

"The SS man would kick viciously at the *kapo* and roar: 'Get these swine moving you lazy oaf. Don't you know that wall's to be finished by 11 o' clock?' The *kapo* would scramble to his feet, pound into the prisoners, lashing them on, faster, faster, faster."

The crematoria and gas chambers were located at Birkenau, where Block 7 was called "Death's Waiting Room". In it there were deaths from dysentery and outbreaks of TB, and typhoid which was spread by body lice. There were also a hospital block, kitchen, canteen, officers' club, and a brothel staffed by young prisoners which was used by the SS and *kapos*. Clients paid two marks, one to the prostitute and one to the Reich.

Warehouses, called "Canada", held crates of prisoners' personal effects, including gold and silver, precious stones and useful clothing.

A typical day entailed waking at dawn in time for the morning roll call, marching to work, hours of hard labour, a body search on returning to camp followed by block inspection and evening roll call.

The prisoners' diet comprised ersatz coffee in the morning, thin vegetable soup for lunch and for dinner a slice of black bread with ersatz margarine and a small piece of sausage. The *kommandant*, officers and guards ate well and the officers' club had champagne, beer and wines. The *kommandant* had a personal staff – cooks, servants, gardeners and drivers – as well as his detached residence, away from the rest.

The first *kommandant*, as noted, had been Rudolph Hoess, replaced in November 1943 by Arthur Liebehenschel who remained in charge until April 1944, when Richard Baer took over. When Auschwitz 3 became a separate entity and was renamed Monowitz, it had its own *kommandant*, Heinrich Schwarz. All four men were executed as war criminals.

It was not the SS guards but "privileged" prisoners who did nearly all the devil's work. Called *Sonderkommando*, they were strong young men selected on arrival, who transported the corpses – sometimes of family and friends – to the crematorium, cleaned the gas chambers, burned the bodies, disposed of the ash and sorted the victims' valuables. Very few of the SS were actively involved in this – no more than two dozen at any one time. The dirty work was done by the *Sonderkommando* who, had they but known it, were merely delaying their own demise.

Chapter 9

The End is Nigh

Late in 1944, all those left in captivity at Auschwitz-Birkenau and Monowitz feared the worst. The Germans were clearly losing the war – that was the good news. The bad news was that they could not afford to leave evidence of their murderous wrongdoing for the Allies to find and punish them for. The prisoners, British POWs included, expected to be exterminated and cremated.

Ron Jones says: "Towards the end, rumours spread like wildfire that we were all going to be killed. The SS couldn't afford to let anyone live and give evidence against them, so they would have to murder everyone. I think that was the cause of all our nightmares, at the time and for years later. We always feared it was going to happen.

"The SS were absolute bastards, they'd do anything. The ordinary German soldiers, the Wehrmacht, were frightened to death of them, just like us and, like us, they knew anything was possible. Those fears, always at the back of our minds, surfaced at the end of November 1944 when, with the Russians closing in, Himmler had the SS blow up the gas chambers and all the crematoria bar one."

Lieutenant General Oswald Pohl ordered Hoess, who had been posted back to Berlin at the end of July 1944, to return to Auschwitz to oversee the cleaning-up operation, but he was unable to get there. In his memoirs Hoess writes: "I immediately attempted to drive to Auschwitz to convince myself that everything important was destroyed as ordered, but I could only get as far as the Oder River, near Ratibor, because of the advance of the Russian tank force.

"On all the roads and streets of Upper Silesia to the west of the Oder I now found columns of prisoners who were suffering terribly as they tried to make their way through the deep snow. There was no food. In most cases the NCOs who were leading this parade of walking dead had no idea which direction they were supposed to go. All they knew was that their final destination was Gross-Rosen [concentration camp]. How they were going to arrive there was a mystery to all of them.

"Using their own initiative, they requisitioned food from the villages, rested for a few hours, then moved on again. There was no thought at all about spending the night in the barns or the schoolhouses since everywhere they were filled to the top with refugees.

"It was easy to follow the route of this ordeal of suffering because every few hundred metres lay the bodies of prisoners who had collapsed or been shot. I gave strict orders to the leaders of these columns not to shoot prisoners who were unable to march any further. They were to hand them over to the *Volksturm* [local militia] in the villages.

"On the streets near Leobschütz I continued to find prisoners who were shot. Since they were still bleeding, they could only have been shot a short time before. As I stopped my car by one of the dead prisoners and got out of the car, I heard pistol shots very close by. I ran towards the sound.

"At that moment I saw a soldier park his motorcycle and then shoot a prisoner who had been leaning against a tree. I yelled at him and asked him what business he had there and what business the prisoners were to him. He laughed at me insolently, looked me directly in the eye and asked me what business I had sticking my nose into this. Without hesitation I pulled out my pistol and shot him dead. He was a sergeant in the air force.

"I saw transports of prisoners frozen stiff in open coal cars. Whole trains of railroad cars were standing abandoned on side rails, out in the open without food or water. There were groups of prisoners completely on their own, whose guards had disappeared. I also met groups of British POWs with no-one guarding them. They were determined not to fall into the hands of the Russians."

Meanwhile back at Auschwitz, without Hoess, the mass burial grounds were levelled and turfed and the ovens, crematoria and gas chambers were destroyed or turned into air raid shelters.

Would all the prisoners be disposed of next? How close did it come? Closer than many may think. Himmler issued instructions that in the event of the enemy approaching, concentration camps were to be evacuated and prisoners moved elsewhere. If this was not possible, they were all to be "liquidated". Camp commanders were told that Hitler held them personally responsible for ensuring no prisoners were left alive to fall into enemy hands.

On 17 January 1945, as the Red Army entered Warsaw, the SS at Auschwitz began evacuating the Jews, who were to be taken to Bergen-Belsen and other concentration camps to the west. The last evening roll call showed 15,317 men and 16,577 women in Birkenau and 10,223 men at Monowitz, and all day on 18 January columns of women and children first, then men, were marched out under SS guard.

Of the 4,500 Jews marched out of Monowitz, nearly all were killed by machine-gunning after scattering during an air attack. Less than 200 survived to continue the murderous march. Ron says: "We were left behind, along with those deemed too ill, weak or young to undertake the march, and work of a sort continued at the factory until 19 January, when the Soviet air force bombed the town of Oswiecim, destroying the power station and leaving the camp and its factories without power."

At that late stage in the war the Russians were on the rampage on all fronts and on the 19th Marshal Ivan Konev's 1st Ukrainian Front took Krakow without a fight. Then, on the afternoon of 27 January a reconnaissance patrol from the 107th Rifle Division emerged from a snowy forest and stumbled upon the most dreadful symbol of man's potential for barbarity.

Auschwitz was unguarded and almost deserted. A week earlier, 58,000 prisoners fit enough to walk had been forced to trudge westwards, away from the Red Army. Mengele escaped to Berlin on 17 January, along with the notes from all his monstrous experiments and IG Farben's civilian workers burned all their records before evacuating in two special trains.

On 20 January SS Obergruppenführer Ernst Schmauser issued an order for the remaining prisoners at Auschwitz to be exterminated. Two hundred women were shot, but only 500 more were murdered before the proximity of the Red Army forced the SS to abandon their grisly work, leaving 7,000 behind. The SS had concentrated on destroying the incriminating evidence, blowing up the crematoria, but it was much too late to hide their appalling criminality. Bodies had been disposed of routinely for four years, but some 600 still lay on the ground, and in the stores there remained 368,820 men's suits, 836,255 women's coats and dresses, 44,000 pairs of shoes and 7.7 tons of human hair.

Of the 300 still alive at Monowitz, 200 more died despite the best efforts of the Red Army medical team.

Richard Baer, the third and last commandant at Auschwitz, was transferred to another camp, Buchenwald, where at what was known as Work Camp Dora, the Germans were again using slave labour in the production of their V2 rockets. He took charge on 1 February 1945 and soon resumed where he had left off, having prisoners bludgeoned to death and staging a mass execution of 162 inmates in March 1945.

Chapter 10

The Death March

On Tuesday 16 January 1945, Russian bombers had made their first night attack on the Buna factory and the following day the German IG Farben staff were told to prepare for a rapid departure. The last evening roll call, on the 17th, reported a total of 67,012 prisoners, made up as follows: Auschwitz-Birkenau 15,317 men and 16,577 women, Monowitz 10,223 men, other sub-camps 22,800 men and 2,095 women.

By this stage, with the enemy almost at the gates, panic had set in among the guards and labourers and some were refusing to work. Their mood was such that police were called in to protect the factory and prevent looting.

The forced march evacuation of the Jews and others (but not the POWs) began on the 19th. The sick, weak and young children were left behind. On the 19th the Russians bombed Oswiecim, destroying the power station, which left the camp without light, as well as food and water.

Ronald Redman was among Ron Jones' colleagues in E715. Of those fraught final days he says: "The factory stopped producing anything and all the civilian workers disappeared. The Jews were marched away, to Belsen we thought, and we demanded from the commandant that we should go too. He said: 'You will not go until I get the order from Berlin'."

Ron Jones says: "We heard on the radio that the Russian army had taken Krakow and you could tell the Germans were terrified of them. Then we could hear the artillery banging away so we knew they were coming and we thought we were going to get released. Instead, the Germans said on Sunday 21 January: 'We're moving out tomorrow.'

"When the time came there was an announcement over the loudspeakers: 'Compounds will be ready to march in one hour.' A big cheer went up. We thought: 'At last we're getting out of this hell-hole.' We had no idea what was about to happen.

"The guards came into our camp and told us to pack up whatever gear we could carry, because they were going to march us out. We could hear the Russians in the distance, we knew they could be only 10 kilometres away, and we had thought we were going to be freed. But there was an order from Hitler that no POWs were to be released to the Russians, who didn't actually liberate the camp for another six days."

Before that, on 25 January, an SS detachment arrived at the camp with orders to kill all the remaining prisoners who could not be evacuated. Two hundred women were quickly shot to death, but the Russians were so close that after blowing up what was left of the crematoria the SS left in a hurry.

On the 27th, at 3.00 p.m., Major Anatoly Shapiro led the first Soviet soldiers to enter the camp. Finding dead bodies everywhere, he declared: "I would like to say to all the people on earth: This should never be repeated – ever."

It was not just Auschwitz-Birkenau and Monowitz that were being evacuated, all the POW camps threatened by the Russians' advance were abandoned at the same time, which meant more than 200,000 prisoners setting out on scores of marches the length and breadth of the Eastern Front.

Of the abrupt departure Ron Jones says: "We didn't have much gear to pack up. The Germans dished out what was left from the remaining food parcels from the store, but that didn't amount to much. I had a little haversack on my back with bits and pieces in it. I didn't have spare socks, just square rags I had to use instead. Basically we had very little to take with us, and virtually no food. There were 560 of us in all, too many for one column, so we were divide into three separate groups, each of which had different routes and experiences.

"Before we left the Russians bombed the factory again and our camp, which was virtually next door, was destroyed."

At this stage of the war, with the Allies advancing on all fronts, and at great pace in the East, the roads back to Germany were packed with refugees, even before the hordes of prisoners from POW and concentration camps added to the confusion and consequent bottlenecks.

Ron Jones says: "The Jews had been marched out before us, and almost as soon as we left the camp we took the same route and passed their dead. I remember seeing their bodies everywhere, poor blighters. Some of them had been kicked to the side of the road to die, others had been shot. We'd started out having a typical British sing-song, but that sight shook us and shut us up for a while.

"Some of the men had made wooden sledges out of the slats in their bunks, and pulled their gear along on those. A Yorkshire man, Walter Booth, had one, but he didn't make it himself. He gave a passer-by a packet of cigarettes for his, and reckoned it saved his life. He put his kit on that sledge and was able to carry more than the rest of us could on our shoulders. I met him years later, at one of our reunions, and he was still on about his bloody sledge. His lasted the distance, but I saw a few that fell apart, useless, after only a few miles.

"It was very noticeable that towards the end of the war, when they realised they were going to lose, all the Germans guards – not the SS mind – became more friendly. It stuck out a mile. There was a lot less pushing you around. They realised that they could be held to account when it was all over and we'd won. We asked them where they were taking us, and they said they didn't know, which turned out to be true. Anywhere west, away from the dreaded Russians, would have been the correct answer. At first we thought we were going to a station to catch a train to another camp, which some did, but that was wrong in our case.

"For the first night they put us in a barn, which was all right. It was quite a while before we were starving. I was on the road for 17 weeks. The distance from Auschwitz to where we ended up, at Regensburg on the Austrian border, is about 400 miles as the crow flies, but we did at least twice that, using country lanes and often doubling back to avoid running into the Allied armies, who were advancing everywhere. All you could do was put your head down and trudge behind the man in front of you. People have called it 'The Long March', or 'The Death March', but we weren't marching, we were just trudging, day after day, herded along by the guards.

"Singing lifted us and really annoyed the Germans. Somebody would start it up and we'd all join in. It was the best way we had to keep our morale up. Near the end, of course, we didn't have the energy, or the inclination for it. By that stage we even stopped talking. I don't suppose any of us said more than half a dozen words a day in those final weeks.

"There were scores of columns like ours, passing through Poland and Germany. We were using the back roads, country lanes really, because the German army and civilian refugees were on the main roads. Where we were, the compacted snow made it like an ice rink underfoot and people fell by the wayside with broken ankles and arms.

"The weather conditions in the winter of 1944-45 were the most severe eastern Europe had known for a generation – it was one of the coldest on record. Temperatures of minus 25 were common and all we could do was huddle together for warmth. It was so bloody cold that your breath would freeze when it made contact with your clothing. It was a blessing that those of us who had been working in the factory still had the cloth gloves they gave us to handle frozen machine parts."

Brian Bishop said: "We'd been on the march two or three days, and were trudging through the snow when suddenly a guard picked up a handful of snow and smashed me in the face with it. I asked the bloke next to me: 'What the hell did he do that for?' He said: 'You should see your nose, it's shining white.' I had frostbite and that was the guard's way of telling me to rub my nose. I got frostbite in both my feet. One big toe is still a mess today, but that wasn't so much from the frostbite. The summer before we left, a German guard had smashed his rifle butt down on my foot because I wouldn't tell him the truth about something.

"It was so cold on that march that it was difficult to have a pee. You'd get your willy out and it would shrivel up and disappear. You'd end up putting it away and piddling down your leg. In some places we were up to our knees in snow. We were marching four abreast. After a time I thought: 'What am I doing, up the front here, flattening the snow for the others behind me?', and I moved further back."

Ron Jones recalls: "We hiked over the Carpathian

Mountains, through Czechoslovakia, down through Saxony, Bohemia and Bavaria and finally to the Austrian border. I wrote everything down on a postcard, where we were and how long it took. The guards locked us in barns at night. After a while they gave us no food at all, no drink. Nothing. To be fair, they had nothing to give.

"All we ate was what the animals had left – what they wouldn't eat. Rotten potatoes and beans. I've heard of lads eating dog and cat stew and even rats. I don't know about that, the only thing like that I can remember is someone saying one morning: 'There's stew over there', so we had some and when we were leaving the farmer whose barn we'd slept in came out raving mad. He'd lost his dog. I wouldn't like to think it was dog stew we'd eaten, but I suppose it was. You'd be surprised what you'll eat when you're literally starving. Starvation really does drag you down to the basest level.

"Different columns experienced different circumstances. I've heard of others on the march eating the horses that had been pulling carts, but there were no horses with us. Others are supposed to have had a visit from the Red Cross, or to have been helped by a group of nuns, but we had none of that either."

Brian Bishop was with a column that ate their horse. He explained: "The nag that was pulling a cart holding the Germans' equipment was dying on its feet and we ended up killing and eating it. I was given a chunk of sinew the size of a matchbox, and I chewed on that all day and all night.

"Another time we stopped at a sugar beet factory and found a big cauldron they used to boil the stuff in. We couldn't find anything else to eat so we got stuck into this sugar beet. I doled it out to all the blokes who wanted it, and at the end there was this mush in the bottom. I wasn't going to waste that and ladled it out into my dixie and ate the lot.

"It was a bloody stupid thing to do. The following morning the pain in my stomach was excruciating. I walked a little way but then just curled up in a ball. The M.O. [medical officer] was further back in the column but someone went to fetch him and he took one look at me and said: 'He's got colic.' I asked him what that was and he told me: 'The same as a horse gets. The only thing we can do for you is to make you walk.' So I had two of the biggest blokes support me, one on each side, making me walk.

"They did it for about a hundred yards and then said: 'Sod this mate, we're knackered, we've got a job to walk ourselves.' So then they strapped both my hands to the back of the horse and cart and I had to walk behind that. Eventually they freed me from the cart, but the pain was still bad until I dumped my load right in the middle of a street somewhere. I was better after that."

Ron Jones says: "Basically, we survived on potatoes. Raw potatoes. At one farm we ripped a couple of chickens apart and ate them raw. Another time I remember kicking a pig out of the way and pinching the potato it had been eating. It was covered in pig muck, but it all went down when you were that hungry. To drink, all we could get was a handful of snow. It makes you wonder how the human body could survive on the scraps we had. Often we were reduced to eating grass or leaves."

Private Alfred Bryant, of The Buffs, remembered the ordeal as follows:

"We walked for the entire day, stopping at intervals but getting nothing to eat. We joined thousands more POWs from various camps until we formed one long mass of darkness against the white snow. That evening we were herded into a very large field, where the snow was about seven feet high and five feet wide round the edge, the column winding round like a python until all the POWs were within the barricade.

"Those that were able to, lay down in the snow to sleep under the stars; the rest had to do as best they could standing up. Frostbite was one of the worst complaints as the only clothing most had was battledress and a pair of clogs. Being one of the lucky ones, able to lie down, I did get some sleep that night, but in the morning the guards came to move us and both companions on either side of me didn't move. One of the guards said to me: 'How is it that your friends are not moving?' A close look showed that they were dead, as were several others in the field. The bodies were left where they were and we were on the march again.

"Again we had nothing to eat and that night we were pushed into a large barn, packed like sardines The lucky ones could squat, and I was one of them. The unlucky ones had to stand and sleep if they could. The next morning the guards came again, and those of us who had managed to survive were marched away. The dead were left behind in the barn."

And so it went on. Private Bryant said: "We were still walking in March. We slept in the open and those that died were left. Regular rations were non-existent and to keep alive we scrumped in any fields we came across. We were getting weaker each day and many of the young lads lost heart.

"One evening after we had stopped it was my turn to see if I could dig for vegetables. The guard saw me and while he was shouting at me, telling me he'd shoot me if I went, a young lad from the column made an attempt to get into the field. The guard shot him in the back and he was left in the field.

"At the end of April we were very weak and almost too

scared to sleep in case we did not wake up again. The lads were dropping like flies. One day a young lad was on his knees praying when a guard came along the road. The lad fell on his face and the guard picked him up and put him on his bicycle and pushed him about two miles along the road towards a house. But before he could reach the house the guard pushed the lad off and said he had died."

In desperation, Mark Mead, a warrant officer in the RAF, struck an expensive bargain: "I came to a house where there was a boy eating a carrot. I called to him through this wrought iron gate, trying to persuade him to give me a carrot. He wouldn't but I kept on: 'Come on, give me a carrot.' He pointed to my wristwatch and said: 'For watch I give you carrot.' So I swapped my 21st birthday present for a carrot. I don't think it was worth it because as soon as I'd eaten the carrot I was hungry again. Another time we raided a boiler in which a farmer had been loading pig food and we put our tins in to scoop some out. Most of us suffered from dysentery after eating that."

Robert Clark, of the 4th Durham Survey Regiment said: "I remember a lady from a farmhouse putting food down for her dog, and when she closed the door I dashed out from the column and took the food from the dog and shared it with a colleague. That shows how desperate our situation was. It wasn't easy to survive." He recalled others eating old fish heads from dustbins.

Ron Jones takes up his story: "One survivor told the *Daily Mirror* that when we passed through Czechoslovakia the people put food out for us on tables. That's a lot of bull. The same fella said he ended up six stone when he got to Regensburg. What, after eating all that Czech food? No way, the poor buggers didn't have any food for themselves."

Brian Bishop did remember getting sustenance from the locals – although he is not entirely sure it was voluntary. He said: "There was only one place where we got food from the local population. We were marching down the main street of this village or small town where people were doing their shopping and I saw some chaps rushing towards the pavement. When I got level with them I saw someone rolling out large circular loaves of bread. I don't know who did it, but it was lovely bread."

Ron says: "Some 230 of us left Auschwitz in our column and there must have been 150 left alive when we got to our final destination, which was Regensburg. Men just fell by the wayside and died, often from dysentery. I saw it happen. They'd stumble and fall. The guards weren't cruel to them, they tried to help them up, but their will to go on and live had gone, so they had to be left there, face down in the snow. In my experience, there was none of the cruelty by the guards that has been spoken of elsewhere. Most of that came from the Hitler Youth kids, who were right little bastards.

"Trevor Manley, who lived near me in Wales, was on the march, in a column just in front of us. I used to see his name written in the barns where we stopped. He developed abscesses on his back, and they shipped him off to hospital straight away. The Germans in their army weren't angels, but they weren't brutes either. There was the occasional bastard, but you get that with any nationality.

"There was one advantage to being on the country lanes. It was how we came across the farms we slept at. In the first six weeks we walked 300 miles, through Poland, Germany and Czechoslovakia, and the ordeal was getting worse by the day. We were absolutely covered in lice. Not a few dozen, I mean hundreds. They were all over you. You tried to keep yourself as clean as possible, to keep them off, but you'd get them in your armpits and wherever your body was a bit warm.

"The longer it went on, you started to find that when you set off in the morning little heaps didn't move. People had died during the night. The men helped one another, it wasn't every man for himself, but for some it just wasn't enough. We knew we were moving west, away from the advancing Russians and towards our own army, but would we get to them or die first? It was all about survival.

"The German guards had no food themselves after a while, and no way to get it. Their supply lines had collapsed, so if there was a crust of bread to be had, it went to them. Real hunger is one of the worst pains a person can experience. Terrible. We were reduced to the level of animals, scavenging for food.

"After two months, with no end in sight, the morale of the men hit rock bottom. More and more were dying. Your pal would have dysentery in the morning, and by the evening he'd be dead. The disease took all the life-force out of you and left nothing. Some guards wouldn't let you stop moving, and if you've got dysentery and you're not allowed to stop, there's only one thing you can do. From that horrible thought you must realise what a state we were in. We were absolutely filthy and stank to high heaven.

"Nevertheless, we all stuck together, thinking: 'We've *got* to make it, got to keep going.' There was a sergeant, a Scot, who was a really big character, and good at going round the lads who were flagging. More than anyone, he was usually able to rouse them and keep them going. I think his name was Andy Porteous."

This was Sergeant Porteous, of the 2nd Scots Guards. In an

affidavit after the war, dated 1 November 1945, he identified the Germans he wanted prosecuted as war criminals. He wrote:

"[From] October 1943 I was with Working Commando E 715 at Auschwitz. On 20 January 1945 the whole Commando set out on a march to the West. The control officer was a Hauptman (captain) whose name was Brandel.

"Brandel was about 5ft 11ins in height, slim build, fresh complexion. He had mousey coloured hair and spoke Russian, French, Czech and Polish. He also understood English, although he did not speak it much. He was of 515 Landschutz Company, with headquarters at Sosnowitz, Upper Silesia.

"In charge of our commando was Feldwebel Meizer, who belonged to the same company. He was about 53 years of age, 5ft 9ins in height, stocky build, about 12 or 13 stone. He was nearly bald with grey hair, had a sallow complexion, was clean shaven and wore spectacles. He had a peculiar monkey-like face with a hole just below the bridge of his nose. His home town [was] Königstadt.

"He was quite well educated and was very dogmatic in his speech. He wore a wound medal as a result of injuries sustained in an air raid on 20 August 1944.

"Also with us was a German guard called Hein, or Heinz, a private soldier. He previously acted as a company clerk. He was very fat, about 16 stone, 5ft 8ins in height, wore very thick steel-rimmed glasses, was probably between 45 and 50 years of age. He had a heavy jaw and was nicknamed 'The Beetle' and also 'The Slug'. He was a baker by trade. I think he worked with his father-in-law at some place near Auschwitz. He used to go off at the weekends and his wife used to visit him at the camp.

"On one occasion on the march, towards the end of February,

after eight prisoners had escaped Meizer, on instruction from Hauptman Brandel, turned the whole commando out of the barns where we were billeted into fields for eight or nine hours as punishment. Together with Captain W.O. Harrison, of the South African Medical Corps, I protested to Meizer, but he said that these were his instructions. I have no doubt that Meizer only acted on instructions as I heard Hauptman Brandel give the order.

"Sometime prior to that I saw Heinz lift the butt of his rifle and strike two men on the back. I told him to stop assaulting them. He ignored me and as he was about to strike one of them again I grasped his rifle. He pushed me away.

"I saw him load his rifle. He pointed it at me and I threw myself on the ground as he fired. He missed me. Another German guard immediately stopped Heinz from taking any further action. Heinz was in a temper at the time and I am convinced that he intended to shoot me.

"I complained to Meizer and he replied that Heinz was mad. As far as I know, no action was taken in regard to that shooting, against Heinz, or in regard to the ill-treatment of the other two prisoners.

"Heinz repeatedly, prior to and after that occasion, threatened to shoot any prisoner who he considered was troublesome."

Sergeant Porteous and others were liberated near Landschutz in Bavaria on 27 April 1945, by a Captain Robertson. The affidavit lodged by Porteous was supported by another, from Private Geoffrey Richard Amery of the Rifle Brigade, dated 12 October 1945. Private Amery wrote:

"I was taken prisoner at Calais on 26 May 1940. I arrived at Stalag V111B Lamsdorf on 26 June 1940 and I was sent to E715 at Auschwitz on 6 April 1944.

"On 19 January the guards and prisoners started to march westwards. We joined up with several other working parties attached to Stalag V111B, as was ours. The column was under the control of an officer whose name I have forgotten. He was a Hauptman.

"In charge of part of the column, comprising members of E715 was Feldwebel Meizer, who had been in charge of the *kommando* at Auschwitz.

"In January 1945 Meizer, for no reason at all, marched 400 men into a field during a blizzard and kept them there for half an hour. Many of them suffered from frostbite in consequence and about six men had to have fingers and toes amputated. This incident took place about 30km from Troppau.

"One day in February 1945 when we were about 200 km north of Prague, two men escaped from the column and by way of reprisal Meizer made the members of E715 spend the whole day, from 7 in the morning until 7 at night, in a field in intense cold and without food. This caused great suffering.

"Feldwebel Meizer belonged to No 3 company, 515 Landschutz. He was about 53 years of age, 5ft 9 ins in height and between 10 and 11 stone in weight. He was nearly bald and what hair he had was grey. His complexion was sallow. I think he had artificial teeth. He wore spectacles for reading and was clean shaven. He had been wounded in an air raid and he wore a wound medal. He seemed to be a well educated man.

"Three days before our column was released by the Americans the guards left the column."

A third affidavit, from Driver F.C. Taylor (2334739), also accused Feldwebel Meiser. Taylor, a Londoner, wrote:

"On Jan 21 1945 we were forced to evacuate E715 by the

Germans, who marched us away from Poland to Germany due to the Russian advance. Some 560 prisoners departed from Auschwitz, destination unknown. We were forced to march by Feldwebel Meiser with a ration of a 2 kilo loaf between 17 men for one week. Water was not available and sleeping conditions in barns were appalling.

"After [already] marching for two weeks, on February 3 1945 we marched 38 kms in a temperature of 28 degrees below. We were made to stand at midday for two hours while Feldwebel Meiser, in charge of the column, ate his dinner in a house nearby. This caused many comrades to suffer from severe frostbite. Captain Harrison, South African Medical Corps, saved many hands and feet by his constant attention. My feet were so septic that I could not get my right boot on.

"Rations for a period between 28 January 1945 and 5 February were 2 kilos of bread between 17 men per day. Other days it was one potato per man."

Incredibly, in view of the damning affidavits against him, the case against Meiser was dropped in May 1946, "for lack of evidence."

Ron Jones resumes: "If anybody dropped, we'd carry them as far as we could, but some were extremely ill and incapable of going any further. They just sat down and the guards, who were out on their feet themselves, couldn't make them get up and move. When that happened, they were dead within an hour. It was only supreme willpower that kept you moving.

"The Russian prisoners, who'd had the worst treatment in the camp, were weakest and couldn't keep up with us, so the guards moved them to the front of the column where the poor devils just collapsed. The Germans left them to die and we passed nine or ten bodies every day."

Andrew Wiseman, an RAF warrant officer, joined the

march from Stalag Luft 3, the camp which was the scene of the film *The Great Escape*. He said: "I think 'march' is the wrong word. It was the long shuffle. As it went on and on, past three months, you began to care less for the others and more for yourself. It really became a personal battle – the survival of the fittest. It was no longer a war between the Allies and Germany, it was you, the individual, fighting for life. You no longer had the strength to look out for anyone else."

Ron Jones was existing on the dregs of his endurance: "There were times when I was in total despair and thought: 'What the hell is the point of going on?' My spirit had just about gone, and I just don't know what kept me going, I haven't a clue. I suppose it was sheer determination that kept me putting one foot in front of the other. The fact that I was a married man made a hell of a difference. I had someone to come home to.

"The frostbite was dreadful. If you feel my hands today, they are always cold, even in the summer. Frostbite left me with bad circulation, that's never been right since. A lot of fellas lost parts of their body. We had a reunion in Croydon one year and I met a fella from Jersey who was in a hell of a mess. He'd lost his nose and one of his ears from frostbite.

"Our boots would be soaking wet from walking through the snow, then they'd lock us in the barns and our feet would freeze in the boots overnight and walking in them next morning would be absolute agony for an hour or so, until they thawed out. You wouldn't dare take your boots off at night. They'd freeze solid and you wouldn't be able to get them on in the morning. Eventually mine rotted, disintegrated completely and fell off. After that I had to wrap my feet in sacks that I found in the barns. We were wearing our uniform tunics, but most of us had no greatcoats or anything like that.

"Given no food, the weight was falling off me all the time and the only reason I'm still alive is what I was able to get for the cigarettes my wife had sent me. I told her they were currency in the camp, you could get almost anything for a few ciggies. I didn't smoke, but in one of my letters home I told Gwladys that cigarettes substituted for money in the camp.

"The smokers were always desperate for a cigarette. I've seen men who were starving give a tin of bully beef for a packet of cigarettes. Now try telling me it's not an addiction. Somebody always had a Bible, which is printed on thin paper, so a desperate smoker would tear a page out of the Bible and go round the edge of the compound, where there was grass, pick out dead clover to substitute for tobacco and make a cigarette that way. We used to call it a 'Holy Smoke'. One of the lads said once: 'Here "Taffy", have a drag', and I took one puff of it and nearly blacked out, but they all smoked it.

"For the real thing, Gwladys used to go to a tobacconist, Smiths in Newport, and send me parcels of 200 at a time. She told me after the war that she'd sent me dozens of parcels, but I only got a few. The Germans pinched the rest. She also used to send me chocolate in parcels, but out of about ten I got four. The Jerries used to help themselves, they were short of everything too. I actually had one of Gwladys's parcels delivered to Bassaleg after I got home, marked return to sender. In the camp I'd go to the factory and swap cigarettes for eggs and white bread with the Polish workers from outside.

"One day a Polish civilian worker who had a Rolex Oyster watch said to me: 'How many cigarettes do I get for this?' It was still in its case. I gave him 200 cigarettes and got a new Rolex, still in its box. I was wearing that watch on my wrist during the march. I had my thumbs in my pack, which was on my back, and a German officer spotted this Rolex. He knew immediately what it was and he kept on at me about it. I thought he was going to take it – an SS man would have done – but he didn't. He just pestered the life out of me: 'I want that watch'. On one occasion he told me we were all going to die on the march anyway, so he might as well let me have it now, rather than later.

"Eventually he came to me with a sack of bread. By this time I was really starving and I couldn't get the watch off quick enough. When you hear kids today saying: 'I'm starving mum', they have no idea what starvation really is. This officer gave me eight or nine bread rolls, so a few of us had a feed for a couple of days. That bread, on its own, tasted like the best Christmas dinner. It probably saved my life.

"On and on we went, food or not. It was sheer purgatory."

Another marcher, Stan Constable, said: "I think the chaps who had been out there from the earliest days and who had spent a few winters in Poland, were used to the severe weather. The ones who felt it more were those who had been captured later, in Crete and North Africa."

One night none of the POWs would ever forget was 13 February 1945, when hundreds of British bombers created a firestorm that turned Dresden, in east Germany into a murderous furnace. Ron Jones says: "The whole sky was blood red, a terrible sight. We thought: 'Some poor buggers are having it.' It was only after I got home that I realised it must have been the fire-bombing of Dresden, that has caused so much controversy since. We'd been in that area.

"Ever since 'Bomber' Harris has been criticised for that because he used incendiaries, not ordinary high explosive bombs and I can understand that viewpoint. I don't think any civilians deserved what happened there.

"I was more fortunate with my health than a lot of the

lads who caught some horrible diseases as a result of the conditions on the march. I knew a guy called Roberts, from Swindon, who was very ill for years afterwards. I was very lucky, I came home reasonably healthy because I was very fit, physically, before I left Britain.

"I was pretty good in the gym. When I got married, in '38, I was doing a lot of weightlifting at the Oxford Gym in Risca. I could pick Gwladys up with one hand and hold her up in the air, like a circus act. I used to work in Rogerstone, and in 1937 we relocated to Cardiff docks and there was no transport, so I cycled back and forth for 12 months, six miles each way. I was a member of the Newport Wheelers cycling club, and we used to ride out every Sunday morning, so I was extremely fit when I got called up and that fitness served me well when core strength became a matter of life and death.

"It seems incredible now, but while we were at our lowest ebb, dropping like flies, the Germans tried to persuade us to fight for them, against the Russians. They handed out a two-page leaflet which claimed the Kremlin was out to conquer the whole of the Western world, including Britain. It said:

"'It is not merely the destruction of Germany and the German race, the fate of Britain, the rest of Europe and eventually the USA is also under threat. This means the fate of your wives, your children and your homes. It also means everything that makes life liveable, lovable and honourable for you.

"'We address ourselves to you regardless of your rank or your nationality. We think our fight has also become your fight. If there are some among you who are willing to join the ranks of the Germans soldiers who fight in this battle, which will decide both the fate of Germany and the fate of your countries, we should like to know it. We invite you to join our ranks.

"'Whether you are willing to fight in the front line or in the service corps, we make you this solemn promise: Whoever as a soldier of his own nation is willing to join the common front for the common cause will be freed immediately after the victory of the present offensive and can return to his own country via Switzerland. All that we have to ask from you is the word of a gentleman not to fight directly or indirectly for the cause of Bolshevik Communism as long as this war continues.

"'At this moment we do not ask you to think of Germany. We ask you to think about your own country. We ask you just to measure the chances which you and your people at home would have to exist in case the Bolshevik Communism onslaught should overpower Europe.

"'Please inform the convoy officer of your decision and you will receive the privileges of our own men, for we expect you to share their duty.

"'Make your decision now!'"

Of this, Ron says: "You had to be really desperate to be tempted by the offer to go and fight for the Germans on the Russian front – they even had special uniforms ready for us. But believe it or not, I heard that a couple of lads actually took them up on it. I'm not sure how true that is, but Cyril Quartermain certainly believed it was, and don't forget we were literally starving and in a hell of a mess, physically. Our mates were dying by the side of us, so maybe one or two fellas felt things couldn't be any worse and did it.

"At around that time, late on in the march, we were in a barn one night and some of the lads went down into a cellar and found some pork hanging there. They wolfed it down in no time. They were sick as dogs after, but didn't they enjoy it at the time!

"Not long after that we stopped in a disused cinema and there was a heart-stopping moment when the German *Feldwebel* (NCO) got up on the stage and said: 'You're all going to die.' He told us there was no hope, that he had no food to give us and so on. He then went on to explain that it wasn't his fault, he was sorry but there was nothing he could do to help. That last bit came as a relief. When he said we were all going to die, we thought they were going to kill us, but he meant we were all going to starve – prisoners and guards alike.

"More of the lads did die right near the end, when the Allies bombed a bridge over the River Danube. To maintain good progress, the guards used to change the 15 or 20 men setting the pace at the front of the column at set intervals. When they'd done their bit, they'd go to the back and others would take over. I'd just gone to the rear and was at the tail end of the column as the lads at the front got on the bridge. We heard the air raid sirens going and had the Germans' permission to scatter whenever that happened, but this time the *Feldwebel* said: 'Don't worry, they won't bomb the bridge, they're heading for the marshalling yards.'

"He was right, but a stray bomb hit the bridge. I don't know how many died. I jumped into the arches beneath the bridge and there were eight of us sheltering there when a section of the bridge came down and buried us. We were stuck for hours before the Jerries got us out.

"My mate Trevor Manley had been working as a coal miner in Katowice, so he was on another march and he got to hear about the bombing, but not who had died. Now me and Trevor were old friends, from the same village, and he got home before me. Gwladys, for obvious reasons, hadn't heard from me for months, so she asked Trevor what he knew, but he didn't tell her about the bridge because he was afraid I might have been one of the dead. I got home a week after him."

After 17 excruciating weeks, the end of the ordeal came about suddenly and unexpectedly on 28 April.

Ron says: "The guards had put us in a barn as usual and there was a lot of artillery fire during the night which suggested the Allies were getting close. It was enough to frighten the Germans and they legged it. In the morning they'd gone. Eventually we broke out of the barn and went looking for food.

"A few of us walked, or more or less crawled, we were in such a state, and came across a hotel called the Grüner Krantz, where the Americans had been billeted. Their food was all compo rations, which they weren't all that keen on and we found about a dozen of these parcels that had been picked at and left, and had a real feast.

"The Americans who left the food had moved on, but now one of their Sherman tanks appeared. It was the advance guard of their 9th Army, God bless them. The tank commander asked: 'Are you boys all right?' and we said: 'We are now!' We were cheering and shouting, but they couldn't give us any food. All they had was bloody chewing gum and cigars! We just stood there, numb, overcome with relief. Free at last! It's difficult to express the joy and exhilaration of freedom when you've been deprived of it for so long. No more guards, no more pushing around.

"The Yanks directed us to a liberation centre, not a hospital, as some have said. We were covered in lice, filthy. We were always covered with them, which was a terrible, debilitating torment. If we could get hold of a pack of matches we'd go all around the seams of our clothes, killing the

142

buggers, but the following morning you were covered in them again. Absolutely crawling with lice. Disgusting.

"This liberation centre had a delousing area where they puffed DDT up your sleeves and everywhere. After that we went to a rest camp and I was there for about a fortnight, recuperating. When we were freed we were finding it difficult just to walk. I'd had the runs for weeks so I had no strength, the weight had dropped off me, leaving me terribly weak. The Americans took all my clothes, which were little more than filthy rags, and rigged me out like a new recruit. They gave me one of their kit bags with everything in it. I came home dressed as an American soldier. I've still got the two blankets they gave me, stamped USA, and their knife, fork and spoon.

"We were with the Yanks for a fortnight, and on the first day they gave us cornflakes topped with peaches for breakfast. We thought that a bit odd, but any food was delicious and heaven-sent after what we'd been through. Then at about 11 in the morning we'd see their lot sitting in the mess hall, dipping something in their coffee. It was donuts, which were unheard of in Britain at that time. We thought what they were doing was disgusting, terrible table manners, but once we tried it, we loved it of course. Dunking donuts. We couldn't get them down quick enough.

"They eventually put us on a Red Cross train which took us via Paris to Le Havre, where there was a fleet of Dakotas to fly us home. That was my first flight in a plane. There were no seats, they were cargo planes, so we had to sit on the floor. One crashed on the runway and some of the lads were killed. What a tragic irony, after surviving the march.

"It wasn't the only tragedy on the way home. On the train journey to Le Havre we pulled up in the sidings in Paris, where some of the men discovered two big vats of fermented grapes, ready to be turned into wine. The boys went out and filled their helmets and whatever they could lay their hands on and got stuck into it. Thank God I was a non-drinker. It was raw juice, not fit for consumption and a few of them died. After enduring all that, they died from drink, how sad is that?

"While we were still back in Regensburg, we heard a hell of a commotion one night. The war had ended, and now that it was all over, I came home to a wonderful woman, Gwladys. I don't think I'd be here today if it wasn't for her. She nursed me back to something like normality."

Ron was one of the lucky ones – or perhaps that should be one of the stronger ones. It is reliably estimated that 2,000 POWs died on the long trek to freedom.

Ron kept a diary on the march, logging its progress each day, but it was stolen, along with other personal effects, before he got home. Instead we reproduce Brian Bishop's log, which is significantly shorter because he spent a whole month in one place, clearing bomb damage:

21 January 1945. Left Auschwitz. Overnight at Neuberun. Distance marched 18 kms.

22 January. Heavy snow. Overnight at Tichau. Distance marched 15 kms.

23 January. More snow. Overnight east of Rybnik. Distance 23 kms.

24 January. Snow. Overnight east of Ratibor. Distance 23 kms.

25 January. Snow. Overnight east of Ratibor. Distance 6 kms.

26 January. Snow. Overnight west of Kreuzendorf. Distance 15 kms.

27 January. No movement.

28 January. Frostbite in both feet. Overnight Kroppau. Distance 32 kms.

29 January. No movement.

30 January. Overnight Sosson [Sudetenland]. Distance 26 kms.

31 January. Overnight Freudenthal. Distance 13 kms.

1 February. No movement.

2 February. Overnight Andersdorf. Distance 32 kms.

3 February. Overnight Deutschlibau. Distance 26 kms.

4 February. Overnight Mahr Schoenberg. Distance 18 kms.

5 February. No movement.

6 February. Overnight east of Schildberg. Distance 22 kms.

7 February. Overnight east of Landskron. Distance 20 kms.

8 February. Overnight east of Landskron. Distance 12 kms.

9, 10, 11 February. No movement.

12 February. Overnight east of Chotzen [Czechoslovakia]. Distance 28 kms.

13 February. No movement.

14 February. Overnight Oberjellen. Distance 12 kms.

15 February. Overnight Hoch Chwojno. Distance 13 kms.

16 February. No movement.

17 February. Overnight Oppatowitz. Distance 19 kms.

18 February. Overnight near Konigratz. Distance 17 kms.

19 February. No movement.

20 February. Overnight Baschnitz. Distance 11 kms.

21 February. Overnight near Hauschnitz. Distance 18 kms.

22 February. No movement.

23 February. Overnight near Sobrotka. Distance 30kms.

24 February. Overnight Repon. Distance marched 14 kms.

25 February. No movement.

26 February. Overnight Kropatsch Wrotitz. Distance 26 kms.

27 February. Overnight Subarsch. Distance 18 kms.

28 February. No movement.

1 March. Overnight Slosein [30 kms from Prague]. Distance 15 kms.

2 March. Overnight east of Schlan. Distance 23 kms.

3 March. No movement.

4 March. Overnight Stern. Distance 11 kms.

5 March. Overnight west of Renton. Distance 24 kms.

6 March. No movement.

7 March. Overnight Willenz. Distance 18 kms.

8 March. Overnight east of Lebens. Distance 19 kms.

9, 10 March. No movement.

11 March. Overnight Deutschkilmes. Distance 21 kms.

12 March. No movement.

13 March. Overnight Gangerhof. Distance 19 kms.

14 March. Overnight near Marienbad. Distance 16 kms.

15 March. No movement.

16 March. Overnight Plan. Distance 16 kms.

17 March. Overnight east of Haid. Distance 16 kms.

18 March. Overnight east of Remmelsberg. Distance 11 kms.

19 March. No movement.

20 March. Overnight Moosbach [Bavaria]. Distance 24 kms.

21 March. No movement.

22 March. Overnight Schanesreith. Distance 16 kms.

23 March. Overnight Theissel. Distance 7 kms.

24 March. No movement.

25 March. To Weiden. Distance 7 kms. At 10.00 hours left by train for Nuremberg. Arrived Nuremberg 03.00 hours. At 10.15 left Nuremberg by train to Regensburg. Arrived 22.30.

26 March until 23 April. Worked in Regensburg clearing bomb damage.

23 April. Heard that the Americans were 28 kms north of us. Left Regensburg at 19.00 hours and marched all night to Mitterhauselbach. Distance 43 kms.

24 April. Overnight Mitterhauselbach.

25 April. Left at 04.30 for Landshut. Distance 30 kms.

26, 27 April. No movement.

28 April. Guards "evacuated."

29 April. SS fighting the Americans 8 kms away.

30 April. Americans arrive in a tank.

1 May. Snowed all day. Lads impatient to get home.

2 May. More snow.

3 May. More snow.

4 May. Heard that Hitler was dead.

5 May. Still waiting [to go home].

6 May. Still waiting.

7 May. Heard that war is over.

8 May. Deloused.

9 May. Deloused again. Allocated plane – when it arrives.

10 May. At 14.45 left for Landshut aerodrome. No planes so returned.

11 May. At 16.30 left Landshut in American Dakota called "Round Robin". At 19.00 arrived at Rheims, France.

12 May. In American camp.

13 May. In American camp.

14 May. Flew in Lancaster bomber to Oakey airfield, near Aylesbury. Arrived 17.00. Deloused again then taken to camp at Hartwell Park.

15 May. At 08.15 join train at Aylesbury. At 10.10 arrived home.

Total distance marched = 836 km.

Brian says: "When I gave Doug Bond a copy of the route my column took and told him it was 500 miles – I logged the distances from signposts along the way – he said his march was more like 800. Some of the others weren't stationary for a month at Regensburg, they had to keep going. We weren't actually in Regensburg itself, we were sleeping on a farm a couple of miles outside the town. The farmer had lost all his stock by the time we left. My pillow was a big sack of potatoes.

"I don't know about the other columns, but in our case we didn't march all day every day. Sometimes we had a couple of days off when we could recover, simply because the roads and paths were blocked by German troops and we had to wait for them to move on before we could. We never actually saw them mind, we were always kept out of the way."

Chapter 11

Liberation Red Army Style

The longer their gruelling march, or rather marches away from Auschwitz went on, the greater the opportunity the POWs had to escape as their guards realised the day of reckoning was approaching. So why didn't they try? The survivors answered the question with a question: Where could they go? They had no idea where they were, they had no maps to guide them, they had no food and no prospect of finding any. Worst of all, both the SS and the Red Army were inclined to shoot first and ask questions later when they came across anyone not part of their particular unit.

The Russians were Britain's allies, but British POWs were correct to be wary of them, as is graphically demonstrated by the experience of Sergeant William Henry Clark, of the RASC. Sergeant Clark, from Horsham, in Sussex said of his escape from the Germans:

"On 2 April 1945 we were strafed by our own planes and during the confusion which ensued I jumped into a ditch and got into the nearby woods, where I sheltered with a friendly Austrian family. SS troops were in the area, and I was hidden by these Austrians.

"On 14 April Russian troops entered the area and visited the house where I was hiding. The Russians ill-treated the family who had sheltered me by striking them and removing all the furniture, stripping the people and removing all their cattle and the fodder etc.

"At a Russian HQ I was taken into a room where there was a Russian officer and three other ranks. I was accused of being a spy, which I denied, whereupon he [the officer] spat in my face. The three soldiers pointed tommy guns at me all the time I was in the room and I had to hold my hands above my head.

"I was in the room about two hours. The Russian officer searched me and found my wallet, which contained all my photographs, my pay book etc. I had about 30 photographs taken of me and my friends, he tore each one up separately and threw the bits in my face, striking me in the face at the same time with his clenched fist. Each time he struck me he called me 'spione' (spy). He then tore up my pay book, hit me in the face again and threw the bits in the fire.

"Having finished searching me, the Russian officer said: 'When we have finished with Europe, having joined up with Tito, to whom we are supplying arms at the present moment, we shall have the whole of Europe, then England and America. He spat in my face again on mentioning the words 'England' and 'America'.

"He then asked for a knife, which was provided by one of the soldiers in the room, and cut my braces and my belt, and cut off all the front buttons on my trousers. I was pushed outside into the street where a lot of Russian soldiers had collected. I was marched down the street, with my hands still over my head, and struck and butted repeatedly and kicked by most of them.

"When I had got about 20 yards from the building the same Russian officer grabbed me by the collar of my tunic and struck me on the back of my neck with a half pick shaft, and rendered me unconscious. While I was unconscious I was thrown into a staff car which contained a Russian major and driven to Gleisdorf, near Graz.

"I recovered consciousness at about 23.30 hours on 14 April and was taken into interview with this same Russian major who had been in the car. He had a Russian soldier with him who spoke a little English. The major wanted to know why I was in British uniform and why I was a prisoner of war, as he said that he understood all Englishmen shot themselves before being taken prisoner.

"He asked me to prove that I was English and I showed him a tattoo on my right forearm, showing a gun with a Union Jack flying over it and the initials RFA (Royal Field Artillery) underneath. This only half convinced him and he produced a large cardboard sheet with the photographs of English and Russian generals and Churchill, Roosevelt and Stalin. I recognised the last three and also Generals Alexander and Montgomery, but was unable to identify any of the Russian generals.

"I was then asked if I should like to join the Red Army Artillery, or become the major's driver. I said that after the treatmernt I had received at Russian hands I was not willing to do this. I was then locked up in a little room at the top of the building and told that the next morning I was to 'go far'.

"The next morning, 15 April, the house had been vacated by the Russians so I forced open the door of my room and walked out into the street, where I was picked up by Cossack troops, who interrogated me. I filled a form to the effect that I was an Englishman. I was then told to return to the Austrian family who had sheltered me until 'clearance' Russian troops arrived who would send me back to Odessa.

"I walked back to my Austrian family, arriving there on 16 April, and remained with them until 4 May. On this day Russian troops again visited the house, I was accused of being a spy and taken to another Russian HQ where celebrations were taking place. Before I got there, the following incidents took place:

"1. On arriving at a large wood, my escort made me kiss him, make the sign of the cross, stand with my back to the woods, facing him, and fired two shots over my head which took my hat off.

"2. I was then taken to a nearby farmhouse, marched into the sitting room and made to sit down – the whole family being in the room too. The Russian soldier then accused me of having slept with the farmer's wife. She denied this and said I was a British soldier. The Russian then struck me in the face and struck the woman too. He then herded the children into one room and the man and his wife into the other and forced them to have intercourse while I looked on, saying to me in German: 'There you are, spy. That is the last you will see.' We left the farmhouse.

"3. I was taken to another farmhouse, where the same thing happened, except that the woman in this house was stubborn and would not do as she was told. The Russian then started firing indiscriminately. The Russian struck me and told me to march out of the door. He then fired two shots over my head when I had gone about 20 yards. Almost immediately there were two other shots down the road. The soldier then turned to the farmers and told them he had meant no harm and not to repeat what had happened. I was taken by a Russian sergeant to Lufitze, where the celebrations were taking place.

"At this Russian H.Q. they insisted that I was an American

and insisted on me having dinner with them. After dinner I asked the Russian captain for papers to prove my identity but he said they were not necessary. I left and on entering the street I was picked up by two Russian soldiers who insisted that I should find them some women, which I refused to do. They then took what remaining papers I had and took me to a farmhouse where they locked me up and said that if I attempted to escape the whole family would be shot. They told me to remain there until 08.00 hours the next morning (5 May), when they said they would collect me and shoot me.

"At about midnight I forced the iron bars of my window, jumped out of the window and made my way back to the Austrian family at Kleinlungitz, where I arrived the next morning at about 07.00 hours on 6 May. I remained here for one day and on 7 May I started out on my way to Graz. I eventually arrived in Graz on 4 June, walking through the woods and occasionally hitch-hiking.

"At Graz I reported to the Russian H.Q., where I was registered with four other English soldiers who eventually came back to Naples with me. I was placed on a train on 4 June and on 5 June I was taken by truck to Klagenfurt, where I arrived the same day. On 6 June I was flown to Udine and on the 8th on to Rome by train. On 9 June it was on by train to Ancona, then by truck to Naples, where I arrived on the 13th."

So much for liberation, Red Army style!

Chapter 12

The Homecoming

On 17 May 1945 Gwladys Jones received another telegram providing better news than the one informing her that her husband was "missing". This one read simply: "Arrived safely. See you soon. Ron."

Some 166,650 British and Commonwealth POWs were repatriated from Germany and, like a lot of them, Ron Jones had mixed feelings about his return home. In many ways travelling in eager anticipation proved more enjoyable than the arrival. For those incarcerated for so long, it was literally a dream come true to be reunited with their families and friends, but the general public were much less welcoming. To put it bluntly, nobody wanted to know them.

Eric Doyle, one of Ron's comrades from E715, expressed their frustration thus: "Our treatment and condition was so bad that it was impossible to explain it to people in Britain."

Ron's long road back to normality began courtesy of the American Air Force. He says: "The Yanks flew us home to Aylesbury, in Buckinghamshire, from where we were taken to Didcot railway station, and I got a train back to Newport. There were crowds of people there, waiting for their menfolk coming home, but not for me. I didn't know what time the train would be leaving Didcot, or what time it would get in to Newport, so Gwladys, who was never 100 per cent healthy, waited for me at home. She suffered from hay fever and asthma, and I used to see her leaning out of the bedroom window, gasping for breath. She didn't complain, she was never a moaner, but she was never what you'd call 100 per cent.

"I got a taxi from Newport station, and because I was in uniform the driver wouldn't take the fare. When I got back to our house in Bassaleg, which was called Rose Mead, they had 'Welcome Home' banners and balloons outside. My whole family was there – absolutely everybody. I think there was 15 all told. To be honest, I wasn't ready for it. I wasn't well enough to cope with the emotion of the occasion. I was thrilled to bits to get home, of course I was, but I was so weak – physically and mentally.

"I could see in their faces that my mother and father were shocked by my appearance. I was in a mess physically and my mother started to cry immediately. How I looked would have been a bit of a surprise anyway, because I was still dressed as a Yankee soldier when I walked in!

"That first night home I went to have a bath and couldn't get in on my own, Glad had to help me in. Doing that, she saw my naked body. I was all skin and bone – not much bigger than one of those Auschwitz Jews – and she started to cry. I said: 'Oh Gwladys, don't cry love. I might be weak but I'm in one piece. I left men out there who are never going to come home.'

"Glad was fantastic. She nursed and cajoled me back to health. We didn't get the counselling the services get today, no help whatsoever in that respect, and for a long time I was in a hell of a state. I used to have blackouts and fall down, without any warning, and I had terrible recurring nightmares, in which I'd be climbing a slippery bank and falling back again and again. Or climbing a high fence and falling off.

"Gwladys built me up on liquids. A lot of Sanatogen, for the iron, rice puddings and stuff like that. Even today, I can't abide the waste of food. It really annoys me and it's something that dates from when I went back to work. In the canteen, fellas would take a piece of bread, wipe their knife and fork on it and throw it away. I used to go berserk. In Auschwitz, the Jews would kill one another for a piece of bread like that. It's something that used to really affect me.

"I don't waste anything. I have a fruit saucepan in the kitchen and any fruit that's left over, or is starting to go on the turn, goes in that pot. I've learned to be pretty self-sufficient from my garden, and apples, greengages and blackberries all go in. That's my dessert every night. When I hear kids say they are starving hungry it makes me smile. If they knew what real starvation was they wouldn't say it.

"When I got back from the war I was a walking skeleton and everybody could see I needed building up. My mother and father were very friendly with the man who ran the Post Office in Rogerstone, Bert Periam, and I'd been home about a fortnight or three weeks when he came to see me. He said 'Bill (my father) sent me to have a chat.' I was unbelievably skinny and he said: 'Ron, I go up to Blackpool for conferences and I've got contacts at a guest house there. I'll make you up a parcel of food, get yourself up there for a couple of weeks, get away from it all.' So that's what I did, with Gwladys of course.

"We had a lovely time, at the pleasure park and wherever. I remember going on a rifle range where if you hit the bull, they took your photograph. Being an ex-soldier, I was a pretty good shot and found it pretty easy to hit the bull. The stallholder said: 'You can bugger off, I'll run out of film!'

"When I came back from Blackpool I had a fat face and a great big tummy and my cousin said: 'Look at you Ron, are you pregnant?' That pot belly soon went though. We couldn't make pigs of ourselves in those days because everything was rationed. For the first ten weeks I had double rations, but after that I was on the same as everyone else. Anyway, I couldn't eat too much because I used to get terribly bloated.

"What made me feel worse when I got home from the war was that Gwladys wanted a baby, which was only natural, she was 28, but I couldn't oblige. I was useless in that department for 12 months, before we had my son, Leighton. We always slept together, despite my nightmares and flashbacks. She would hold me and cuddle me until I settled. We were a wonderful pair and we had a very happy life. A lot of fellas came home to find their wives had been having affairs or even babies with other men.

"I was in the same hut out there as an Anglo-Italian fella from Cardiff. He was a dark and swarthy guy – a real Mediterranean type – but he went grey overnight. He got a letter from his parents, saying his wife had had a baby by somebody back home. He was in a terrible state, we had to hold him down to stop him harming himself. And he was a hell of a nice fella. He wasn't the only one, but I know all about him because he was in our room."

In common with many former comrades, Ron kept his story to himself, speaking only to close family about his experiences for over 50 years. He says: "Most people weren't interested, and anyway I wasn't inclined to talk about it and to bring back all those horrible memories."

Denis Avey says: "Many former prisoners were made to feel they had let the side down by being captured at all. No one ever said it straight out, but we felt under suspicion. Instead of being victims of Nazi forced labour programmes, it was as if we had unwittingly helped the German war effort. We weren't treated as returning heroes at any rate. We had done what we could to sabotage work at IG Farben and had suffered as much as any who served. We had also witnessed humanity's darkest chapter and come home with nothing we could talk about. Nothing anyone could understand, at least."

Brian Bishop had a similar experience: "After the war, people were only interested in heroes. If you escaped from a prison camp, then you became a hero. If you didn't escape, then you became forgotten. In Auschwitz it was practically impossible to escape as every bush had a soldier hiding behind it. You got fed up with people bragging about what they did in the Army, and I didn't feel my experiences mattered that much."

Arthur Gifford-England, a Somerset man who served in the Royal Engineers said: "I didn't talk about it for a long time. No one believed that we were at Auschwitz and no one believed what we had seen."

They didn't talk about it, but the camp dominated their thoughts. Ron says: "For years I had terrible nightmares and blackouts. I've spoken to others when we had our reunions and they all said the same. I reckon the nightmares were the result of thinking that we might be next for the gas chamber. We were always afraid that they'd stick us in there if their situation became desperate.

"People back in England didn't understand it – Gwladys didn't. Friends and family wanted to talk about it, but I wouldn't, it was something I just wanted to forget. You couldn't explain to people what we went through. We talked about it amongst ourselves at our reunions, that was our emotional release. I never told anybody else, but I was in a terrible state.

"There's more talked about Auschwitz now, 70 years later, than ever there was back then. Young people, especially, are well informed. I know of schools who take their pupils to Poland to teach them all about it. Some of them came to see me and said: 'We had a good look at where you'd been, Ron.' They were very understanding.

"A few years ago I told my nephew, Philip, my story. He told his sister-in-law, who is a teacher in Cwmbrân, and she had her pupils put on a play that they called *The Embroidery*, which was about me. They put it on stage at their school, in Llantarnam, and had me along as guest of honour, which was lovely.

"I've spoken to a lot of the other fellas, and it took us all about four or five years to recover fully. There's no doubt we suffered from what they now call Post Traumatic Stress Disorder. The lads back from the Falklands, the Gulf War and Afghanistan get counselling, we didn't. Our mental state was totally ignored. When we got home they gave us ten weeks leave and double rations to build us up again, and a bit of food was all we needed, as far as the Army and the Government were concerned. Nobody came to see me to discuss how I was, nothing. The authorities didn't want to know."

For Ron, the long road to recovery began in Cardiff. He says: "When I got back I had to go for a medical at the Ministry of Pensions and they regraded me from A1 to B4. My feet, in particular, were in a terrible mess. My boots had fallen apart and I had sacks wrapped around my feet towards the end of the march. Because of that, the arches had gone for good and my calves have never been the same, either.

"When I was fit enough I was sent to Pangbourne, near Reading, to join up with the Royal Engineers. I couldn't go back to the Borderers or the Welch Regiment because with my fitness downgraded to B4 I was no good to the infantry. Meanwhile, my father was working as a blacksmith with my old firm, Guest Keen, and Sid Birchall, the personnel manager, sent for him one day and said: 'I hear Ron is home.' My father told him I was, and Sid said: 'I suppose he'd like to come out of the Army, wouldn't he?' I suppose Sid was feeling a bit guilty about letting me get called up in the first place.

"With a job waiting, I was only at Pangbourne for about a month. We were allowed home on leave at weekends, and I could go back on the midnight train, as long as I was on parade at 9.00 a.m. One Monday morning I walked on to the parade ground and the sergeant major said to me: 'Corporal Jones, what are you doing here?' I thought I was in trouble and told him I'd just got back from a weekend pass. He said: 'There's a letter for you in the office.' It was my discharge papers. GKN had got me out."

Brian Bishop was in the Regular Army, so there was no automatic demob for him. He describes his return to England as follows: "The Yanks flew us to Rheims in France. We had three days there and then we were flown home in Lancasters. We were supposed to land in Kent, but it was too busy there and we ended up somewhere near Aylesbury.

"The Army sent me for re-training down near Brighton. It was for weapons training, but with my experience I could do it all with my eyes shut. I remember them teaching us how to use hand grenades. There was this great big net, we were all given six grenades each and we had to throw them into the net. If we got all six in, we passed. I got my six in the net, fine, then the bloke next to me got five in but the other hit the edge and fell out. He was disqualified. He said: 'Blimey I blew up God knows how many Germans with bloody hand grenades and I get failed back here. The first five would have done the job in any case.'

"I had a bit of an attitude because of the war and being a prisoner, and I thought it was all a waste of time, so I used to go AWOL from that camp. I used to clear off into Brighton. I'd turn up the following morning and get into trouble, but at that time I didn't really care what I did. The last time I did it I was told: 'Right, you've got to go and see the trick-cyclist.' I thought: 'What the bloody hell is a trick-cyclist?' I hadn't a clue. Anyway, I went where they sent me and I was called into this room by a big fat Jewish guy, which I thought was a bit ironic. Cor he was a size – not like those in the camp. He asked me a few questions which I answered, then said he was sending me to a hospital in Dartford. I asked why and he said I was psycho-neurotic, I suppose that's the equivalent of what today they call Post Traumatic Stress Disorder.

"I was shipped off with two other fellas to this hospital in Dartford, which was next to a well-known lunatic asylum. We had to go and see a psychiatrist. I was there for three months, but I got in more trouble, for going missing a couple of times. Then I got called into the office one day in January 1946 and was told I was being discharged from the Army. I wasn't happy about that. My father had been in the Services for over 20 years and fought in both World Wars, I wanted to beat that but was kicked out after less than eight years.

"Because I was a regular soldier I got my backpay from the war before I left the Army but no compensation for slave labour. As a regular they put me on a pension of ten shillings a week. But when I was having psychiatric treatment I had to go to West Hammersmith Hospital and I got fed up with that so they decided to send me to another hospital in Surrey.

"I didn't think I needed treatment. I had a good job and I wanted to keep it. My attitude was: 'What do I need to go to hospital for?' I didn't accept that I was ill, but when I left hospital for the last time a nurse said to me: 'I hope you're better now, because you were the most ill-mannered pig I ever met.' I was shocked. I thought: 'Who, me? I've never been ill-mannered in my life.' I had been, of course, I just didn't realise it.

"When I refused to go back to hospital the first thing the Army did was stop my pension. That was that, they never bothered with me again and I've never had the pension since."

For Ron Jones it was demob time – a routine which was the same for hundreds of thousands. He says "I was given a railway pass down to Taunton, where they rigged me out in civvies. There was no end of us, all in a line. We dumped our uniforms and the demob suits we all got instead were ordinary, at best. All the same colour, and not very good quality. Once I got home, I couldn't wait to get my own clothes on and I never wore that suit again. They gave us trilby hats, underclothes, the full kit.

"I got back at 9 o' clock that night, knocked on the front door and gave my wife another shock. She didn't know about my discharge. I had a week off and then went back to Guest Keen where, first of all I had to go and see

Birchall, the personnel manager, who said: 'I'll give a job that involves light work to start with.' He probably thought he owed me after the cock-up that got me in the Army in the first place.

"Two days before I was due to start back, I received a letter from the War Office. I'd had a decent secondary education and they had found a place for me at Pontypridd, to train to become a teacher. I'd have loved that, but I couldn't do it because I'd committed myself to rejoin my old firm, as a qualified tradesman, and it was a bloody good job. The wire drawers were the elite of the works in those days. We were on piece work and we reckoned on earning £1 a day on a five-day week. So we were on £5 a week while qualified fitters and electricians were only getting £2.50. They used to class us as the snobs of the works. We were very well off – Glad said it was like being married to a millionaire! I couldn't give up a job like that to go training to become a teacher, and I went back in the first week of January 1946. I was on light duties for six months, then they gave me my old job back, with the seniority I'd have been entitled to if I'd never been away.

"The firm were very good to me. For all the time I was abroad, in the Army, they paid the rent for Glad. In fairness, it wasn't Birchall who was responsible for me getting called up, it was his typist who put my reserved occupation form in the incoming mail instead of outgoing. I played hell about it at the time, but what was done was done. What could I do about it afterwards? They couldn't give me those years back.

"I was working again, but that doesn't mean I was right, either physically or in the head. I was on the night shift sometimes so Gwladys would be in bed when I got home, and without her standing there to reassure me I couldn't walk up the stairs normally. I used to walk up backwards. My nerves were shot to pieces and when I was washing at the handbasin I was looking from side to side all the time. I was always afraid of someone creeping up on me.

"Gwladys had to put up with a lot in those early years after the war – probably too much – but she was tremendously loyal and supportive. I wouldn't have come through it but for her. I was living on my nerves all the time and used to get into terrible rages. I grabbed her by the hair one day and shook her in temper. Our doctor, Desmond Hull, knew us both well – we were at school together – and he said to Gwladys: 'Get hold of his head and shake him to teach him a lesson.' She did, and I never did it again. I was in a hell of a state and needed that shock to come to my senses, but I still had those awful tempers, which isn't me. I was never that kind of fella pre-Auschwitz. Our life was terrible for five years or so."

Ron was by no means alone in abusing his nearest and dearest. It was a common manifestation of the returning POWs' psychological problems. Brian Bishop was married not long after the war and admits: "I must have been hell to live with. Everything got on my nerves. I was easy-going before the war but being a prisoner all that time really affected me and had made me awkward and a bit of a rebel. I know there were times when my wife was scared of my temper. She never knew what sort of mood I would be in. On some days nothing was right and I remember I used to shout at my daughter just for drumming her fingers on the table. Mind you, she was a sod and I think she used to do it knowing it would wind me up.

"It was a long time before I was really right again, but I

was able to hold down good jobs in the electronics trade. The Signals had given me a good grounding there."

Ron says: "What didn't help my mental rages was an incident a couple of years after I'd got back when somebody in the works nicked my signet ring. I managed to keep it throughout the war, even when I had to hide it up my arse to keep the Italians from having it, only to lose it among 'friends'. Working, we used to wear heavy gloves, with steel ribbing, because we were handling hot wire. When I put them on, I'd take the ring off and put it somewhere safe. Somebody must have seen me do it and stole it. Gwladys went mad. She went and bought me another one straightaway.

"For years my nerves were so bad that I couldn't sit still for any length of time. It was Gwladys who eventually cured that. She used to embroider tablecloths and one day she'd done a corner of one and I was sat opposite her, fidgeting. Suddenly she tossed me the tablecloth and said: 'Do that, see if it will keep you still for a while.' It worked. I knew how to sew, my mother had been a dressmaker and she used to give me a halfpenny to sew buttons and buttonholes on for her. That way I'd become good with a needle, so now I had a go at Glad's hobby and found it was good therapy. I started making tablecloths, and became so good at it that I've done dozens over the years, sold some and given others as wedding presents, birthday presents and so on. That definitely helped.

"It still took me five or six years to get back to being what I would call a 'normal' man and before I did we moved house, to the three-bed end of terrace where I've lived ever since. We moved here in 1948. I had the keys from the council on my birthday, April 30, and we moved in on Glad's birthday, May 5. It was a brand new council house that had just been built.

The rent was 19 shillings [95p] per week. Later we bought it, for £6,000 in 1980, when I retired."

Ron was relieved to discover that he was by no means alone in experiencing mental issues: "I've spoken to fellas about this at our reunions and 90 per cent of them said they were the same. I know of men who never got over what amounted to a nervous breakdown. One old friend was still living a nightmare when he died, at 78, and from what I've read, we were all suffering the same when we got home. Back then, nobody had a clue what it was, or what to do to cure it.

Brian Bishop's nightmares often featured a crying baby who was picked up by the feet by an SS man and killed by smashing his head against a wall. "I had that one for years," he said.

Brian was given an allowance to visit a psychiatrist but found the sessions of little benefit. It took ten years for his mental state to improve, during which time he did not realise that he was ill.

Ron says: "In the Sixties I met Cyril Quartermain, from E715, and his wife, Lily, at a reunion in Croydon and Lily asked me: 'Do you still get nightmares, Ron?' I said: 'Thank God no, I finished with that years ago.' Lily told me: 'Cyril does, even now.'

"I think I was fortunate that I got back to work so quickly after the war. That stabilised my life. Some of the other POWs had shocking problems when they came home, much worse than me. Arthur Dodd was one. But I came home to a good wife who looked after me, I went back to work, on light duties at first, and had my old job back within a year. That gave me the grounding I needed.

"Poor old Arthur had a terrible time when he came home.

166

He arrived back at his house and his father had remarried to a woman from Liverpool. They'd had another child in his absence, and they didn't want to know him so he left home. What a homecoming. Disgraceful. Thank God I never had anything like that."

Back in "Civvy Street", in 1946, Ron became the first person in his village to own a car. "I hadn't even passed my driving test," he says. "My brother-in-law Harry, the zoo keeper from Dudley, taught me how to drive in an Austin 8 and I also had a friend who was a garage owner, so I became used to the convenience of running around in his car, as a passenger, and I said to Gwladys one day: 'I've got to have a car.'

"I picked up the local paper one night and read about the new Austin Devon. I knew the Austin people in Newport, so I went in there just after Christmas and asked about buying one. The salesman started to laugh and I said: 'I'm not laughing, I want that car.' He explained: 'You won't get one of those for a year or two. There's a long waiting list, and doctors and their like will get first choice.'

"In the corner of the garage there was this Austin 8 and I said: 'Whose is that?' The guy said: 'That's just come back from the makers, in Longbridge, it belongs to the garage owner's wife, and she's just had it serviced.' I asked him if she'd sell it and he said: 'I don't know', so I told him: 'Go and ask her.' He came back and told me: 'You can have it for 350 quid.'

"I didn't wait for a bus, I ran all the way home, got the cash and went straight back for the car. It was a lot of money then, but I had the cash in the flat. That came about because Gwladys worked for a company called Alcan during the War, she didn't believe in banks and kept all her earnings in shoe boxes under the bed. So I had the 350 quid and couldn't get into town quick enough.

"I kept the car in a friend's garage and Harry came down on holiday and taught me to drive it. When I went into Newport to take my test, I pulled up outside the test centre and who should come out but one of my officers from the Army. 'Good God... Jonesy!' he said. He was the examiner. He told me to drive up the road a bit, we had a chat about old times and he signed my licence without me taking the test!"

To the delight of Ron and Gwladys, their son, Leighton, was born in 1947 and grew up making them proud of his success in life. Ron says: "I hope the mental problem I had in his early years never affected him, and I don't think it did. He's a clever bugger – he takes after his mother. The local village school wasn't very good, so we sent him to Rougemont, which is a private prep school. From there, one of his teachers, Mrs Evans, phoned one day and suggested Leighton should go to public school. I said: 'I don't know about that.'

"All I was interested in was Leighton passing the 11-plus to get into grammar school because there is a really good one just down the road, in Bassaleg. But Mrs Evans said: 'He's ideal material for public school', and she gave me a list of six. I picked out three and took him to Christ's College, Brecon, Hereford Cathedral School and Haberdasher's, at Monmouth on three successive Saturdays. He passed the entrance exam for all three and had the choice of them.

"Leighton was only ten-and-a-half at the time, but we left it up to him, and he said: 'I'd like to go to the one at Monmouth, dad', so that's where he went, on a scholarship. At 16 he had 13 O levels and two A levels, and Leighton wasn't a swotter, he was just a natural when it came to education. He was offered a place at Cambridge University but didn't want to go there. His careers master recommended Liverpool, so he went there and ended up with an honours degree in Economics. When he left he went on to become a director at Marconi, where he had £1m-worth of shares, and travelled all over the world so, all things considered, I don't think my post-war problems held him back."

A proud father with a loving wife and his old job back, Ron's recovery was slow but sure. "I carried on working for Guest Keen, always as a wire drawer, until I was 63. Ninety per cent of what I did was for the motor industry – push rods, back axles and plugs, all that sort of thing. A lot of the machines also made smaller stuff – screws and nails. Eventually they found a way to draw the wire on the same machine that was producing the nuts and bolts, so that caused redundancies. Somebody said: 'What about letting the old boys go, they've been here years', so they gave four of us a golden handshake. That was in 1980, when I was 63.

"I came home and said to Glad: 'What am I going to do?' I'd always been a busy, active man, but I needn't have worried, I was very lucky. I had a brother, Les, who had his own painting and decorating business, and whenever he was busy I helped him out. Les had a twin brother, Mel, and they both died from lung cancer. Too much smoking I reckon.

"When I wasn't painting with Les I was still busy. I'd been retired three weeks when there was a knock on the door one morning and it was Chris Blight, my nephew, from Cook and Blight estate agents. His mother and I had always been the two in the two families who got on best. We were very alike and good friends. Anyway, Chris said: 'Mum tells me you've retired Uncle Ron.' I told him I had and he said: 'Come and do a few odd jobs for me.' I took him up on the offer and Glad said: 'You're putting more bloody hours in now than when you had a full-time job!'

"I started putting up and taking down 'For Sale' boards and doing other chores for Chris in 1980 and at 96 I'm still doing it two days a week, more than 30 years later!

"Glad died in July 2005 and I was very bitter about that. She was a lovely, kind-hearted woman who lived a blameless life, and that she should go with cancer while some of those bastards I saw in Auschwitz lived longer really tested my religious faith. We were together just over 70 years, married for 68, and of course I really miss her. I don't like being on my own, but I've got used to it.

"I do feel that the war robbed me of a lot. Robbed me and Gwladys. I was 23 when I got called up and went away and 28 when I got back. After that I wasn't right, mentally, for about five years, so the war robbed me and Gwladys of what I'd call the romantic years of marriage. I often think of that when I see young couples showing their love, making a fuss of one another. We didn't have that – the romance of youth. Don't get me wrong, Glad was a wonderful wife, couldn't have been better, but we did lose out in that way."

Brian Bishop didn't have a wife to come back to after the War, but he soon acquired one – after a courtship of just 17 days. He explained: "When I was in Libya I used to go out on patrols, looking for the Germans. When I came back one day some of my gang were having an argument, so I went over to see what was going on. The row was over the fact that they had nothing to eat apart from a big tin of bully beef. I said I had a large tin of hard tack biscuits in my vehicle and I went to get it.

"On top of the packaging there was a piece of paper, inviting anyone looking for a pen friend to contact Maud

Turnbull at her address in Edinburgh. I kept that note throughout my captivity and after the war I found it and wrote to her. She replied, saying 'Why don't you come up to Edinburgh', so I did. Seventeen days after that we got married, on 7 November 1945. She already had a baby girl, who we brought up together. She's in her seventies now."

Chapter 13

Are You Sure?

Ron Jones was by no means the first, but at this late stage he will undoubtedly be the last survivor of Monowitz block E715 to tell his story. A large part of his motivation to do so now, 68 years after gaining his freedom, is to dispute some of the tales told by his comrades, in the belief that exaggeration, or inaccuracy, are manna from hell to the Holocaust deniers.

Ron says: "Some of my fellow POWs at Auschwitz have painted themselves as heroes, for whatever reason, and what these people have said needs to be examined in detail." There are three accounts in particular which detail events which differ from his own recollections.

1 Charles Coward
"I've got his book and he's the biggest liar that ever walked the earth. When he came home, he told everybody he'd been in the Jews' camp and freed a lot of them. He told all sorts of lies like that. I had a phone call once from a vicar in London, Roger Ryan, who wanted to come to see me. He said: 'I'm researching an article about your old sergeant, Coward.' I said: 'Oh, that bloody liar.' When the vicar came here, I proved to him how many lies Coward had told. The vicar

Charles Coward, whose tales of derring-do in Auschwitz were made into a film, in which his part was played by Dirk Bogarde. Self-aggrandising nonsense, according to Ron Jones. *(Wiener Library)*

Charles Coward honoured by the television programme *This Is Your Life*. His claims have since been widely discredited. *(BBC)*

Row upon row of barracks at Birkenau, in which Jewish prisoners were made to live like animals. *(Auschwitz-Birkenau State Museum)*

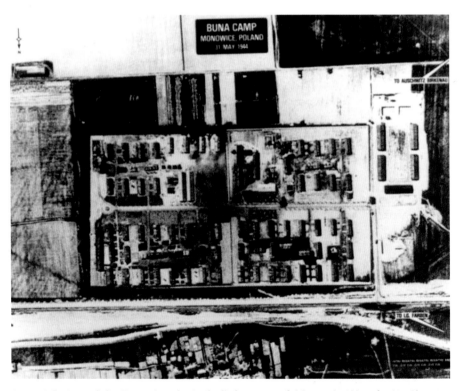

An aerial view of the Buna (synthetic fuel) factory and Monowitz (Auschwitz 3) camp from film taken in 1944 by an American reconnaissance plane. *(National Archives, Washington)*

Three monsters share a joke during a break from the devil's work. From the left: Richard Baer, camp commandant, Doctor Jozef Mengele and Baer's predecessor, Rudolph Hoess.
(United States Holocaust Memorial Museum)

Heinrich Himmler (right), head of the SS, in discussion with IG Farben engineer Maximillian Faust. *(Vad Yashem)*

A canister of Zyklon B, the gas that was used to exterminate Jews and others the Germans deemed "unworthy of life". *(Auschwitz-Birkenau State Museum)*

SS men and female auxiliaries enjoy some leisure time while their victims burn.

Arthur Liebehenschel, the second commandant at Auschwitz, who was in charge from December 1943 until May 1944. He was executed by hanging at Krakow in January 1948.

Richard Baer, the third commandant at Auschwitz (May 1944 to February 1945).

Rudolph Hoess's execution by hanging at the camp. *(Auschwitz-Birkenau State Museum)*

IG Farben staff indicted for war crimes at Nuremberg. *(Auschwitz-Birkenau State Museum)*

IG Farben staff in the dock at Nuremberg in 1947. The court found that Auschwitz was paid for and owned by the company and that their use of slave labour was a crime against humanity, but by 1951 all those jailed had been released and most were soon back in executive positions in German industry. *(Auschwitz-Birkenau State Museum)*

Ernst Bartels, appointed to liquidate IG Farben, who insisted British POWs had no claim to compensation for their slave labour.   *(BBC)*

Benjamin Ferencz, the United States's executive prosecutor at the Nuremberg war crimes trials, who maintains that British POWs were entitled to the compensation they have never received.   *(BBC)*

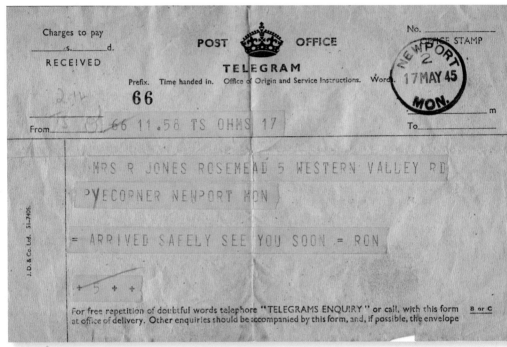

The news Gwladys Jones had waited three long years to receive. Ron has been repatriated at the end of the war and is on his way home.

(Author's collection)

then went to visit a man who's dead now, we'll call him Dave, who told him exactly the same. The vicar told me he'd get back to me about it, but I never heard anything more from him.

"Coward was a sergeant in the Royal Artillery when he arrived at Auschwitz in 1943. He was promoted to company sergeant-major in there – heaven knows how that happened – and he enjoyed comparative freedom of movement as the Germans' so-called 'Man of Confidence' and the British POWs' Red Cross trustee.

"In his book *The Password is Courage* (Souvenir Press, 1954) his biographer, who wrote under the pen name John Castle, told the story of Coward's capture by the Germans in France, how he is supposed to have been given the Iron Cross and his alleged swap with a Jewish prisoner in the extermination camp. To me, nearly all of it is literally unbelievable.

"The story starts with Coward's wounding and capture at Calais in 1940. Fair enough, but then comes the nonsense about the Germans giving him a medal by mistake. It's all absolute rubbish. Coward was wearing his khaki uniform, the Germans wore grey. Do you think nobody would have spotted the difference? Not the medical orderlies who carried him into the field hospital, the soldiers in the next beds, the doctors or the visiting general and his entourage? It's all lies.

"He said he was present when Leslie Reynolds was shot but I don't remember that. I do remember that there were three of us present, including me, and he wasn't one."

In his book, the incident is described as if Coward was an eye witness, as follows:

"'Die verfluchten Englander' muttered the German to Coward. 'They are lazy pigs. I will make them work, you will see.'

"Coward said clearly: 'You lay a hand on one of those men and there'll be trouble, unteroffizier.'

"The man sneered back and elbowed his way into the men. A young English corporal named Reynolds was angrily refusing to climb the steel pylon in that cold weather unless [he] had rubber boots and sufficiently thick gloves.

"'Climb!' shrieked the unteroffizier. 'Climb!' A foam flecked his lips. Reynolds shrugged. 'I'm going back to the other chaps,' he said quietly.

"'Watch it,' warned Coward. 'I don't like the look of this rat – he's dangerous.'

"The corporal laughed grimly. 'It's only bluster, he wouldn't dare.'

"He began to walk away from the group. Coward saw a pistol appear in the German's hand and shouted: 'Look out man!'

"Reynolds turned and stared with open mouth as the gun thundered. He stood quite still for a moment, a small, dark stain appearing on the breast of his khaki tunic. Then he cried 'Christ, he's shot me!' and crumbled in a heap on the frozen ground.

"The Britishers rushed forward to where he lay, but he was dead. Coward knelt beside him, then looked long at the unteroffizier, who now stood with the smoking pistol in his hand, clearly shaken by the results of his choler.

"'You yellow, dirty swine,' said Coward deliberately."

Detailed, if a trifle melodramatic stuff, yet in the affidavit he submitted to the War Crimes Tribunal at Nuremberg, dated 24 July 1947, he does not suggest that he was present when Reynolds was shot. In this document he states: "The British prisoners of war were treated better than any other nationality working at IG. Still, many incidents occurred which cost the lives of our prisoners of war. [Records show that only Reynolds was killed].

"One German non-commissioned officer used to threaten to shoot all of us. He would beat British prisoners of war at the IG Farben plant or at the camp. [None of the other British POWs has said this.] At times it happened that IG civilian workers used to beat some of our prisoners.

"In the winter of 1943-44 a civilian foreman of IG Farben ordered five prisoners of war to climb an ice-covered iron girder. Under the circumstances it was almost impossible to climb the girder, especially since the men did not have proper boots. The men refused to obey the order. Thereupon the German guard shot and killed one of the five British prisoners of war."

Ron Jones snorts: "Rubbish. The description and the conversation are all made up.

"Coward definitely wasn't there. The man was a fantasist.

"I've got a photograph of Coward with Eamonn Andrews, who used to present the television programme *This Is Your Life*. He was on it in October 1960, talking about what he'd done during the war. I was absolutely disgusted. Coward died in 1976, without being exposed. He gave evidence at the Nuremberg trials, mentioning how he'd released Jews. It was all lies. Another thing he said was that he had a handcart and that he used to go into the works and bring back the bodies of the Jews who had died. I never saw him with a handcart.

"Many have called him a liar. Everyone knew exactly what was going on in the camp because we all used to talk about it. Nearly every conversation was about what was happening to the Jews. There was not much else to talk about, after all. There were no secrets in there and we'd have known all about it at the time.

"I've got a letter that was published in the *Daily Mail* in which Coward is accused of stealing another prisoner's greatcoat. That tells you what he was really like."

The letter in question, from Liam Hillman of Stockton-on-Tees, states:

"My grandfather, Sergeant William Hillman (Royal Engineers), and my eldest uncle, Private William Hillman (The Buffs), both had the misfortune to be incarcerated with Sergeant-major Charlie Coward for much of World War 2. My grandfather would say little about his wartime experiences, but did have a thing or two to say about Coward.

"Coward was promoted to sergeant-major in the prison camp only so that he could avoid going out on the working parties, and the 'hero' stole my uncle Bill's greatcoat in the middle of winter. After the war ended, he falsely claimed to have broken out of Stalag V111B, broken into Auschwitz, broken out of Auschwitz and broken back into Stalag V111B. He was later taken to the Nuremberg War Crimes Tribunal as a witness. One wonders how many innocent Germans were wrongfully prosecuted with the help of 'witnesses' of his calibre.

"My grandfather and uncle are dead now, but when I asked my father about Charlie Coward he concurred with what they told me as a boy. He added my grandfather and another former Stalag V111B prisoner, 'Darkie' Rowe, were involved in a BBC programme in the late Forties or early Fifties which showed Coward for what he truly was – a liar and a thief. Unfortunately, he also seems to have been Teflon-coated, as his false accounts are still mistaken for the truth in some quarters."

Of Coward's status as sergeant-major, Brian Bishop says: "A lot of people in there promoted themselves. There were a lot of corporals who were only what we called 'stalag corporals', who were privates but promoted themselves to get better jobs and an easier time. I was one of those. I don't know if Charlie did that, but I definitely remember him wearing a sergeant-major's crown on his arm."

In his book, Coward claimed to have smuggled guns and dynamite into Auschwitz. A more convincing version is given by Yisrael Gutman, in *Anatomy of the Auschwitz Death Camp*, which was published in association with the United States Holocaust Memorial Museum. Gutman writes: "In October 1944 Sonderkommando prisoners staged a doomed uprising. Explosives were smuggled in by Jewish women workers from a factory. Their uprising and subsequent attempt to escape, which ended with the murder of all participants, was the only significant act of resistance of its kind in the history of the camp."

Ron Jones says: "You can read about this at the Holocaust Memorial Museum. I bet Coward heard of it and claimed the credit for himself. That would have been just like him."

Coward also alleged that he smuggled himself into the extermination camp, Birkenau, by bribing a guard, to see an English prisoner – a Jewish doctor who was seriously ill. His book says he did this by swapping places with a Jewish inmate at the death camp. The alleged switch is explained as follows:

"While working with a digging detail, Coward had plenty of opportunity to get his hands and face thoroughly grimed. A little before six in the evening he mentioned to the feldwebel in charge that it was necessary to visit another party... turned up his coat collar to avoid recognition and made his way to the factory cellars. It had not been difficult to find an inmate willing to change identities for a night and enjoy a good rest.

Approaching the inmate's kapo... was more nerve-wracking... but the lure of cigarettes tipped the scales. For such a prize the kapo would have committed murder six times over. With the prospect of 50 and a promise of 20 more on Coward's safe return, his decision could not be in doubt.

"Soon he [Coward] could hear from overhead the shouted orders for the gangs of workers to form up for their march back to their camps. There were sounds of someone descending the stone stairs and he struck a match, revealing the inmate and his kapo. The cigarettes changed hands and he stripped off his clothes, reaching out for the pyjama tunic.

"In the crush of men who had appeared from their tasks, like rats from their holes, no one had noticed. He [Coward] began to stride after the kapo, then, remembering his new identity, fell back to a scuffle, dragging his clogs along the floor and drooping his head.... Jostling his way into their midst, Coward did his best to ape their movements, hanging his arms straight down and keeping his eyes on the feet of the man in front. His arrival occasioned no comment."

Coward describes in detail the appalling conditions in Birkenau and how he couldn't find the English doctor. The switch back from slave worker to POW is explained like this:

"The high point of danger came as they [the Jewish work party] slowly approached the main gates. He hung his head as low as he could.... The queue moved gradually forward, he could hear the voices of the guards counting loudly. He was level with the gates... then through. Other parties were already beginning to work as they entered the factory. He slipped from his rank and moved over beside the kapo.... The kapo gave a barely perceptible nod and in the next instant Coward had whipped through the door and was clattering down the steps. There was no doubt in his mind that he [the

Jewish inmate] would be waiting. Stripping off the pyjama suit and wooden clogs, feeling again the warmth and cleanness of his own khaki and the familiar fit of his boots, Coward wanted to shout with delight...

"In a corner of the huge yard of the factory the British working party had just arrived on a digging detail.... With his coat collar turned up and his face smeared with clay to hide his incriminating stubble from the guards, Coward worked with his men all day."

The alleged swap with a Jewish prisoner was supposedly intended to rescue Karel Sperber, a British naval officer who was Jewish, of Czech origin. Sperber, who was in Monowitz, not Birkenau, died in 1957. Before doing so, he said he had no knowledge of any attempt to rescue him.

Ron Jones poses the question: "Would he [Sperber] not have come forward and thanked Coward after the publication of his book, which came out in 1954?" Ron says: "As far as I know, none of it happened. Nobody I knew in there ever heard of it, and we would have. Coward loved to talk about himself and what he'd done and we'd have known all right."

Doug Bond, a Londoner in E715, who died in December 2009, agreed. Asked for his recollection of Coward, he told the National Ex-Prisoner of War Association: "I have read and heard many of his exploits, also got to know him as camp leader of E715 at Auschwitz, where I was also a POW. Personally, I think he had a very vivid imagination. I think he based his book and film on other POWs' experiences.

"As a camp leader at E715 he would have had very little contact with the Jewish community as he did not go out to work like we did at the local IG Farben factory. I think we had more contact with them, working alongside."

In Duncan Little's book *Allies in Auschwitz* (Clairview Books, 2010), Doug returns to the subject and says: "He [Coward] was the man in charge of the camp, so he couldn't afford to go missing, could he? When we were on parade he was always there. He was always on parade when the German officer came on parade, so he could never afford to go missing really. I used to talk to Charlie Coward all the time and he never mentioned it [the swap]."

Another former POW, Ronald Redman, said: "My first recollections of Charles Coward were on being transferred to Auschwitz E715. He was appointed senior British POW to liaise with the German commandant. After a short time he organised an evening concert dominated by himself."

It would seem Coward was not exactly "politically correct", and not above mimicking the suffering Jews, as Redman adds: "He impersonated a typical Jewish prisoner in genuine pyjama suit, cap and clogs. Although rather cruel, he mimed all the nervous shuffling and cap-doffing mannerisms to a T and I think the German guards observing were most amused. He must have studied the Jewish prisoners to a fine detail.

"When the bombing of Auschwitz began and life was very uncomfortable I think Charlie returned to Stalag V111B at Lamsdorf, using his authority."

The compulsory questionnaire Coward completed upon rejoining the Army, dated 14 April 1945, states that he was detained in E715 from September 1943 until "some time in 1944." Of his experiences he wrote only:

"On 21 January 1944 I escaped from E715 Auschwitz with two Jews from the concentration lager, but gave myself up on train to Vienna after 12 hours, so that I could engage in conversation with 2 Gestapo officials, whilst the 2 Jews could jump the train. On this occasion I had no passport, was sent back to Auschwitz. Was not punished because was not reported missing. Escaped again whilst in Hanover about 4 April 1945."

Brian Bishop has mixed feelings about Coward. He is grateful for the help he received from the "Man of Confidence", but dismissive of the claim that he exchanged places with a Jewish inmate. Brian said: "Everything Charlie said he would do for me in the camp he did, and he did a bloody good job looking after our Red Cross parcels when the Germans were after them all the time. I used to get in trouble with the guards for little things I did to wind them up and Charlie would intercede for me and sort it out. He wasn't a bullshitter in that respect.

"Where I definitely don't believe him is his claim to have broken into the Jews' camp. He was the fittest looking fella you could wish to see. How could he possibly pass himself off as a starving six-stone Jew? Among that lot he would have stuck out like a sore thumb.

"I got on all right with him but he did have a good relationship with the Germans and I heard a rumour that he profited from some of the gold teeth extracted from the dead Jews, getting it sent to Switzerland. I don't know if that was true, he wasn't going to admit it, was he?"

Classified documents on Coward held by British Intelligence, which should reveal the full story, are not due to be released until 2020.

2 Denis Avey

At the age of 91, Avey was named a Hero of the Holocaust for helping to save the life of an Auschwitz inmate. He received a medal inscribed "For Services to Humanity", and had his heroic activities in the camp described in an authorized biography which is remarkably similar to Charles Coward's.

In April 2012, the BBC broadcast a programme, *Witness to Auschwitz*, which cast doubt on key parts of it, posing the question: "It's an heroic tale, but is it believable?" Ron Jones asks the same question.

Avey, like Ron, was captured in North Africa but he escaped, only to be recaptured in Greece. Again like Ron, he had a rough time as a POW in Italy before ending up in Poland. It's in Auschwitz that their stories differ.

Avey claims to have broken into the Jews' camp and talks of "the ghastly stench, the nightmares, the prayers, the crying, the screaming, it was murder." He said he entered this hell-hole to gain first hand evidence of the Nazi atrocities.

Like Ron Jones, Avey was made to work for IG Farben, alongside the Jews, building the synthetic rubber factory. Of that experience he says: "When I saw them [the Jews] first of all, I couldn't believe it. I thought I was seeing ghosts. There was death in their faces. The poor devils... it was ghastly being with them. I used to watch Jews coming into the camp, especially Hungarian Jews, who were big chaps. Thirteen stone when they started work, but with the lack of food they had – you couldn't call it food – if they lasted three months it was quite some time for them to live.

"A lot of our fellas built up a defence mechanism, and accepted it, but that was not me, I was very angry."

Communication with the Jewish inmates was forbidden, but went on nevertheless when the guards weren't looking, and Avey won his "Hero of the Holocaust" award for helping one by the name of Ernst, who had a sister in England. Avey says he got a message to her, asking for cigarettes, which he smuggled into the Jews' camp. After the war, Ernst testified that Avey's actions helped to save his life: "I got 200 cigarettes and a bar of chocolate to him," Avey says. "He said I saved his life because he was able to get thick soles on his boots (in exchange for the cigarettes) and on the Death March that saved him."

It was a chance conversation with another Jew that Avey says gave him the idea to break into their camp. "I can't even explain why I did this," he says. "I chalked an algebraic formula on pipework. I'd just finished it and a stripey (the POWs' name for Jewish inmates) came up behind me and said: 'Have you got a cigarette?' He saw this formula and said: 'I know that formula', and that's how we got talking."

The Jew, who Avey knew as Hans, was of similar height and Avey said this gave him his idea. If he could swap places with Hans for the night, he could become a witness to the Nazi atrocities from inside Auschwitz proper and provide the evidence needed to bring the perpetrators to justice.

"To tell me something is no good," Avey explains. "That's all right, but it doesn't prove anything. If I witness something, then it's a different situation. So I realised I had to witness how they were living, how they were treated."

In order to change camps, from E715 to the Jews' quarters and back again, Avey would have to swap clothes with Hans and bribe the *kapo* in charge of Hans's working party. Avey says: "The *kapo* I bribed. All he had to do was turn his head. I said that if he did that, I'd give him more cigarettes when I came out.

"I had to be absolutely certain that my hair was shaved because at the *appelplatz*, which was the counting area, the *kapo* counted and the SS counted and the *kapo* would shout 'hats off' and you had to whip your hat off and stand to attention."

According to Avey, a couple of his friends agreed to look after Hans in E715, and in the Jews' Monowitz camp Avey also had help. He says: "They took me to a bed – well, they called it a bed for want of a better word. It was a slot where people were supposed to sleep head to toe. The stench in that warm room was ghastly. There was always noise going on, there were nightmares, there were prayers, there was crying and screaming. It was murder. Nevertheless, I got to know what I wanted. I got to see the treatment inside."

Incredibly, according to the television programme, Avey repeated the swap several months later, but a third attempt had to be abandoned. The programme called it "an heroic tale", but posed the question: "Is it believable?" and, in looking for an answer, turned to Dr Piotr Setkiewicz, the chief historian at the Auschwitz-Birkenau Memorial and Museum, and an acknowledged expert on the IG Farben labour camp.

Dr Setkiewicz pointed out that the Jews' appalling treatment meant their general appearance was strikingly different from the POWs. He said: "The British prisoners received the same kind of food as the other workers at IG Farben, nevertheless their situation was better because they received food parcels from the Red Cross. They had better clothes and they were not beaten by the guards, so their situation was many times better."

Apart from the difference in appearance, there were other factors which would make the exchange very difficult. Bribing a *kapo* was fraught with danger. There was no guarantee he would deliver. And inside Monowitz desperate inmates acted as spies, ready to report anything unusual in the hope of better treatment. Dr Setkiewicz said: "There was an overwhelming fear and lack of trust between people. If you tried to talk to somebody, you could not be sure what kind of person he or she was, friendly or not."

For the doctor, for Ron Jones and others, there are unanswered questions about how Avey managed to pull off such an exchange under these conditions. Brian Bishop says he has questions why he didn't hear the story at the time: "This Hans had to go into a barrack room where 20 men were sleeping. I don't think that was practical or possible – not with British soldiers especially. It would have been all round the camp in no time."

Further questions exist about why, if Avey wanted to bear witness to what went on, he waited so long to talk about it? He says that straight after the war, "I was asked [by the Army] if I would like to relate any of my POW experiences. I told them about Auschwitz and as I described it to them I could see the glazed-eye syndrome. I could see they obviously didn't believe me. They hadn't had the knowledge or experience. I thought: 'That's it, finished.' I walked out of the office and from that day I thought people had had a bad war and didn't want to know about my experiences."

He finally spoke out in 2001, but in this first account, for the Imperial War Museum, some facts did not match up. He told his interviewer, Lyn Smith, that it was not Monowitz he had entered and it wasn't Hans with whom he made the swap. He said he had gone into Birkenau in an exchange with Ernst.

Ernst was the Jewish inmate Avey had helped to survive with smuggled cigarettes from his sister.

The POW camp E715 was miles from Birkenau. So what about Hans and Monowitz? Avey says: "Obviously after 50 years I say things that are possibly wrong because I haven't properly understood you or haven't properly made myself understood. That's it. It's quite simple."

Rob Broomby, the BBC journalist who wrote Avey's book, says: "I think you've got to see that with a 92-year-old man you cannot really subject his entire testimony to the kind of forensic analysis you might use with a politician on the *Today* programme. We shouldn't beat about the bush, what's remarkable about Denis's whole story is not what he's forgotten, not the details that have occasionally got confused in that fog of war. It's just how much he can recall. I am the first person to go through that story forensically with him and I am absolutely convinced we've got that story right."

Others are anything but convinced. Of the British POW accommodation in E715, Avey says: "Icicles hung from the barracks ceiling in winter and mosquitoes swarmed in the warmer months." Ron counters: "I don't recognise any of that. I was never really that cold in our hut and don't remember any mozzies."

Avey says of the POWs' football matches: "I played two games on the right wing for the South African team, I scored in the final and we won. I fancy there were machine guns set up to stop us getting too frisky." Ron shakes his head at this. "The word 'fancy' is right. There were no machine guns, and who was going to get 'frisky' wearing only football kit? Were we going to attack the Germans with our boots?"

Avey, like Coward, claims to have smuggled himself into Birkenau. In his case, it was said to have come about through relationships he had with two Jewish prisoners, called Ernst and Hans. Like Coward, he says he swapped places with Hans. In his book *The Man Who Broke Into Auschwitz* (Hodder & Stoughton, 2011) Avey says:

"If we could organise an exchange, he [Hans] could come into the British camp overnight to rest. He'd get better food and more of it, possibly even eggs. The swap took weeks of meticulous planning and observation. I studied the movements of the Jewish prisoners, I knew where and when they would gather to march back to their camp, learned to copy their weariness, the stoop, the shambling gait. I taught myself to walk in the crude wooden clogs they wore.

"One of the 'stripeys' (Jewish prisoners) pointed me towards an older kapo who, I was told, was less brutal than the rest. I managed to get him onside with a bribe of 50 cigarettes – 25 now and 25 when I had returned successfully from the swap... When the time was right I hacked at my hair with a pair of old scissors and then shaved off the rest with a blunt razor. As the shift neared its end, I smeared dirt on my face, especially on my cheeks and under my eyes, to gain the grey pallor of exhaustion. I was ready... I had to see for myself what was going on. I had to get myself in there...

"Evening was approaching and I knew the British POWs would soon start to assemble 50 yards away from the 'stripeys' for the march back to E715. I could see that the Jewish work kommandos were getting ready to form their own column for the trudge back to their camp and I made my move.

"People were milling around so, taking advantage of the end-of-day confusion, I strode purposefully towards a wooden shed tucked away in the contractor's yard.... As soon as I was hidden inside I pulled off my heavy boots and got the coarse wooden clogs ready for a speedy exchange. Hans saw me go into the hut and followed rapidly on my heels.... For him, the chance of a safer night and a bit more food was worth the risk.

"Hans pulled off his infested top and tossed it to me. In return I gave him my military tunic. I pulled on his blue striped outfit, the smell of filth and human decay rose from the weave.... Then I adopted the hangdog expression that I had observed, dropped my shoulders and with my eyes cast downwards I left the hut and hobbled towards the Jewish column that was forming up. There I edged myself into the middle of a rank, coughing as I went so I could hide my accent behind a croaking voice if anyone spoke to me...

"Adrenalin pumped through my veins as I listened to the rhythmic drone of counting.... My pulse was racing inside a body that had to ooze hopelessness.... I had to bear witness and nothing must get in my way.... It was still light when we passed through the gate and I saw the sign bearing the cruel promise 'Arbeit Macht Frei' – work sets you free. I didn't know then that the irony of those words would scream across the decades. This was Auschwitz 3 – Monowitz.

"The swap called for a lot of luck, but I was disappointed with what I learned. There were many questions I still couldn't answer, but I had seen it, and that was a start."

Ron says: "The Jews were in such dreadful condition that they couldn't stand up straight, they were permanently hunched over, and when we returned to our huts after work we were all individually searched and required to stand bolt upright while it was done. None of the Jews I saw could have passed that close inspection."

Interviewed for this book, Brian Bishop said: "I never knew Avey in the camp, but I was told about his book and the BBC journalist who wrote it [Rob Broomby] phoned me about it. I was dismissive about the whole thing and Broomby said: 'How can you be when you've never read it?' I told him I'd been given the details of what was in the book and thought it was an unlikely story. Anyway, he sent me a copy and it was just as I thought. When I read it, it made me laugh. It's called *The Man Who Broke Into Auschwitz*. I can't believe he "broke into" anywhere. What he claims to have done is sneak from one camp into another, and I find even that hard to accept. Still, at least Broomby sending it saved me the few quid it would have cost to buy the book!

"A lot of ex-POWs died before Avey came out with his story, but there's still a few of us left. Like me and Ron Jones, Doug Bond was sceptical too.

"When we got bombed, the bomb that killed our lads fell about 50 yards from where I was laying in the sick bay. Avey describes how he dug out the men who were injured and the book reads as if he did it all on his own. When he talks about the 38 graves being dug in the town, you'd think he did all that, too."

Ron agrees. "Brian is right," he says. "We'd have known about it if Avey had got into the Jews' camp. We were like one big family, with no secrets from each other, and something like that would have gone around like wildfire. It didn't. To be honest, I never even heard Avey's name mentioned at any of our reunions after the war.

"If people could see the situation in there the way we saw it, nobody would ever believe these claims. I knew Coward and Avey, they were both fit and strong in comparison with those poor Jews, who were all at death's door and could never have passed inspection as POWs. And how could Coward and Avey make themselves look like six-stone Jews? It just doesn't seem possible.

"I can see it now, every time we walked back into camp we were ramrod straight with our hands high above our heads, ready to be searched, and the guards ran their hands down our bodies in a thorough check. The Jews were in such a state they walked like cripples. None of them could have stood erect, as we had to.

"Coward said he broke into the death camp and Avey said he walked under the *Arbeit Macht Frei* sign. There was only one sign like that, at Auschwitz 1, but neither of them is saying he went there."

In both the *New Statesman* and the *Daily Mail* questions have been raised about Avey's account. As Guy Walters wrote: "Avey's story is reaching a huge audience.... He [Avey] says: 'I can't really believe that people would believe what I did.' The trouble is that increasing numbers of people don't believe him. They include former Auschwitz prisoners, historians and Jewish organisations – and they all doubt very much that he broke into Auschwitz. Dr Piotr Setkiewicz, the head historian at Auschwitz, said he did not believe Mr Avey's story of the swap."

Walters makes the point that the World Jewish Congress had asked Avey's publishers to verify the historical accuracy of the book and quotes their spokesman as saying: "We are deeply concerned about the charge that a significant part of Mr Avey's story – that he supposedly smuggled himself into the Auschwitz-Buna concentration camp – is exaggerated if not completely fabricated."

Walters also points out that Yad Vashem, Israel's official memorial to the Jewish victims of the Holocaust, felt unable to honour Avey with Righteous Among the Nations, awarded to Gentiles who saved Jews during the War, because it could not back up his claims. He writes: "Former prisoners at Auschwitz and at camp E715 have also strongly disputed Mr Avey's story, arguing that the swap would have been impossible. The idea that the two men could have simply switched columns twice, without being seen by German guards, is implausible."

Sam Pivnik is a Polish Jew who was a prisoner at Auschwitz until January 1945. He says: "Avey's story seems to me highly unlikely. Swapping places with an Auschwitz Jew wasn't just risking his own life, but those of everyone else in his block, and he was taking a huge risk that he wouldn't be informed on. It isn't a risk that I would have taken. Prisoners in Auschwitz were so desperate you couldn't take the risk of trusting them."

Walters picked up on various inconsistencies in Avey's story, observing "In his book he writes that he swapped places with a Dutch-Jewish inmate called Hans and smuggled himself from the British POW camp into the part of the death camp known as Auschwitz 3. However, in an interview he gave to the *Daily Mail*, Mr Avey claimed to have swapped with Ernst Lobethal, the man to whom he smuggled cigarettes.

"In his book Mr Avey also writes of passing under the infamous 'Arbeit Macht Frei' sign as he entered Auschwitz 3. There was no such sign there, it was at the Auschwitz 1 camp, some six miles away."

Avey claims the clothes he borrowed from the Jewish inmate were infested with lice. This detail is doubted by Sam Pivnik, who says: "We were made to be scrupulously clean at all times in Auschwitz 3 work camps, and you risked a severe beating if you got dirty. The SS were terrified of typhus outbreaks and the prisoners' uniforms, bedding and barracks were endlessly disinfected and deloused."

Even Ingrid Lobet, the daughter of Ernst Lobethal, who Avey claims to have swapped with, rejects the story. "I don't believe this happened," she says. "Where is the detail in what he saw that can't be gleaned from the vaguest Holocaust account? The Jews looked half-starving, the British did not. Most of the Jews spoke only Yiddish. How is some starving, Yiddish-speaking Jew going to be mistaken for a British POW while in POW barracks? Did he [Avey] memorise the switched survivor's number in German so that he could respond to it at roll call?"

Of the close resemblance between Avey's story and that first told by Charles Coward in 1954, Walters says: "In a post-war trial Coward gave testimony – now widely discredited by Holocaust scholars – in which he claimed to have smuggled himself into Auschwitz by swapping places with a Jewish inmate. The chance that two British POWs both independently thought up the life-endangering idea to swap places with an inmate of Auschwitz for the night stretches credibility to breaking point.

"The similarity between the two tales also raises the question why Mr Avey took so long to speak about his wartime experiences. In July 2001 Mr Avey gave a five-hour interview to the Imperial War Museum in which he spoke about his incarceration as well as the psychological impact of the war and his problem with nightmares. Not once in this interview did Mr Avey talk about smuggling himself into Monowitz.

"In 2004 and 2005 Avey was interviewed by the journalist Diarmuid Jeffreys for his book *Hell's Cartel*. He again failed to talk about the swap. Only in 2009, in an interview with the BBC journalist Rob Broomby, did Mr Avey first mention that he had smuggled himself into Auschwitz. Rob Broomby went on to co-write the book that has now appeared.

"Mr Broomby has explained that Mr Avey left it so long to tell the story because he suffered from Post Traumatic Stress Disorder when he came back from the war. Why then was he able to talk about all those other experiences of the war in the preceding years?"

Brian Bishop asks: "Why does he start telling this story now? I don't understand why all these stories are coming out now. It looks like they're waiting for everybody to die and then no one can contradict them."

In April 2011, when asked why he did not mention the swap to the Imperial War Museum, Avey said: "I don't know why I didn't choose to establish it then. But what I wrote in the book is the truth. I don't have to defend it. I don't mind what anybody says, I don't mind if they doubt my word, I know what I've done."

Avey's story came under further scrutiny from Guy Walters in the *New Statesman* on 17 November 2011, when he wrote: "In a taped interview given to the Imperial War Museum in July 2001, Avey claimed that he had gained entry to Auschwitz-Birkenau by swapping places with an unnamed 'stripey' – as British prisoners of war called the Jewish inmates on account of their striped uniforms – and had been accompanied by a Jew called Ernst. However, in the published book, Avey claims that he broke into Auschwitz-Monowitz (a camp about four miles from Birkenau), swapped places with a Dutch Jew called Hans, and that the man who accompanied him was not 'Ernst'.

"The catalogue of problems with Avey's story was highlighted by myself... in the pages of the *Daily Mail* some seven months ago. Furthermore, we informed Avey's publishers, Hodder and Stoughton, in May of the existence of no fewer than eight differing versions Avey has given of his celebrated 'swap'." Walters concludes: "It is almost impossible to take *The Man Who Broke into Auschwitz* at face value."

In August 2012 Ron Jones was approached by a representative of the Holocaust Memorial Museum, in America, who subsequently flew from Washington to film him for a new exhibit. Ron says: "This man told me they had only been able to find two ex POWs from Auschwitz still alive. One was Brian Bishop, down in Somerset, and I was the other. When I mentioned Denis Avey he said he doubted Avey's story and didn't want to bother with him. Brian Bishop had told him the same as me: that he couldn't believe it happened. So he interviewed just the two of us – me and Brian."

3 Arthur Dodd

Dodd's authorized biography, *Spectator in Hell* (Summersdale, 1998) was written by Colin Rushton. Dodd, from Northwich, in Cheshire, was younger than Ron Jones – only 19 when the war started. He was trained as a mechanic, and therefore the two men had their engineering background in common. Ditto their capture in North Africa. Ron says: "I knew Arthur in the camp and he was a good man. His book is accurate in most respects, but I struggle with his story about breaking out to fight with the partisans on three nights in succession. I wouldn't have thought that was possible.

"In the book he says he was approached by a Pole from outside the camp who got him out of Monowitz, under the wire. Once outside and clear he says he joined four other British POWs who had done the same, and they met a partisan leader called Alex, who explained that his group had learned of the importance of an electrical installation at IG Farben and were going to blow it up. Arthur and his four colleagues were needed to get the explosives into the camp. Agreeing to do so, they carried boxes of explosives, batteries, sticks of gelignite and rolls of wire back in the way they had come. The POWs then watched from a safe distance as the Poles blew up the installation.

"Dodd and the others stayed overnight with the partisans, and were "somewhat alarmed" when Alex said they would be going back to the factory to lay more explosives and finish the job."

The book describes the incident as follows:

"Alex announced that they would be going back to IG Farben the next night. Although it [the electrical installation] had been badly damaged it had not been destroyed. The five British lads thought such a mission was suicide, and said so. They were convinced the factory would be swarming with guards as a consequence of their success. On their way back to the camp, laden again with explosives, Arthur was convinced that he would be either killed in the next few hours or captured and beaten to within an inch of his life.

"As it turned out, the mission was as successful as the previous night, and Arthur was astonished at there being no reception committee waiting for them. Once they were safely back at their makeshift camp, Arthur and the other lads again brought up with Alex the matter of their escape. They were 'less than impressed' with his answer. 'Gentlemen (Alex said), very rare have I ten good men to do work. We must do as much damage as we can. One more task. Then you go. I help you.'

"On the third night they were loaded up again and set off with their Polish comrades. Before long Arthur realised they were heading back to the factory. He could not believe they were going to the installation for a third consecutive night. Once more they scrambled under the wire, laid the charges and retired some distance away. Again they were unchallenged. By the time they left IG Farben that night they had not only destroyed what was left of the installation, they had also effectively sabotaged the preparations the Germans had made in the past 48 hours to rebuild it. The site was so badly damaged it would be difficult to build anything there for some time.

"On their return, Alex again told them they must do one more job. 'You will escape (afterwards) tomorrow,' he told them. They left the copse and travelled back towards Auschwitz, this time moving further to the east of Monowitz. As they neared the camp it was clear that they were approaching one of the Jewish sectors and Arthur was reminded of a rumour he had heard some time earlier of a planned mass break-out.

"Suddenly, when they were still some 100 yards from the wire, powerful searchlights were switched on, blinding the men and lighting up the area as if it were mid-afternoon. Within seconds a blanket of machine-gun fire opened up on them. As they ran, each in turn stumbled and fell before scrambling back to their feet and carrying on. After a couple of minutes, the machine-gun fire receded behind them and they fell to the ground exhausted.

"Arthur thought through what had happened on the previous nights and it was obvious that the plan to destroy the electrical installation was part of a plan to reduce the amount of lighting available to the Germans at the time of the break-out. In this they had failed."

The book suggests that the last, abortive raid deliberately coincided with the uprising in Birkenau in which the sonderkommandos attacked the SS and destroyed Crematorium 1V. It is alleged that 70 SS and Wehrmacht guards were killed.

What is said to have followed borders on the incredible. Of Dodd's escape bid, the book says: "The three British POWs decided to set off, but they had no idea where they were, and so no idea where to go. They decided they would walk by night and rest during the day.

"Their plan to keep out of sight during the day worked well, they never once saw nor heard anybody, [but] after a few days of little if anything to eat, Arthur was as downhearted as he could remember being. One morning they stood on the brow of a hill and looked down on the valley below. To the left was a small village. They decided that they had no choice but to go into the village and give themselves up. The alternative was to starve to death.

"They had passed road signs indicating that they were now in Czechoslovakia. They were close to the first of the buildings when they were confronted by a policeman carrying a gun. The officer led them to the village hall where they admitted to being escaping British POWs from Auschwitz. The officer then immediately called the German authorities. They had expected to be picked up within a few hours but by the end of the day there was still no sign of the Germans. They bedded down for the night and waited again the next day.

"As it happened two full weeks passed before the Germans arrived. Arriving back at Monowitz, they shook each other's hand, fully expecting that this would be the last time they would see each other. They were, however, left at the gate and told to return to their huts and await further orders. There was only one other man in the hut as Arthur entered and he hardly raised an eyebrow at his appearance. "How did it go then?" he asked casually. It suddenly dawned on Arthur that nobody was aware that they had in fact escaped. Why?

"There could be only one reason and Arthur went to leave the hut to warn his Geordie friends before they let the cat out of the bag. He didn't get as far as the door when one of them came rushing in. 'Arthur,' he said, quietly but urgently, 'keep your mouth shut. Everybody thinks we've been on a working party!'

"'I know,' Arthur replied. 'It can only mean one thing. It's a Wehrmacht cover up. If the SS get wind of the fact we escaped, we won't be the only ones in for the high jump. Some senior German officers will be in trouble, too.' [The Geordie said]: 'You're right! They're going to pretend nothing's happened!'"

For Ron Jones, this account is very difficult to tally with his own experiences: "We were counted all the time, morning, noon and night, to make sure we were all there. If the count was one under, or one over, they'd do it over and over again to find out why. The guards always found out.

"Arthur says when he went to meet the Poles there were four other POWs there from our camp. How did they all do it? We were counted every night. You could maybe double up and cover up for one missing, but I can't see how you could cover up for five.

"Arthur also says that having only partially destroyed the gantry the first night, they went back the next night to complete the job. There was a garrison of 3,000 SS men at Auschwitz at the time. I would have thought that after the first raid there was a guard put on that vital piece of equipment.

"When they were caught and the Wehrmacht brought them back to the camp the Germans told them to carry on as normal and they'd forget about it because they didn't want the SS to find out? I don't buy that. That's a load of balls.

Brian Bishop says flatly: "Dodd is another liar. He was in the same part of the camp as me, and he is supposed to have got out and joined up with the Polish resistance fighters. He never did anything like that. He is supposed to have been away for three days and the Germans never missed him. I don't think so."

Significantly, none of the heroic exploits claimed by Coward, Avey or Dodd are mentioned either in the official history of the Auschwitz work camps, published by the Auschwitz-Birkenau State Museum, or in *Anatomy of the Auschwitz Death Camp*, the encyclopedic reference work published in association with the United States Holocaust Memorial Museum.

Chapter 14

The Culprits

The Jews are the eternal enemies of the German people and must be exterminated. All the Jews within our reach must be annihilated during the war. If we do not succeed in destroying the biological foundation of Jewry now, then one day the Jews will destroy the German people.
(Heinrich Himmler, Reichsführer SS, to Rudolph Hoess, first commandant at Auschwitz, summer 1941)

There is no doubt that this is probably the greatest and most horrible crime ever committed in the whole history of the world. It is clear that all concerned in this crime who may fall into our hands, including the people who only obeyed orders by carrying out the butcheries, should be put to death.
(Winston Churchill to Anthony Eden, July 1944)

It was well known after the War that the task allocated to the many Nazi concentration camps, of which Auschwitz was the biggest, was to exterminate European Jewry, and other "undesirables" not to Hitler's liking. Given that this was their raison d'être, the trials of those who undertook the annihilation left much to be desired. Justice was not seen to be done.

At the Nuremberg War Crimes Trial at the end of September 1946 it was found that the SS was a criminal organisation and international legal status was given to courts trying members as war criminals guilty of crimes against humanity. This was later reaffirmed by a resolution of the General Assembly of the newly instituted United Nations.

With this in mind, it is a disgraceful fact that only 789 SS men and 200 female guards who served at Auschwitz ever faced prosecution. According to German figures, 7,200 SS men and women served at Auschwitz at one time or another. The average garrison strength was around 3,000 and so, in effect, the entire staff was replaced twice. The largest number on site at any one time was 4,552 in January 1945, shortly before liberation. Approximately 1,500 of the 7,000 were called away to fight on the Eastern Front in the Waffen SS, and it is thought that up to half of these may have died, which leaves more than 6,000 members of the Auschwitz SS surviving the war. Some were captured by the Russians, who probably executed them straight away, without trial, but at least 5,500 escaped to the West.

In *Auschwitz: The Nazis and the Final Solution*, Laurence Rees writes: "It was not only Germany that failed to prosecute in substantial numbers those SS members who had worked at Auschwitz. This was a collective failure of the international community (with the possible exception of the Polish courts, who tried a remarkable 673 out of the 789 Auschwitz staff ever to face justice)."

Why did so few of the murderers receive the punishment they deserved? A lack of will, by Britain more than her Allies, is the uncomfortable answer. In December 1945 the British Prime Minister, Clement Attlee, wrote to the Secretary of State for War expressing concern at the lack of "drive and energy" being shown in the hunt for, and prosecution of, German war criminals. Consequently the Attorney General,

Sir Hartley Shawcross, called for an "accelerated war crimes programme", noting that "There are tens of thousands of Germans responsible for millions of murders. We must set ourselves an absolute minimum of prosecuting at least ten per cent of those criminals in the British zone. That is about 2,000 people. I am setting an irreducible minimum that we try 500 cases by 30 April 1946."

Attlee was not satisfied, and pointed out that this objective "would surely have the effect of leaving a large number of criminals unpunished and at large." The Prime Minister was clearly right, but even the modest target that he deemed inadequate was never met. Twelve months after the end of the War, the British stopped investigating cases in which their own nationals were not directly involved, leaving it to other countries whose people had been murdered to search for the culprits.

Laurence Rees concludes: "Prosecutions were hindered not just by lack of consistency between nations about what conduct constituted a 'crime' in Auschwitz, but also by the division caused by the Cold War and, it must be said, by a clear lack of will.

"Despite the Nuremberg trials stating that the SS was a 'criminal' organisation in its entirety, no attempt was ever made to enforce the view that the mere act of working in the SS at Auschwitz was a war crime – a view that popular opinion would surely have supported.

"A conviction and sentence, however minimal, for every SS man who was there would have sent a clear message for the future. It did not happen. Around 85 per cent of the SS who served at Auschwitz and survived the war escaped scot-free.

"When Himmler set in train the development of the gas

chambers in order to distance the SS from the psychological 'burden' of shooting people in cold blood, he could scarcely have predicted that it would have this additional benefit for the Nazis; this method of murder meant that the vast majority of the SS who served at Auschwitz could escape punishment after the war by claiming successfully that they had not been directly part of the extermination process."

With Britain taking a back seat, it was the Poles who tracked down and indicted the Auschwitz staff. Between 1946 and 1948 at least 1,000 members of the SS were extradited to Poland. Between 11 and 29 March 1947 the camp's first commandant, Hoess, was brought to trial in Warsaw, then from 24 November to 16 December that year 40 members of the Auschwitz staff were tried in Krakow. The trials attracted huge, global interest, making a horrified world fully aware of the exact nature of the camp's murderous business.

Hoess, the first and longest-serving commandant, had been honoured by Hitler in April 1943, when he was awarded the Cross of Merit First Class with Swords for his contribution to the Final Solution. He went on the run in April 1945, first to the island of Sylt, where he joined Naval Intelligence under a false name, Franz Lang, before seeking anonymity as a farm worker near Flensburg, where he was finally arrested on 11 March 1946, after a tip off. He was taken to Nuremberg, as a witness at the main war crimes trial, then handed over to the Polish authorities in Warsaw on 25 May 1946. From there on 30 July it was back to Krakow, where he was imprisoned and wrote his autobiography before being tried and hanged near Crematorium 1 at Auschwitz on 16 April 1947.

One would like to hear what the Holocaust deniers have to say about the following extract from his memoirs, written in longhand, shortly before his execution:

"I am unable to recall when the destruction of the Jews began, perhaps not until January 1942. At first we dealt with the Jews from Upper Silesia. These Jews were arrested by the Gestapo from Katowice and transported via the Auschwitz-Dziediez railroad. As far as I can recall, these transports never numbered more than a thousand persons.

"A detachment of SS from the camp took charge of them at the railroad ramp, and the officer in charge marched them to the bunker in two groups. This is what we called the extermination installation. The Jews had to undress at the bunker and were told that they would have to go into the delousing rooms. All of the rooms – there were five of them – were filled at the same time. The airtight doors were screwed tight and the contents of the gas cylinders emptied into the rooms through special hatches.

"After half an hour the doors were opened and the bodies were pulled out. They were then moved using small carts on special tracks to the ditches. The clothing was brought by trucks to the sorting place.

"All of the work was done by a special contingent of Jews (the *Sonderkommando*). They had to help those who were about to die with the undressing, the filling up of the bunkers, the clearing of the bunkers, removal of the bodies, as well as digging the mass graves and finally covering the graves with earth. These Jews were housed separately from the other prisoners and they themselves were to be killed after each large extermination action.

"An order specified that the gold teeth were to be pulled from the mouths of the bodies, and the hair was to be cut from the dead women. This work was also carried out by special groups of Jews. Supervising the extermination at that time was the camp commander, Captain Hans Aumeier, or the duty officer, Sergeant Major Gerhard Palitzsch.

"The sick who could not be brought to the gassing rooms were simply killed with small-calibre weapons by shooting them in the back of the neck."

Scarcely less culpable than Hoess was his deputy, Aumeier who typically wrote in December 1942: "Only able-bodied Poles should be sent here, in order to avoid as far as possible any useless burden on the camp and the transport system. Mentally deficient persons, idiots, cripples, and the sick must be removed as quickly as possible by liquidation, so as to lighten the load on the camp."

At the Krakow trial of 40 SS men, Aumeier was one of 23 condemned to death. Six received life sentences, seven got 15 years and three were sentenced to ten, five and three years. One was acquitted. They were accused of: conspiracy to wage aggressive war; crimes against peace; war crimes; and crimes against humanity.

More explicitly, the accusations concerned: the creation of camp conditions which caused the confined prisoners to lose their health and their lives; systematic starvation, forced hard labour, inhumane camp punishment, medical experiments on prisoners which caused illnesses, crippling or death; the use of deadly effective Phenol injections and death of prisoners by means of torture, executions, hanging, suffocation and gassing; immoral treatment of prisoners, humiliation of human dignity, arousal of the lowest of human instinct for their fight for survival; killing of all sense of decency and making a mockery of the female sense of dignity; mass murder of the Soviet POWs in the camp, which was contrary to the Hague Convention of 1907; the overburdening of prisoners with forced labour, excessive workload for the purpose of capitalistic war aggression and the mass murders which resulted from labour under these conditions; mass robbery of possessions, clothing, shoes, tools, jewellery, money and other valuable objects from the individuals arriving at the camp, these supplies stored for the enrichment of the economy of the German Reich and its citizens; systematic plundering, the extraction of gold from the teeth of deceased and murdered prisoners, which was turned over to the German Reichsbank; cutting the hair of females and their corpses for delivery to German industry to be used as raw material, as was the ashes left from the cremated bones of the victims, used as artificial manure.

The only defendant acquitted of all charges was Hans Munch, an SS doctor, whose successful defence was based around numerous testimonials from former prisoners. Artur Liebehenschel, the second of the three Auschwitz commandants, and 20 others, including Aumeier, were hanged at Krakow on 24 January 1948.

Richard Baer, the last commandant, evaded justice until December 1960, living under a false name and working in forestry. He died in detention in Frankfurt in July 1963, while awaiting trial. Josef Kramer, who served at Auschwitz as adjutant to Hoess, was sentenced to death by the British for crimes committed elsewhere, as commandant at the Bergen-Belsen concentration camp. His appeal for clemency to Field Marshal Montgomery fell on suitably deaf ears and he was hanged along with his lover, Irma Grese, at Hameln prison on 13 December 1945.

Astonishingly, at his trial Kramer's lawyer, Major T.C.M. Winwood, offered the following plea for leniency: "He was dealing with the dregs of the ghettos of Eastern Europe", while Grese's lawyer portrayed her as a "scapegoat", contending that since the camp was a prison, corporal punishment was "reasonable in the circumstances."

The summing up by the British Judge Advocate-General, C.L. Stirling, also provoked international outrage. He told the military tribunal judging the cases that much of the evidence was "vague", and said the court "would have to be satisfied that a person on the staff of Auschwitz or Belsen was guilty of deliberately committing a war crime; just being a member of the staff itself was not enough to justify a conviction."

Two decades after the War, what became known as the Second Auschwitz Trial was staged in Frankfurt, between December 1963 and August 1965. This saw 360 eyewitnesses tell their appalling stories, brought home to the German public, who had spent the previous 20 years forgetting this hideous stain on their history, through television and newspaper reports. Of the 22 defendants, 17 were convicted but only six received the maximum penalty of life imprisonment. Some were sentenced to only three years and three were acquitted.

Trial records show that in all, 602 individuals who had served at Auschwitz were prosecuted, of whom 590 received prison sentences. The most common sentence was three years – the punishment for 32 per cent.

One of the most notorious Auschwitz monsters of them all, Adolf Eichmann, escaped from captivity in 1945 and lived anonymously in Germany until 1950, when he emigrated to Argentina. Agents of Israel's Mossad secret service tracked him down there ten years later and spirited him back to Israel, where he was tried and hanged at Ramla prison on 31 May 1962.

The worst of all those working at the camp has to be Josef Mengele, whose medical experiments on Birkenau prisoners – often on children and without anaesthetic – defy belief. Mengele was a qualified doctor but a stranger to the Hippocratic oath. He was particularly interested in identical twins. In one experiment two were sewn together to create conjoined twins. Gangrene resulted. On one evening alone he killed 14 twins. Children would return to the block screaming in pain after enduring his "experiments".

Eva Moses Kor and her twin sister Miriam were 10 years old in 1944 when they became subjects of Mengele. Eva said: "Three times a week both of my arms would be tied to restrict the blood flow. They took a lot of blood from my left arm – sometimes enough until we fainted. At the same time they were taking blood, they would give me a minimum of five injections into my right arm. After one of these injections I became extremely ill and Mengele came in next morning with four other doctors.

"He looked at my fever chart and said, laughing: 'Too bad she is so young, she has only two weeks to live.' I would fade in and out of consciousness and, in a semi-conscious state of mind, I would keep telling myself: 'I must survive'. They were waiting for me to die. If I had, my twin sister would have been rushed immediately to Mengele's lab, killed with an injection to the heart, and then Mengele would have done comparative autopsies."

The perverted reasoning was explained by Myklos Nyiszli, a prison doctor who worked alongside Mengele, who said: "This phenomenon was unique in world medical history. Two brothers died together and it was possible to perform autopsies on both. Where, under normal circumstances, can one find twin brothers who died at the same place at the same time?"

When not carving up twins, Mengele would attempt to change eye colour by injecting chemicals into children's eyes, sterilize young girls with horrific doses of radiation and amputate limbs unnecessarily, all without anaesthetic.

A former Auschwitz prisoner, Alex Dekel, said: "Mengele ran a butcher's shop. Major surgeries were performed without anaesthesia. I witnessed a stomach operation. Mengele was removing pieces from the stomach without any anaesthetic. Another time it was a heart, again without anaesthesia. It was horrifying. Mengele was a doctor who became mad because of the power he was given. Nobody ever questioned him: Why did this one die? The patients did not count. He professed to do what he did in the name of science, but it was madness on his part."

Another of Mengele's functions was to supervise the initial selections to which all prisoners were subjected on arrival at the ramp on the railway spur that served the camp. There he played God, deciding who was to live and who would go directly to the gas chambers. Each selection took only seconds, based upon a prisoner's ability to work. Typically, on one occasion when a mother fought to keep her daughter, assaulting an SS man trying to separate them, Mengele drew his pistol and shot both mother and child, then sent the whole trainload of Jews straight to the gas chambers, shouting: 'Away with this shit.' Exceptions to such treatment were twins, dwarfs and those with physical abnormalities who he was also interested in.

Born in Bavaria in March 1911, to a well-to-do family, Mengele qualified as a doctor and gained a degree in Anthropology at the University of Munich. The first hint of the wickedness to follow came in 1937, at the Institute of Hereditary Biology and Racial Hygiene in Frankfurt, where he developed his interest in twins.

Also in 1937 he joined the Nazi party and by the

following year he was in the SS, where he volunteered for the medical section of their combat arm, the Waffen SS. Mengele distinguished himself on the Russian front, and was awarded the Iron Cross First Class for pulling two soldiers from a burning tank. Wounded and rendered unfit for active service, he was posted to the Economy and Administration Office of the SS, in Berlin, where he was promoted to the rank of captain shortly before moving to Auschwitz in May 1943.

His first job there was medical officer at the so-called Gypsy Family Camp. When this was liquidated and all its inmates gassed, in August 1944, Mengele became chief medical officer at Birkenau. Contrary to popular belief, he was not chief of all the medical staff at Auschwitz. His superior in that role was Eduard Wirths.

Mengele was only at Auschwitz for 20 months, but in that relatively short space of time he came to personify cruelty at its worst, and his name is better known than any of the three camp commandants. This is due, in part, to the endless, high profile attempts to find and apprehend him after the war.

When the SS abandoned Auschwitz in January 1945 he worked at other camps briefly before joining a Wehrmacht medical unit a week before the war ended. Captured by the Americans, he was mistakenly released in June 1945 and found work, and anonymity, as a farmhand in Bavaria, where he remained, unnoticed, until May 1949. The Odessa escape network then took him to the Nazi haven that was Argentina. In Buenos Aires, where Nazis enjoyed the patronage of the Perons, he lived comfortably, practising medicine, and keeping company with Adolf Eichmann, among others.

However the Israeli Mossad agents who captured Eichmann were also on Mengele's trail, and in fear of the same fate he moved to Paraguay, where the dictator, Alfredo Stroessner, was another Nazi sympathiser. Later he moved again, to Brazil, where he lived in a suburb of Sao Paulo for the rest of his life.

Mengele died in February 1979 when he drowned, probably after suffering a stroke, while swimming in the Atlantic. He was buried in Brazil under the alias Wolfgang Gerhard whose ID card he had been using. After widespread scepticism about "Gerhard's" true identity, a DNA test was performed in 1992 and confirmed that the body was Mengele's. He had evaded justice for 34 years, and to the end of his life showed no remorse.

Ron Jones says: "I followed all the trials closely and have continued to keep up to date with everything to do with the camp. I can't comprehend why more of the sadists and killers weren't caught and punished after the war. A hell of a lot of them got away with it, which is scandalous. We were told at the time that getting proof was the problem, but I can't accept that. They didn't try hard enough. It was said at the Nuremberg trials that just being a member of the SS was a criminal act. Bearing that in mind, all the SS were tattooed with their blood group, so proving membership can't have been that difficult."

Chapter 15

The Testimony

The most contemporaneous evidence of the evil that occurred in the camp was provided by statements from prisoners for the Nuremberg trials. Six British POWs were called as prosecution witnesses, and typical of their evidence was an affidavit, sworn by Fred Davison, of the RASC, on 19 July 1947.

Fred, from Sunderland, was a spirited character who, when captured and asked for his profession, told his interrogator he was a "brothel-keeper's assistant". Sadly that spirit and his health were broken at Auschwitz and he died in 1963, aged only 46.

In his sworn affidavit he said:

"I was captured on 8 April 1941, near Tobruk. After my capture I was sent to Italy, then to Lamsdorf, Stalag V111B, and finally to Auschwitz. I remained at Auschwitz until 19 January 1945, having arrived there about the beginning of September 1943. At the end we were marched from Auschwitz, through Czechoslovakia, to a place near Regensburg, where we were freed by the Americans.

"When we were first told that we were going to Auschwitz, they said we were to work for IG Farben, which was a paint factory. When we arrived we found it was a petrol (synthetic) factory. When we protested that this was war work, which prisoners didn't have to perform, the German commandant, who was a member of the German Army, pounded on the table and, pointing to his revolver, said: 'This is my Geneva Convention.'

"I was assigned to work at carrying pipes to be used to make the compressors necessary for the production of the oil. In this assignment I would work in all different parts of the factory. Although it was forbidden, I often talked to the inmates, the foreign workers and even the *kapos* and German civilians who were foremen and *meisters* (supervisors).

"The condition of the Jews, who we called 'stripeys' because of the striped pyjamas they used to wear, was very poor. These pyjamas, which were practically their only clothing, were made of a material which resembled sacking. They had no socks and wore wooden clogs instead of shoes.

"In the wintertime some of them would have striped coats made of the same material. These clothes were never enough to keep them warm in the winter months. They would die of exposure. I would see the dead every day. From those which I alone witnessed, there were about five a day dying of the cold. There must have been many others from the rest of the factory.

"From what I saw, I would say that a reasonably healthy inmate arriving in the month of October could not hope to live through to the end of the winter. Of course it wasn't the clothing alone that was killing the inmates. Their food was very bad. We used to get soup at midday which was like water, and which tasted so bad that the British boys, even though they were inadequately fed themselves, would give away to the inmates.

"Also, the inmates... would be murdered in the streets in the factory grounds. I have seen the bodies hundreds of times. Moreover I have actually seen the murders being committed on four or five different occasions.

"The Farben civilians would never stop or attempt to prevent the SS or *kapos* from beating or killing the inmates. As a matter of fact, they would often help them. For example, the inmates were forced to carry hundredweight bags of cement. It would take four men to put the bag on the back of one. If the inmate couldn't carry it, or couldn't go along quickly enough to satisfy the *meister*, they would beat the inmate with sticks or iron bars, or punch them with their fists and kick them. In addition, they would tell the SS that the inmate was a bad worker and the SS would often go into them with revolvers and hit them on the head.

"I have seen them beaten to death with iron bars and murdered on the premises.

"Even apart from the beatings, I saw inmates collapse every day on the road and in the factory. Every night they used to be carried back to the camp on planks of wood. The administration building was a sort of main road along which these bodies would be carried on the way to the camp.

"Very shortly after I arrived, I heard about the inmates being sent to the gas chambers. I didn't believe it at first. I spoke about it to two or three *kapos*, who told me that every Thursday the inmates would be lined up and doctors would pass down the line and pick out the inmates, all of whom had been stripped, who they thought were not fit to continue working. The *kapos* said that those selected as unfit were told that they were going to be transferred, but actually it meant the gas chambers.

"The *kapos* were mostly German convicts who were given

charge of a group of inmates for the purpose of the work details. Sometimes the *kapos* were regular inmates who had earned the chance of being a *kapo* by having worked in the crematoria.

"It was common, everyday knowledge about the gas chambers. All the civilian *meisters* in the factory knew about it, and of course the inmates themselves constantly thought about going to the gas chambers and about their friends who had already been sent.

"It was not unusual for the Farben foremen and *meisters* to threaten the inmates that if they didn't work harder they would be sent to the gas chambers. Some of the Farben officials that I knew personally... had knowledge of the gassings because they spoke about it. [They were] supervisor Bertram, a rough fellow who liked to use his revolver all the time, supervisor Kratsch who, although not as bad as Bertram, was definitely a Nazi, and supervisors Weiss and Streuber. They all carried revolvers.

"When I tried to find out why they were gassing the Jews, they expressed the opinion that there were too many Jews, and it was a good thing to get rid of them.

"I got to know a number of the inmates fairly well. I used to see them practically every day and, when I could, I would slip them some food which I had. One was a Greek and one was from Holland. You could see they were getting weaker and thinner all the time. One day the Greek did not show up. The Dutchman said he had been taken to the gas chambers.

"However, we all knew this would happen because the previous week Strauber, the Farben supervisor, had watched the Greek work and could see that the man could hardly stand. He turned away from him and said: 'He is *kaput* – in another week he will be in the gas chamber.'

"There was a hospital in the camp for concentration camp inmates. I don't know whether they would try to get anybody well again. The main thing was to find out whether they could work again soon. The inmates told me that no one could stay in the hospital longer than a fortnight, and that if they couldn't get well in that time they might as well die.

"Although we were treated much better than the inmates, since we had our own doctors in the camp, the Germans used to get us to work even though we may have been sick. They only allowed a certain percentage to be sick at any time. I remember one time when more than the allotted percentage were sick, the plant doctor came down to our camp and made a very quick examination of all the patients, and in all cases that he thought could go to work he crossed the names off the sick list.

"The next day the German camp guards came to our hospital and called out all those whose names had been crossed off the list to come out into the square. It made no difference whether the patients were bed patients or not. I was one of the bed patients, in with 'flu. Although it was November, and quite cold out, some of the patients had to go out even before they put shoes on. I had a shirt, trousers and shoes on, but no coat.

"We thought we would be in the square for just a few minutes and return to the hospital. Instead we were marched off under guard to work. Usually we would bring part of our food ration to work with us for the midday meal, but this time, since we were coming from the hospital, we didn't even have food to eat during the day.

"The progress of the work was inspected from time to time by IG Farben engineers. It would be completely impossible for those engineers and inspectors, or anybody else who visited the plant, not to observe the conditions. The inmates working all over the place... were obviously dying on their feet. Only sheer will power kept them going. I still can't understand why more of them didn't die. They were all definitely as thin as rails. Anybody watching them work could see that they were doing so with their last bit of strength, and that they couldn't possibly continue that way without dropping from exhaustion."

Incredibly, in March 1948, eight months after his deposition, Fred received a letter from Kurt Streuber, one of the bullying, revolver-carrying IG supervisors he had identified for the war crimes court. With no trace of shame, and no apology, Streuber wrote to say he was now a police chief in his home town, Bad Kosen, which was then in the old East Germany. His opening sentence was: "My dear friend Fred, you will be astonished to get some sign of life from your workmates from Auschwitz." Streuber continued: "We have got over the war well here, and I hope that you also, dear Fred, have got over everything." Fred certainly hadn't, and chose not to reply.

Another trial witness was Leonard Dales, of the Lincolnshire Regiment. In his affidavit he stated the following:

"From North Africa I was brought to Sicily, then to Italy, then to Germany and finally, at the end of August 1943 to Auschwitz. I worked for the IG Farben Company at Auschwitz until January 1945, when I was taken on the 'March'.

"We were under the supervision of Stalag V111B when we first came to Auschwitz. V111B later changed [its name] to Teschen. From 1943 to 1944 we were housed at Camp 8, under IG Farben plant territory. During January-February 1944 we were moved to Camp 6, which was closer to the factory. Camp 6 was about 300 yards from the camp in which the concentration camp inmates were who worked for IG Farben.

"At the IG Farben factory I had the position of labourer to the German pipe engineer. In this capacity I had work details to perform in all parts of the factory, and had excellent opportunity to observe working conditions and the conditions of the inmates and foreign workers.

"In the morning the SS used to march the concentration camp inmates into the factory grounds and divide them up among the various '*meisters*' of IG Farben and the different contractor firms working for Farben. We came in at about 6.30 and at that time many of the inmates were already there.

"Once they were assigned to the different '*meisters*', they became the slaves of each respective '*meister*'. Those German foremen had the power of life and death over the slaves assigned, and could order them to do various tasks.

"In order to obtain compliance, these Farben foremen would sometimes beat the inmates. A much more effective way of making the inmates do their every command was to threaten them that they would be reported to the SS guards and be sent to the gas chambers.

"The German civilians often used to joke about the fact that the ultimate fate of all the Jews would be the gas chamber. Uppermost in the minds of all the Jews was the ever-present possibility of being gassed.

"I recall one incident which was pretty typical. One of our boys tossed a cigarette to a Jew who was loading some pipes. He scrambled down to get the cigarette and in doing so he badly lacerated his leg. He didn't seem so much hurt as scared when he said: 'I guess this is the end. It means the gas chamber for me.'

"After that inmate went back to the lager that night he disappeared and was never again seen by any of us at the factory.

"One Dutch Jew who had worked in the camp where the crematoria were [Birkenau] described the operation of the gas chambers to me. He said that the victims were given a piece of soap and a towel to give them the impression that they were going to have a shower. Many times when they realised what was happening, terrible scenes would take place, but they were forced into the gas chambers at pistol point by the SS.

"This man told me that he didn't think he would ever get out alive, but that he knew the British POWs would, and he wanted us to be able to tell the rest of the world what had happened at the concentration camp. In describing the procedure, he mentioned that the valuables were all taken from the Jews, and even the gold from their teeth was removed.

"Of all the groups that worked at the Farben factory, the ones treated the worst by far were the Jews. Their general appearance was shocking. They were haggard, drawn and weak, with pale faces and scrawny arms and legs. They wore striped pyjamas in all weather. Their shoes were wooden clogs. The food they received at the plant was soup. This was almost plain water with a few pieces of cabbage or turnip floating in it.

"When we received our soup, which was thicker, our so-called better soup wasn't edible and we used to divide it among the other inmates who fought and scrambled to get some of it. They did hard labour, which included digging ditches, carrying cables and carrying cement sacks which were heavier than their own weight.

"I still don't know how they were able to work at the

pace they did and carry those weights in the broken-down condition they were in. They worked harder than they were really capable of out of the fear that if they appeared weak or unable to work, they would be exterminated.

"Many of them, regardless of their will, didn't have the strength to carry on, and just collapsed. It was a common occurrence at night to see some carried by other inmates and others in wheelbarrows.

"I was told by a young Polish Jew, although I didn't see it myself, that at night, when the inmates returned to their camp, there was a 'selection' process at the gates. An SS man would pick out those who were weaker and copy down their tattooed number. Those whose numbers were taken would be exterminated in the gas chambers.

"Everyone who was at IG Auschwitz, or who visited, must have known about the gassings that took place since everyone there knew about it and it would have been almost impossible to avoid hearing it. Certainly everyone who visited the factory would know that the Jews were being starved to death, since that required nothing more than to look at them."

A flavour of the proceedings at Nuremberg is provided by the following edited transcript of courtroom exchanges between Reg Hartland, from Worcester, who did the same work as Ron Jones, and a Dr Gierlichs, the defence counsel for Carl Krauch, Chairman of the IG Farben Board, who was on trial for war crimes:

Question [from Gierlich]: In Auschwitz you worked in Shop 797. Can you tell me what kind of a job that was?

Answer [from Hartland]: It was a general workshop for the benzine plant. It contained lathes, drills, and all the necessary machinery.

Q: In what capacity did you work there?

A: I worked on the tires which were filtering beds for the benzine, helping to put in the filters for these tires.

Q: Did you know that no gasoline was ever produced in Auschwitz?

A: Yes there was. Definitely.

Q: You know then that gasoline was produced in Auschwitz?

A: Yes.

Q: You maintain that assertion, even if I put it to you that the gasoline production at Auschwitz never came to operation?

A: It definitely did because there was quite a celebration when the first tankload of benzine was sent off, I believe to Russia. Trucks were decorated with garlands and many high officials came down. There was quite a celebration over it.

Q: You mention a few incidents, amongst which you mention the shooting of Corporal Reynolds. Were you present when your comrade was shot?

A: No.

Q: Your statement on this point is only what was reported to you from third parties?

A: It was obvious. I saw the body, but I wasn't present when the shooting took place.

Q: From the reports you were given, do you know where this incident occurred?

A: Not exactly. It was in the factory, but I don't know the exact location.

Q: Perhaps you would remember it if I put it to you that this incident occurred near a pipe bridge and that the German sergeant shot your comrade because your comrade did not comply with an order, and refused to obey it three times in succession, contrary to the other prisoners of war who did obey the order?

A: As far as I remember, at the time the bridge was covered in ice and snow and he refused to go up until he had ample protection. Some of the other British prisoners had such things as lifebelts to secure them to the bridge while they were working. Corporal Reynolds hadn't got one of those and refused to go up until he had one. The result was he was shot.

Q: Did you hear anything about the fact that the German sergeant who shot your comrade, after he had asked him three times to comply with the order, was put before a court martial and punished for his conduct?

A: I did not.

Q: You mention another incident in which one of your English comrades was stabbed. Can you give me the name of that other person?

A: His name was Campbell. He was a Scotsman.

Q: Can you give me any more detail about this incident?

A: I don't know many details, I only know it was the same *unteroffizier* that stabbed Campbell. He was the same man that shot Corporal Reynolds.

Q: Were you present?

A: No.

Q: You speak of the fact that the inmates were beaten by the SS and the *kapos* and that they were also beaten by the Farben foremen. Can you give me the names of those Farben foremen?

A: No, I didn't know the names.

Q: In Department 797, in which you worked, did anything like that happen?

A: Not actually in the workshop, but in the surrounding outer shops there were cases of that.

Q: So the Germans with whom you worked did not participate in such incidents?

A: Some did, yes, but not in the main workshop.

Q: And the names of those, you no longer remember?

A: No. I didn't know them. I wasn't that interested.

Q: You also mention that inmates were beaten to death and then taken away in a wheelbarrow. But who is to be charged with such conduct – previously you mention *kapos*, SS and foremen. Please specify?

A: All three were just as responsible – *kapos*, SS men and the German *meisters*.

Q: I should like to define my question a little more. Did you see a German *meister* beat one of the inmates to death?

A: Yes.

Q: But you cannot give me the name of that *meister*?

A: No.

Q: Can you give me the department in which he worked?

A: Attached to 797 workshop.

Q: You speak of the fact that many of the inmates had sores for which they appeared to receive little or no medical treatment?

A: Yes. They weren't bandaged up. They were running sores. They were like that for weeks at a time and when we spoke to these fellows, and asked them why they did not have medical treatment, they appeared to be afraid of reporting these matters. They all seemed of the same opinion, that if they were sick and therefore no longer fit for work, they would end up at the gas chamber.

Chapter 16

Auschwitz Revisited

Auschwitz today is possibly the bleakest, most dispiriting place on earth. Coachloads make the journey every day – some 1.4 million visitors in 2011. Holocaust survivors come in pilgrimage, Germans by way of atonement, some others out of morbid curiosity. What they all find is a manifestation of evil so chilling that it leaves even the most committed atheist intoning: "Thank Heaven it wasn't me."

The first shocking aspect of the place to strike new visitors is the sheer size of the Birkenau death camp, preserved in eerie perpetuity, with its row after row of wooden barracks stretching as far as the eye can see. The mind boggles and the body shudders. This truly was extermination on an industrial scale.

No birds sing in an unrelentingly melancholy atmosphere, no flowers bloom in earth poisoned for all time by the ashes of the poor souls slaughtered by beating, gunshot or in the gas chambers.

Passing under the greatest lie of all time, *"Arbeit Macht Frei"* (Work Will Make You Free) at the gate, causes the hardiest soul to shiver, and tears well over the macabre exhibits that follow.

At the gas chambers up-to-date signs convey the information that "Corpses were stripped of gold teeth, hair, ear-rings and then transported to the crematory. Victims' personal documents were destroyed." By way of confirmation, huge glass cases are full of old, battered suitcases, clothes, hair and spectacles harvested from those who would be in no further need of them.

On they trudge in horrified, silent disbelief, coach parties and solitary visitors alike, past searingly sad photographs of some of the 232,000 children who perished, past the wall where prisoners were routinely shot before the use of Zyklon B, past the ovens of the crematoria.

There is the grim reminder that too many of the culprits all but got away with their terrible criminality. For example, Doctor Horst Schumann, who conducted agonising sterilisation and castration experiments on inmates, escaped justice at the War's end and worked in a hospital in Sudan until 1962. When he was finally apprehended and put on trial, in 1970, he served little more than a year in prison before he was released on medical grounds. Freed because he was supposedly at death's door, he lived for another 11 years.

Ron Jones knew it was all there, of course, and never wanted to return, but he has done so twice, at the instigation of others. The first occasion was in 1999. Ron says: "My nephew, Chris Blight, an estate agent in Newport, had arranged and booked the trip for the two of us as a surprise and I didn't want to disappoint him. He'd tipped off the local paper, *The Newport Argus*, who sent a reporter and a photographer, and also HTV Wales, who also covered it and showed it on their news bulletins.

"I wasn't keen because the place had only bad memories for me, and I didn't want them awakened after all those years. Nothing good happened there, did it, so why re-live it?" It was a rhetorical question.

But, with great reluctance, Ron did go back. He says: "Chris had a friend who picked us up at the airport in Krakow, and the following day he drove us out to Auschwitz. He had a camera with him and when I asked him why he said: 'Where I live, half the people don't believe the camp existed.' And his house was near Katowice, just a few miles away!

"I was right about the old memories, it all came flooding back and I was very emotional, really choked up, especially thinking about young Reynolds. I could see his shooting all over again, as if it was yesterday. That poor, poor man.

"The Nazis had demolished Monowitz village to build the factory and the sub-camps for the Jews and POWs, but the Poles have rebuilt the village next to the old works site. One of the factories was still in use, with the old walls topped with barbed wire still around it. I'd read that the Russians had knocked it all down, but there it still was, still in operation. Just looking at it gave me the shivers. I could see all those poor emaciated Jews stumbling about and smell that dreadful stench.

"I couldn't sleep that night and for weeks later the old nightmares were back to haunt me. I was right all along, it was a mistake to go." Nevertheless he went back in September 2013, at the invitation of the BBC television programme *The One Show*, who screened a biopic the following month.

Brian Bishop went back in 2007, also as a guest of the BBC. But unlike Ron, he had no regrets. "I was there for three days and thoroughly enjoyed it," he said. "I didn't have any flashbacks or anything like that. I was disappointed, though, that I couldn't find where our camp had been. It had gone completely. Also, I expected to find the gasometer I'd worked on, but our guide told me they'd pulled it down two years earlier."

Ron says: "It was because I wanted to forget it all that I avoided POW reunions at first, but eventually I went to a couple. My interest was stirred by a fella by the name of Jeffrey Howe. I was a member of the British Legion and I picked up their magazine one day and he was asking anyone who had been in E715 to contact him, so I wrote and he organised a get-together at the British Legion club in Croydon. There was quite a crowd of us at that first one, but I only went twice. I don't think Charlie Coward, Denis Avey or Arthur Dodd went. I don't remember seeing them, anyway.

"On the second occasion we went to a holiday camp on Hayling Island, down by Portsmouth. I took Glad and we had a good time, dancing to a nice orchestra. I'd say there were 50 or 60 ex-POWs there, but not just from Auschwitz, from other camps, too.

"Sam Kydd, the old actor, came to one of the local 'dos' we had, at the British Legion hall in Clytha. He'd been a POW in the war and we had a good chat, comparing our experiences. He wrote a book about his time in camp. The British Legion have done a lot of good work for ex-military people. If I was ever in trouble, I know they'd be the first to help, but fortunately I've never had to ask. It's been more a case of what I've been able to do for them. I've done charity work on their behalf for more than 50 years and they've given me a solid gold badge and membership for life.

"I know it will seem strange to some people, but my experience in Auschwitz hasn't left me with ill feeling towards the Germans. I've been back to Germany on holiday and I've always found them all right. They've always been very nice towards me. Mind you, I haven't told anybody over there about what happened, I wouldn't bring that up in front of people who had nothing to do with it.

"I went to grammar school, so I learned the basics of French and Latin, which give you a bit of Italian, and from being in Germany I picked up a bit of German, too. So I could always get by wherever I went on holiday. One year we went to the old Yugoslavia and in the hotel we met two families from Austria, so we got talking. We made friends with them and went to restaurants and out dancing together. We got on fine.

"Basically, I found the German and Austrian people were pretty much like us, I never had any bother with them at all."

Chapter 17

Unfinished Business

Of the 4.58 million POWs pressed into forced labour for
the Germans in the Second World War, only 3.42 million
survived, and the fact that British POWs at Auschwitz were
not compensated for what they suffered as slave labourers,
in the same way that wartime prisoners of the Japanese
eventually were, has long been an deeply-felt grievance for
Ron Jones, who has seen nearly all his old comrades from
E715 die without receiving a penny.

In Ron's case the resentment is greatly exacerbated by the
fact that his Army pay was withheld throughout his sojourn
as a POW, and has never been paid. To add insult to injury,
on his return home he was issued with document WOP 2367,
chasing him for unpaid income tax. It read in part as follows:

"You may be asked to complete a statement, showing
whether you received any pay or working pay during captivity.
You may also be asked to produce any documents in your
possession which relate to your account with the Detaining
Power, credit balance, or status (including any evidence of
recognition by the Detaining Power as a protected person) or
any receipt for currency which was surrendered or impounded
from you during captivity."

In plain language, POWs were expected to pay income tax.

The issue has been a *cause célèbre* for the National Ex-Prisoners of War Association, whose embittered president, Les Allan, said in an interview for this book: "When it comes to money, and what they've done us out of, the British Government could give lessons to the mafia."

Charles Rollings, in *Prisoner of War*, summarised the situation like this:

"British ex-POWs had it harder than their brethren from the Commonwealth and the United States. Some of these countries showed their appreciation by striking a medal for ex-POWs, and almost all gave them a pension, an additional disability allowance, free medical treatment, retraining and the opportunity to go to university. As they had technically served abroad during the war, they had also paid less income tax and thus accrued some savings.

"The British, on the other hand, were well and truly shafted. Officers had had a third of their salary deducted to pay for the 'hospitality' they had received from their captors. The Treasury pocketed the money. NCOs and other ranks, who had been systematically underpaid – if they were paid at all – while undertaking forced labour for the enemy, likewise received no recompense."

Rollings concluded: "The indifference of the British government and the failure of the Axis countries to publicly acknowledge and apologise for the treatment of prisoners of war remains a very sore point to this day."

Les Allan, who is 94, was captured at Dunkirk and spent the next five years as a prisoner of war. He has been campaigning for compensation for his members for half his life, only to be balked and frustrated at every turn. The only former POW from the European theatre, as distinct from prisoners of the Japanese, to get any money is Denis

Avey, who received £10,000. This is despite the fact that the Germans put up £1m for the purpose.

"That was back in 2006, and with accrued interest it would be worth a fortune today," Les says. "Where did the money go? I'm told it disappeared into central funds. We certainly didn't get it, as was intended."

Understandably resentful, he quotes with disgust what Britain's Deputy Prime Minister, Clement Attlee, said on the subject in 1944. Attlee was responding to a motion tabled by 150 MPs of all political persuasions, which read as follows:

"This House, being conscious of the disquiet felt by relatives of prisoners of war, and believing that the present system of divided responsibility is unsatisfactory, urges that a senior minister should be designated to co-ordinate and be responsible for all action in connection with prisoners of war and to answer questions."

Attlee's reply was brief and dismissive. He said: "The wrongs it is sought to right are largely illusory."

In October 2012 Les and his association were pushing the government for recognition of the service given by men taken prisoner by the Germans before D Day (6 June 1944). "We've given up on the money," Les explained. "What we want is the French-German campaign medal that has been denied to all those who were captured before D Day. We played our part before then, and by refusing us the medal, the government are giving the impression that everyone before then was a coward."

Ron Jones says: "Because of that attitude, all I've got is a Prisoner of War medal. Not the North Africa campaign medal."

Why had the Ex-Prisoners of War Association finally given up the fight for compensation? "Because we've been blocked at every turn," Les Allan said. "First there was the statement that ex-POWs were not eligible, only other slave workers, then when the Germans were agreed that we were, the government persistently refused to back us and we gave up in around 2006. Denis Avey was the only one to get a penny, and good luck to him. It was down to his sheer bloody-minded persistence."

The Association had made strenuous efforts on behalf of the Britains imprisoned at Auschwitz, pursuing claims under the German Forced Labour Compensation Scheme, which was established in 2000. This was a fund financed 50-50 by German companies, some of whom had used slave labour, and the German government. Initially, nearly 4.5 billion euros was paid to 1.7m forced labourers of the Third Reich who were still alive. These were one-off payments of between 2,500 and 7,500 euros. None was paid to British POWs.

Even now, Ron Jones has not entirely given up hope. The issue has been raised in Parliament on his behalf, to no avail, but nearly 70 years after the event he is still not prepared to let the matter drop and, regarding it as a point of principle, he continues to raise the subject with his local MP, Newport's Paul Flynn.

It has been tried before, at much higher level, without success. The following is an edited version of a letter sent by Flight Lieutenant Michael Roth, a former POW, to the Prime Minister, Margaret Thatcher, in July 1979:

"I was commissioned in the RAF (pilot 39175) in 1936. I was shot down and taken prisoner on 10 May 1940 and was a POW until 7 May 1945.

"While we were prisoners we had a third of our pay deducted and withheld by Cox and Kings, Lloyds Bank, Pall Mall. I still have an account there. After the war the manager of that bank informed me that the amount withheld was in a separate account and could not be released without instructions from the Treasury. We were income-taxed on this third we did not receive, as well as the remaining two-thirds of our pay!

"I hope you can understand my consternation at this breach of good faith.

"I have made inquiries regarding this awful and ruthless matter, and have been informed by the bank that all records have been destroyed and nothing can be done. My question was: Who received the pay I earned? It was in a separate account at the close of the war. Where did it go? It appears to have been, to put it forthrightly, connivingly filched by the Treasury.

"No records? We did have a war. That needs no recording, and I have my personal service record history from the Air Ministry. This destruction of so-called records does not eradicate the debt.

"Other members of the Commonwealth Forces were not so penalised. On the basis of common fairness, why were the English?

"At the war's end there was no conceivable way that any records as to what the Germans had paid us or not paid us could have been available. The money held on our behalf by our banks should have been automatically released to us – we had earned it.

"According to the conditions of service laid down in King's Regulations and Air Council Instructions, all officers were in lieu of part of their pay entitled to a ration allowance of six shillings-a-day if one did not receive food or rations from the Air Force. This, while we were prisoners, was not paid.

"The Germans did not give us the equivalent of their

'barrack behind-the-front-line troops', as laid down in the Geneva Convention. What they did give us would not have supported our lives. We were able to occasionally buy a bulk issue of old potatoes with the token marks in lieu of rations from either the Germans or the British in 1940-41.

"For the first year of captivity we were paid once a month token money by the German Accounting Officer. After the first year there were no more money parades. We were, in fact, financially penalised for being taken prisoner.

"It is surely time this horrible injustice was rectified.

"All records have, it appears, conveniently gone into the shredder, but the debt still remains. Who got the money placed in separate accounts and held by our banks? No one knows. But those who earned it did not get their rightfully earned pay.

"Was it for this we endured what we endured? The question of what happened to our pay has never been answered. Where did it go? Who got it? Someone did."

Michael Roth died without getting an answer.

Central to the issue is the fact that the alleged cost of the POWs' accommodation, food, the handling of mail etc was automatically deducted at source from the prisoners' pay, with the intention that the detaining powers would be reimbursed at the end of the war. In the case of those held by the Germans, however, the deductions far outweighed the value of the "services" provided. Be that as it may, in 1945 the two governments waived their claims. The British Treasury, however, chose not to pay the prisoners back, it simply kept the money.

The payment of compensation has been similarly inequitable. By the end of 1986 West Germany had paid 61 billion DM to victims of the Nazis, nearly all of them concentration camp victims, but hardship suffered in a prisoner of war camp was specifically excluded. There was no compensation for the British prisoners of war and the POWs themselves did not lodge any claims.

As part of her *Heart of the Matter* television series, Joan Bakewell examined their case in a BBC documentary, entitled *Unfinished Business*, when one of her principal witnesses was Fred Murray, an E715 POW whose case mirrors that of Ron Jones. Fred, like Ron, was captured in North Africa, imprisoned in Italy and ended up at Auschwitz, working for IG Farben. Again like Ron, Fred was graded A1 fit when he joined the Army, but was invalided out after the War.

Both men were plagued by abscesses in the camp but were still forced to work long hours, with the result that their health deteriorated. Then, during the Death March that followed the closure of Auschwitz, both suffered frostbite to their hands and feet. Neither man recovered fully.

Fred Murray told Joan Bakewell: "Underneath your feet you've got pads. Well I haven't any more, just the bones, and every time I walk, I walk on bones, which is why I can't walk far. That's the result of the frostbite and the marching. Week after week we marched every day, which is a long way to walk on frostbitten feet. Every night we slept in barns and all we had to eat was pig-swill. Of course that didn't do my stomach any good and it didn't do me any good, it just kept you going."

Health broken, Fred was demobbed with his medical category downgraded from A1 to C7. Within three months of his return home he was hospitalized, and he was never fit enough to hold down a job for any length of time. "I was always ill," he explained. "My stomach was always bad and my feet got worse and worse. They wouldn't operate on my stomach and I was told there was nothing that could be done for my feet, so I just had to keep going. I had a nervous breakdown for a year. That was really rough, I wouldn't wish that on anybody. I couldn't even write my name or tie my tie. I used to get on the phone to my wife, crying all the time."

Fred, like Ron, didn't get a war pension and was reliant on his wife, Jessie, to nurse him through his illnesses. In 1988 money was too tight to afford the special shoes he needed, which cost £50. Jessie approached an organisation called The Soldiers and Sailors Families Association, whose local representative was the former Bishop of Grantham. He said: "I went to see them and sure enough, Fred's feet were absolutely crippled and there were signs of osteoarthritis in his spine because of the way he walked. I got in touch with his regimental association, the East Yorks, who provided the £50. Mrs Murray had been in the ATS, so I asked them if they would provide the road fund licence for their clapped out car, which they did.

"Obviously the first thing I'd asked Fred was: 'What about your war pension?' He said: 'I haven't got a pension because I wasn't wounded.' He left the army in 1945 and on his discharge papers it said: 'multiple abscesses, peptic ulcers and frostbitten hands and feet.' And that counted as not being wounded. I think there must have been a lot of men treated like that.

"How it happened that men coming out of the Army with that sort of medical category weren't given a pension form I just can't imagine. Whether it was incompetence or that the officer discharging them didn't realise what was needed I don't know, but the British government of the day have got a bit to answer for."

In Joan Bakewell's programme, a powerful case for the

British prisoners in E715 getting compensation, was presented by Benjamin Ferencz, the United States' Executive Prosecutor at the Nuremberg war crimes trials. After Nuremberg, Ferencz filed 163,000 claims for Jewish property seized by the Nazis and later he headed the Jewish Claims Conference, convened to deal with Germany's reparations to Jews.

Of IG Farben he said: "At Nuremberg we thought this was a company that should answer for its deeds and we put the leading Farben directors on trial. The court confirmed that the conditions were as we had described them, based upon German documents, which was our primary source of information, and that all those who worked there were being terribly abused. This ran the entire gamut of different types of employees – it was not only the Jews but the Poles, the French and the prisoners of war. They had to answer for those crimes and there was a general conviction for them – for having used slave labour in a most inhumane and illegal way.

"That was the primary thrust of the IG Farben trial. It did not deal with compensation for any of the survivors or any personal financial liability on the part of the defendants. It was basically a criminal trial. Unfortunately, no one spoke on their [the POWs] behalf. It costs money to bring a lawsuit in Germany. The British POWs appeared at the Nuremberg trial to testify against the IG Farben directors who they'd worked for, but no test case was brought on their behalf, so no compensation was ever considered or given.

"From a moral point of view and a human point of view, anyone with such an interest should be entitled to compensation from the party that injured them. That's a fundamental principle of law and should be applicable to POWs as well. They shouldn't lose those rights simply because they happened to be serving their country. But there's a difference between what is legally possible in a court of law in Germany and what is morally desirable."

Ferencz had no doubts that the POWs, like the Jews, were used as slave labour: "All of the big German industrial firms did the same, they used their connections with the SS to recruit whatever labour they could get. Concentration camp labour was eagerly sought after and the industries had to build camps to make sure that they wouldn't escape. That was one of the requirements, and they had to train the guards. The SS were in charge, but the industrial leaders themselves had to define what the work would be and to make sure conditions were such that the prisoners couldn't escape.

"All over Germany and the occupied territories, wherever IG Farben, Krupp, Siemens, Daimler Benz or any of the other German companies had a factory, they would build a small slave labour camp or concentration camp. The working conditions varied from camp to camp. In general, they were horrendous. Some people survived, but the working conditions were to extract the maximum labour at minimal cost in terms of food, nourishment etc.

"I negotiated slave labour settlements with many of the companies. Invariably they all took the line that it didn't happen. It never happened. Then when you presented them with the documentation and said: 'Look, we have your requisitions here,' it was: 'Well, we were forced to do it.' I said: 'But you weren't forced, you had to fight for it, I have the correspondence.' Then it was: 'Oh yes, but the working conditions were so fine that I don't know why they should be complaining. We had a lot of people tell us how happy they were to work for us.' I'd say: 'How come? Everybody I've talked to tells me it was terrible.'

"Their reply to that was: 'Well, it's true, but it was much

better than they would have had otherwise. Otherwise they would have gone directly to the gas chambers, so in effect we saved their lives, so why are they coming to us and asking us to compensate them? We're the ones who saved their lives.'

"That was essentially the position taken invariably, by all of German industry. It's enough to make you sick. In fact there is a legal obligation on the part of the German government to deal with this issue for British POWs. And that is not generally recognised. There was a provision written into the contractual agreements between the Allies and the West German government in 1954 whereby IG Farben would be liquidated but that its obligations would be met, and that even after liquidation those obligations would have to be paid. It didn't define those obligations.

"In fact IG Farben wasn't liquidated. The Allies, including the British and the Americans, looked the other way and let it go. But in the 'Four Plus Two' agreement in 1990, which was the equivalent of a peace treaty, this question of compensation came up again and a provision was written in where the German government said: 'We're aware of the obligations of IG Farben after liquidation and the obligation to take care of any claims against IG Farben and we will try to deal with that.'

"So they've left a little tag onto which to hang these claims, and I would certainly have exploited that if I was concerned with pursuing it."

Ron Jones says: "I was never paid by the Army for the time I was a POW, and haven't been compensated for what I endured in Auschwitz. I'm bloody angry about that. The day I got captured in North Africa, my wages stopped and I assumed that when I got home, all my back pay would be handed over as a bounty. Was it hell."

Les Allan explained why as follows: "Our pay was withheld because our government paid the German POWs for the work they did and it was assumed that the Germans paid us, which they didn't. So not only were we POWs, we paid for the privilege!"

Ron says: "I've been to see my MP, Paul Flynn, about it three times and he brought my case up in Parliament, asking what happened to my wages. He was told I wasn't entitled to them because the Germans had paid us. They didn't of course, we never received a penny. I've heard talk that prisoners at other camps received something called *Lagergeld* to buy soap and stuff, but I never had any money in all the time I was a POW.

"My friend Trevor Manley, worked in a coalmine near Katowice, and he was never paid either. Unfortunately the issue seems to have been clouded by the fact that some POWs who were held elsewhere did get this *Lagergeld*. I knew a guy called Charlie French, from Portsmouth, who did. He worked in a coalmine somewhere in Czechoslovakia, and he got this *lager* money. When he came home after the war he was able to exchange it for sterling.

"So the problem is that some got it, others didn't, and how can those who didn't get it prove they didn't?" Brian Bishop also saw none of the *Lagergeld*.

Ron Jones says: "When we got back, there was a letter pinned up in the local British Legion, stating that anybody who had worked as slave labour for the Germans should apply for compensation. Trevor did, but when he said he had worked in a mine as a British POW they discounted his application straight away. He died a couple of years ago, still resenting that treatment.

"Because I'd worked in Auschwitz they took an interest. I

exchanged letters, back and forth, for all of two years. Then eventually they said: 'You're not entitled, you were a British prisoner of war and the Germans paid you to work.' It seemed all they were interested in was compensating the Jews. The German government allocated billions to compensate the ones who were still alive for their slave labour. Nothing went to POWs as far as I know. We were particularly aggrieved in 2001, when the Government agreed to pay servicemen who had been prisoners of the Japanese £10,000 each by way of compensation.

"I know that because one of my neighbours in Bassaleg, Paul Pembridge, was a prisoner of the Japanese and he had his £10,000, paid to him by the British Government

"Let's be honest, our POWs held by the Japanese were treated far worse than we were by the Germans. I lost half my teeth through malnutrition, but nobody mistreated me like the Japs did those poor lads. It was that bloody march when the camp was disbanded that our crowd deserved compensation for. A lot of us died, for God's sake and others were ruined for the rest of their lives.

"People seem to think that because we were POWs we just lounged about like the ones you see on television, in *Colditz* or *The Great Escape*. No way. There was no lounging, just the opposite – we were bloody slave labourers, forced to work without pay! On that basis, we were entitled to compensation just as much as the men who were prisoners of the Japanese."

In their winter 2006 newsletter the National Ex-Prisoner of War Association reported: "Some of you sent claims to this body, especially those who spent time in concentration camps such as Auschwitz, and all were rejected on the grounds that prisoners of war were not considered eligible. However, member Denis Avey appealed against his decision and fought it all the way until September this year, when he succeeded in overturning the initial rejection of his claim for compensation for imprisonment in E715 at Auschwitz.

"The appeals body concluded that 'the applicant had been subjected to forced labour in a concentration camp, or in another place of confinement under comparable conditions as defined under the Foundation Act. The appeals body therefore decides to reverse the initial decision'."

The newsletter added: "The maximum amount payable to applicants classed as slave labour is 15,000 Euros. Denis now has a good cause for celebration this Christmas, and we congratulate him on his persistence and success.

"I suggest that if you feel your claim was unfairly rejected you write to the International Organisation for Migration in London."

Ron Jones says: "I saw Paul Flynn at Newport County in November 2011 and asked him if there was any sign of my missing pay after all these years. He laughed and said: 'No, it's still at the War Office [now the Defence Ministry], accumulating!' Perhaps he thinks it's funny, but I certainly don't. The German POWs were not only treated a hell of a lot better than we were, they got paid, too, so they had money to go home with."

Anthony Beevor, in *The Second World War*, says of the 1945 General Election: "The Prime Minister [Winston Churchill] had received warnings that things might not go his way, largely because of votes in the armed forces, whose men wanted to do away with the past, both the harsh years of the 1930s and the war itself.

"At a dinner in London a few weeks before, when Churchill had talked about the election campaign, General William Slim, back from Burma, had said to him: 'Well Prime

Minister, I know one thing. My army won't be voting for you.'

"For most soldiers and NCOs the military hierarchy bore too close a resemblance to the class system. An army captain who had asked one of his sergeants how he was going to vote, received the reply: 'Socialist sir, because I'm fed up with taking orders from ruddy officers.'

"When the votes were counted it became clear that the armed forces had voted overwhelmingly for the Labour Party and for change. Churchill's greatest fault was to have shown no taste for social reform, during either the war or the campaign."

Ron Jones was one of The Great Disillusioned. He says: "I've never thought much of politicians, and their failure to get me the money I'm owed certainly hasn't changed that. There was a General Election at the end of the War, but I didn't vote. To be honest, I never have. It doesn't interest me. Whoever is in Parliament, the fate of the working man doesn't really change. Gwladys used to go on at me about it, but I've never voted. If I had in 1945, I'd probably have been like a lot the servicemen and voted against Churchill, because I was bloody annoyed at the way his government treated us.

"Nowadays, when they come home from the Falklands, the Gulf or Afghanistan, the lads all get counselling, compensation and whatever. I got bugger all. Nobody came to see me to ask if I was coping all right, there was no contact, nothing. I was given ten weeks leave, and after that the Army sent me back to Pangbourne and the Royal Engineers as if nothing had happened. I was really annoyed about that.

"Ordinary people locally were much more concerned. The congregation from the chapel where Gwladys played the organ all came to see how I was, but I got nothing from the

War Office or the Army. Not even a letter. I'm sure that sort of thing was why so many from the services voted against Churchill and got him out."

The reason, or rather convenient excuse, given by the Germans for the delay in addressing the issue of compensation was that no formal peace treaty had been signed at the end of the War because the division of Germany into Communist East and democratic West denied the former state full national sovereignty and therefore collective responsibility. Instead, the Potsdam Conference in August 1945 agreed "provisional" terms that would be finalised by a peace agreement for Germany, to be accepted by the government of Germany "when a government adequate for the purpose is established".

In November 1951 Norbert Wollheim, a former Monowitz inmate, sued IG Farben for 10,000 DM as compensation for suffering he endured as a slave labourer building their factory. In a court judgement delivered two years later, he was awarded the full sum, which was widely seen as a precedent.

Faced with the prospect of thousands of such claims, the IG Farben board sought an agreement with a Jewish organisation representing former prisoners, and in 1954 the company's receiver at the time, Walter Schmidt, started negotiating with the Jewish Material Claims Conference. Initially, IG offered 10 million marks to cover all future claims. Herbert Schoenfeld, acting for the Jews, demanded 100 million marks, based on 10,000 each for 10,000 former prisoners, and after much haggling, the figure arrived at in February 1957 was 30 million marks.

Schmidt, for IG, insisted that the sum agreed should not be considered as compensation or damages in the legal sense as the company admitted no such obligations. The money was a gesture of goodwill to former "employees". Payment was made only to 6,500 Jews, their negotiators refusing to share the fund with Poles and other slave labourers, including the British POWs.

At an appeals court, a Polish claim was rejected as "premature", because according to the London Agreement of 1953, the Federal Republic of Germany had first to sign a peace treaty and also to settle all its debts to foreign countries before dealing with private individuals. Incredibly, after awarding them nothing, the Frankfurt court even charged the Poles 331,000 marks in costs.

It was more than 30 years before this moral injustice was properly addressed. After the fall of the Berlin Wall the governments of the FDR and DDR wanted to form a unified state, and in order to do so they were prepared to meet the terms agreed at Potsdam, which included compensation for wartime slave workers. Reunification came about on 3 October 1990, since when the issue has remained on the agenda.

The new German constitution provided for those who, before partition, had assets in East Germany and had had them confiscated by the Communists, enabling them to claim them back. Now IG Farben shareholders had to decide whether to end the company's liquidation and claim those assets.

When the company sought to recover its assets from East Germany, two ex-POWs, Alan Hicks and Albert Lougher, went for compensation. They failed.

In 1990 Joan Bakewell asked Ernst Bartels, the new liquidator for IG Farben, if they would be compensating British POWs. Evasiveness personified, he replied: "That's impossible because we believe that the English prisoners have no claim against IG Farben. They could only have a claim against the German government." Pressed on the subject, he added: "When they worked in the IG Farben factories they had no working contracts with IG Farben, they were sent by the German government to our factories with the order to work."

It was put to Bartels that the company had a contract with the German government of that time, and was therefore responsible for the workers, but again he denied it, saying: "No, only the German government was responsible. They sent the prisoners to us and the prisoners worked under the observation of the German soldiers."

Asked why British POWs could not have the same compensation paid to the Jews, he said: "The fate of the Jews was much more cruel than what the English soldiers had to suffer. The English soldiers had their own camp in which they lived from where they went every day to the factory. Their camp was near the IG Farben factory.

"The Jews had to march seven kilometres every morning from the concentration camp to the IG Farben factory and seven kilometres back in the evening. They had almost nothing to eat and they were very weak. So they suffered much more than the English prisoners. Later on, IG Farben proposed to the Nazi government that they make a small concentration camp within their factories, so that the Jewish concentration camp prisoners did not have to walk 14 kilometres every day."

Bartels was seeking to liquidate a company that was, in effect, a trust for what remained of IG Farben's assets, most of which had long since been sold off to four major German corporations: Bayer, Hoechst, Agfa and BASF. Negotiations dragged on, the company's lawyers blaming compensation claims for delaying dissolution and the distribution of its remaining assets to its victims.

There was a breakthrough in December 1999, when the German government agreed to release a fund of 4.5m dollars to compensate the slave workers. The money came half from the government and half from the 6,300 companies involved, although the latter demanded guarantees that they would not be sued again in the future.

Chancellor Gerhard Schroeder's chief negotiator for the fund, Otto Lambsdorff, said: "I must apologise to those for whom our work took too long. The delays were, and are painful because we will no longer reach many of the victims who died."

To their continued disgrace, IG Farben did not contribute to the fund. It did, however, pay 500,000 DM (£160,000 at the time) into a foundation for former captive labourers of the Nazis. In 2001 the company's latest liquidator, Otto Bernhardt, announced that it would be formally wound up in 2003, and on 10 November that year the liquidator filed for bankruptcy. If it's dead, however, it won't lie down and in 2012 the company was still in existence, as a "corporation in liquidation".

There is an annual meeting every year, in Frankfurt, those in attendance running the gauntlet of hundreds of protestors.

Bibliography

The number of books published on Auschwitz is enormous. Of great value to the author as reference works were the following:

Yisrael Gutman and Michael Berenbaum, *Anatomy of the Auschwitz Death Camp* (Indiana University Press, 1944).

John Cornwell, *Hitler's Scientists* (Penguin, 2004).

Duncan Little, *Allies in Auschwitz* (Clairview, 2010).

Piotr Setkiewicz, *The History of Auschwitz IG Farben Work Camps* (Auschwitz-Birkenau State Museum, 2006).

Barbara U. Cherish, *The Auschwitz Kommandant* (The History Press, 2009).

Colin Rushton, *Spectator in Hell* (Summersdale, 1998).

John Castle, *The Password is Courage* (Souvenir Press, 1954).

Denis Avey and Rob Broomby, *The Man Who Broke into Auschwitz* (Hodder & Stoughton, 2011), quoted here by kind permission of Hodder & Stoughton Limited.

Rudolph Hoess, *Death Dealer: The Memoirs of Rudolph Hoess* (Da Capo Press, 1996).

Laurence Rees, *Auschwitz* (BBC Books, 2005), quoted here by kind permission of The Random House Limited.

Ian Kershaw, *The End* (Penguin, 2011).

Max Hastings, *Finest Years: Churchill as Warlord* (Harper Press, 2009).

Frederick Taylor, *Exorcising Hitler* (Bloomsbury, 2011).

Andrew Roberts, *The Storm of War* (Penguin, 2009).

Antony Beevor, *The Second World War* (Weidenfeld & Nicholson, 2012).

Charles Rollings, *Prisoner of War* (Ebury Press, 2008), quoted here by kind permission of The Random House Limited.

Richard J. Evans *The Third Reich at War* (Penguin, 2008).

David S. Wyman, *The Abandonment of the Jews: America and the Holocaust* (Pantheon Books, 1986).

Also the following television programmes:
The Long March To Freedom (Yesterday Channel, SkyTV).
The Heart of the Matter (BBC Television).